…ghes and **Katie Wood**

with additional material by Paul Dummett

…herine **Walter**

Navigate

Coursebook

with video and Oxford Online Skills

A2 Elementary

OXFORD

UNIVERSITY PRESS

Contents

Oxford 3000™ *Navigate* has been based on the Oxford 3000 to ensure that learners are only covering the most relevant vocabulary.

1 Your world

1.1 Multicultural cities

GOALS ■ Talk about countries, nationalities and languages ■ Describe people using the verb *to be*

Vocabulary & Speaking countries, nationalities and languages

1 Work with a partner. Look at the photos and answer the questions.
  1 Which countries are cities a–d in?
  2 What is the nationality of people from these countries?
  3 What are the languages in these cities?

a London

b San Francisco

c Melbourne

d Dubai

2 Work with a partner. Turn to page 126 and check your answers to exercise 1.

3 Work with a partner. Are the words in the box countries (C), nationalities (N) and/or languages (L)?

Arabic *L*	Jamaica	Spanish
Chinese	Mexican	the UAE
English	Pakistani	

4a Work with a partner. Complete the table.

Country	Nationality	Main language
Mexico	1 _____	2 _____
the USA	American	3 _____
Italy	4 _____	Italian
China	5 _____	6 _____
Vietnam	Vietnamese	7 _____
Turkey	Turkish	Turkish
the UK	8 _____	English
Poland	9 _____	10 _____
Pakistan	11 _____	Urdu
the UAE	Emirati	12 _____
France	13 _____	French
Greece	Greek	14 _____

b 1.1))) Listen and check your answers.

c 1.1))) Listen again and mark the stress on each word. Practise saying the words with a partner.

● Mexico   ● American

5 Work in small groups. Take turns to think of things you have from around the world and to guess what it is.
  A *It's Italian.*
  B *Your car?*
  A *No.*
  C *Your bag?*
  A *Yes!*

Grammar & Listening present simple to be

6a **1.2**))) Listen to Godwin talking about his life in London. Write the countries, nationalities and languages that you hear.

b Compare your list with a partner.

c Work with a partner. Complete the factfile.

FACTFILE

Name Godwin

Nationality Nigerian

Married/Single Married

Wife's name Sylvie

Wife's nationality
Half-¹_____
Mother is French;
Father is from ²_____

Number of children Two

Nationality of children ³_____

Language at home ⁴_____

Home North London

Nationality of neighbours Iraqi

Near his house ⁵_____ supermarket;
Lebanese ⁶_____

Work ⁷_____ organization

Nationality of boss ⁸_____

Interests
Football and playing the saxophone

d **1.2**))) Listen again and check your answers.

7a Work with a partner. Underline the verbs from the interview.
1 *Is / Are / Am* you from London?
2 My name *is / are / am* Godwin.
3 I *'s / 're / 'm* from Nigeria.
4 Our two children were born in England, so they *'s / 're / 'm* British.
5 The neighbours *is / are / am* a family from Iraq.
6 The restaurant across the road *is / are / am* Lebanese.
7 My boss *isn't / aren't / 'm not* American.

b **1.3**))) Listen, check and repeat.

8 Work with a partner. Complete the rules in the Grammar focus box. Use exercise **7a** to help you.

GRAMMAR FOCUS verb *to be*

Positive (+)

I	¹_____	(am)	
He/She/It	's	(is)	from Nigeria.
You/We/They	²_____	(are)	

Negative (−)

I	'm not	(am not)	
He/She/It	's not/³_____	(is not)	American.
You/We/They	're not/aren't	⁴(_____)	

Yes/No Questions (?)			Short answers
Am	I		Yes, I **am**. No, I ⁶_____.
Is	he/she/it	late? Italian?	Yes, he/she/it ⁷_____. No, he/she/it **isn't**.
⁵_____	you/we/they		Yes, you/we/they **are**. No, you/we/they ⁸_____.

→ Grammar Reference **page 136**

9 **1.4**))) Godwin is at his first saxophone class. Listen to the conversation. What do we find out about Andy and Murielle?

10a Work with a partner. Look at the conversation between the teacher (T), Godwin (G) and Murielle (M) and complete the conversation using the words in the box.

Are from I'm introduce Is meet This too ~~What's~~

T ¹ *What's* your name?
G Hi, I'm Godwin.
T ²_____ you a student?
G No, I'm not. I have a job.
T Where are you ³_____?
G I'm from Nigeria, but London's my home now.
T ⁴_____ it your first class?
G Yes, it is.
T Let me ⁵_____ you to the other students.
    ⁶_____ is Murielle. She's a student here ⁷_____.
G Hi, Murielle. Nice to ⁸_____ you. ⁹_____ Godwin.
M Nice to meet you, ¹⁰_____.

b **1.4**))) Listen again and check your answers.

11 Work in small groups. Take turns to practise the conversation in exercise **10a** using your own names and countries.

1.2 Family

Reading & Grammar possessive determiners

1 Work with a partner. Look at the photo of some children from a village in India. What is special about them?

2 Read the article and check your ideas.

3 Work with a partner and answer the questions.
1 Why are the people in Kodinhi not typical?
2 Are people in Kodinhi happy to have twins?
3 Why are there a lot of twins in Kodinhi?

4 Work in small groups. Answer the questions.
1 Do you have twins in your family? Are any of your friends twins?
2 Is it good or bad to be a twin? Why?

5 Look at the highlighted words in the article and complete the information in the Grammar focus box.

GRAMMAR FOCUS personal pronouns and possessive determiners

Personal pronoun	Possessive determiner
I	1 _____
you	your
he	2 _____
she	her
it	3 _____
we	4 _____
they	5 _____

→ Grammar Reference page 137

6a Underline the correct options.
1 *She / Her* friends are Italian.
2 Where's *you / your* wife from?
3 *I / My* have a big family.
4 Are *they / their* twins?
5 *He / His* brother is a teacher.
6 This is *we / our* house.

b Compare your answers with a partner.

TWIN VILLAGE

Kodinhi is a small village in Kerala in south India. It's a typical village, but its people are not typical. Two thousand families live here and 290 families have twins. In India seven babies in 1,000 are twins, but in Kodinhi, forty-five babies in 1,000 are twins.

Mohammed Rāshin's family is from Kodinhi. He and his wife have seven boys. Four of their sons are twins. Mohammed says, 'My wife and I are very happy with our family. Everyone in the village is happy.'

But why are there so many twins in Kodinhi? How is it possible? No one really has an answer, but the village doctor says it isn't genetic; he thinks it's something in the water or the food.

■ **typical** a good example of something that's usual, normal, average
■ **genetic** things that come from your parents, like blue eyes or brown hair

7 Complete the sentences using the words in the box.

~~their~~ his her our its my your

1 a They have a house in Kodinhi.
   b Kodinhi is _their_ home.
2 a We have seven children – all boys.
   b All _____ children are boys.
3 a Mohammed and Suhara are the parents.
   b Mohammed is the father; Suhara is _____ wife.
4 a You have a big family.
   b _____ family is big.
5 a Suhara's friend has twin girls.
   b _____ friend has twin girls.
6 a Many people know about the twins in Kodinhi.
   b Kodinhi is famous for _____ twins.
7 a I have twin sisters.
   b _____ sisters are twins.

Vocabulary & Speaking family

8 Work with a partner. Make a list of all the family members you can think of.
father, wife, ...

9a Match a male word to a female word.

Male		Female
1	brother *c*	a stepmother
2	son	b grandmother
3	husband	c sister
4	father	d sister-in-law
5	uncle	e niece
6	grandfather	f daughter
7	grandson	g mother
8	nephew	h granddaughter
9	stepfather	i aunt
10	brother-in-law	j wife

b **1.5**))) Listen, check and repeat.

c Work with a partner. Choose the correct word.
1 She is the mother of six *child / children*.
2 My uncle and aunt have a daughter, Anna. She is my *cousin / sister*.
3 My *brother / brother-in-law* is a doctor. He and my sister have three children and they all live in Seattle.
4 My *parents / grandparents* have two sons – me and my brother.
5 My father is dead. My mother is now married to Didier. So he's my *stepfather / half-brother*.

10 Work with a partner. Talk about three people in your family.
My brother is married to Marianna. She's a teacher.

Grammar & Speaking possessive *'s*

11 **1.6**))) Listen and complete the family tree.

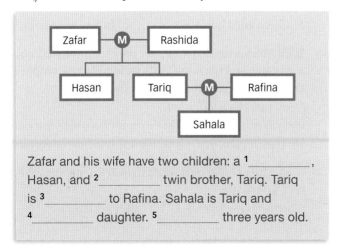

Zafar and his wife have two children: a ¹_____, Hasan, and ²_____ twin brother, Tariq. Tariq is ³_____ to Rafina. Sahala is Tariq and ⁴_____ daughter. ⁵_____ three years old.

12 Read the Grammar focus box and complete sentences 1–6 about the family in exercise **11**.

GRAMMAR FOCUS possessive *'s*

We use the possessive *'s* to show that something belongs to someone.
Rafina is Sahala's mother. (= Rafina is her mother)
Her husband's name is Tariq. (= His name is Tariq)
Hasan is Zafar and Rashida's son. (= Hasan is their son)

Note: *'s* is also a contraction of *is*.
My name's Marta. (= My name is Marta.)
It's a Spanish name. (= It is a Spanish name.)

→ Grammar Reference page 137

1 Zafar is _____ husband.
2 Hasan is _____ brother.
3 Rafina is Tariq's _____.
4 Their _____ name is Sahala.
5 Sahala is Zafar's _____.
6 Rashida is _____ grandmother.

PRONUNCIATION similar sounding words

13a **1.7**))) Listen to the phrases and sentences. Is the pronunciation of the highlighted words the same (S) or different (D)?
1 Zafar's wife — Zafar's a doctor.
2 their daughter — They're happy.
3 I'm his son. — He's my father.
4 Is he your brother? — You're right.
5 She's our teacher. — Are you married?

b **1.7**))) Listen again and repeat.

14a **TASK** Draw your family tree or invent one.

b Work with a partner. Take turns to describe the people in your family tree and to ask questions about your partner's family.
A *My uncle's name is Lester. He is my mother's brother.*
B *How old is he?*

▶ VOX POPS VIDEO 1

1.3   Vocabulary and skills development

GOALS ■ Understand positive and negative contractions   ■ Use regular and irregular plural nouns

Listening & Speaking   positive and negative contractions

1a   Write the names of three people you know.

b   Work with a partner. Take turns to talk about the people in exercise **1a**.

Kirit is my brother. He's 25. He's a nurse.

2   **1.8**))) Read and listen to the information in the Unlock the code box about positive and negative contractions.

> 🔒 **UNLOCK THE CODE**
> positive and negative contractions
>
> - When we speak, we often use contractions, e.g. *I'm, she isn't*, etc. It is important to understand the difference between the positive and negative forms of the verb.
> - The verb *to be* is not stressed in positive sentences.
>
>   *He's Australian.   I'm Chinese.*
> - In negative sentences *not, isn't* and *aren't* are stressed.
>
>   *She's not Polish.   It isn't my family name.   They aren't friends.*

3   **1.9**))) Listen and <u>underline</u> the contraction you hear.

1   *I'm / I'm not* Russian.
2   *It's / It isn't* an Arabic name.
3   *That's / That's not* a girl's name.
4   *They're / They aren't* brothers.
5   *It's / It's not* the same.
6   *She's / She isn't* French.
7   *It's / It's not* a long name.
8   *He's / He isn't* married.

4   **1.10**))) Listen and complete the sentences with the words you hear.

1   It _____ a female name.
2   Their name _____ Spanish.
3   She _____ called Sarah.
4   His family name _____ Ramirez.
5   That _____ a boy's name.
6   My name _____ very long.
7   Their family _____ large.
8   He _____ my friend.

5a   Match the names to the nationalities.

1 Li Na	a	Turkish
2 Antalek Tamás	b	Chinese
3 Bülent Sadik	c	Hungarian
4 Manuela García Gómez	d	Spanish

b   **1.11**))) Listen and check your answers.

c   **1.11**))) Listen again. Tick (✓) the pairs of countries that have something the same, and cross (✗) the ones that are different.

1   Turkey and China   3   Spain and Hungary
2   China and Hungary   4   Turkey and Spain

6a   **TASK**   Work with a partner. Use the prompts to talk about your name and the names of your friends and family.

My name's ... , but my friends/family call me ...
I have two/three/four names.
In my family, no one has/some people have the same name.
My aunt/brother has a long/short/funny/interesting name.

b   Work with another partner. Tell them three things about your first partner.

Alberto has five names ...

10   ⊙ⁿ Oxford 3000™

Vocabulary & Speaking regular and irregular plural nouns

7a Work with a partner. Read part of a magazine article about names. What do you find out about titles and names?

What's in a title or name?

Titles and names can tell us a lot about people. For example, in English there is one title for men, *Mr*, and three for women – *Mrs* for a married woman, *Miss* for a single woman and *Ms* for both. In some countries, for example Greece, wives can have their husband's last names after they are married, but in other countries they have their own names. In Iceland, most last names have *-sson* or *-dottir* at the end, for example Gunnarsson or Guomundsdottir. A person's last name is their father's first name with *-sson* or *-dottir*. If a man is called Magnus Einarsson and his son is called Jon and his daughter is called Kristen, then Jon's and Kristin's last name is not Einarsson. Jon's last name is Magnusson and Kristin's last name is Magnusdottir.

b Work with a partner. What's special about names in your language or other languages you know?

c Read the article again and complete the table. Compare your answers with a partner.

Regular (singular)	Regular (plural)	Irregular (singular)	Irregular (plural)
¹ _a name_	names	a man	³ _____
a country	² _____	⁴ _____	women
		a person	⁵ _____

d **1.12**))) Listen, check and repeat.

8 Read the information in the Vocabulary focus box about regular and irregular plural nouns.

> ### VOCABULARY FOCUS regular and irregular plural nouns
>
> **Regular nouns**
> 1 To talk about more than one noun, we usually add *-s*.
>   *name → names   cousin → cousins*
> 2 With nouns that end in *-ch*, *-sh*, *-ss*, *-s*, *-x*, *-z*, we add *-es*.
>   *brush → brushes   box → boxes*
> 3 With nouns that end in a consonant + *-y*, we take away the *-y* and add *-ies*.
>   *country → countries   family → families*
>
> **Irregular nouns**
> 1 Some nouns are irregular in the plural.
>   *child → children   person → people*
>   *man → men   woman → women*
> 2 Some nouns that end in *-f* or *-fe*, have plurals in *-ves*.
>   *wife → wives   half → halves   knife → knives*
> 3 We don't add *-s* to irregular nouns.

9 Work with a partner. Take turns to ask and answer questions about singular and plural nouns. Student A, turn to page 126. Student B, turn to page 131.

10a Look at the photos for one minute.

b Close your books and write down all the things you can remember. Use *a*, *an*, or a number before the thing(s). Compare your list with a partner.

five pencils

c Open your books and check your lists.

1.4 Speaking and writing

GOALS ■ Ask for personal information and check you understand ■ Write a personal profile

Listening & Speaking asking for personal information and checking you understand

1 Work with a partner. Look at the advert and answer the questions.

1 What is the course?
2 Who is it for?
3 When and where is it?

2 **1.13**))) Listen to a conversation between a student and a receptionist. Complete the form.

⊕ Eastfield Adult College

Name	¹ _Antonio_ Russo
Nationality	² _____
Job	³ _____
Type of website (please circle)	⁴ Business / Fun
Email address	⁵ _____

3a **1.14**))) Listen to the first part of the conversation again and complete the receptionist's questions.

1 _____ your name?
2 _____ your nationality?
3 _____ your job?
4 _____ the website for business or for fun?
5 _____ your email address?

b Check your answers in the Language for speaking (1) box.

> **LANGUAGE FOR SPEAKING (1)** asking for personal information
>
> *What's your name?*   *What's your nationality?*
> *What's your job?*   *What's your email address?*

c **1.15**))) Listen to the questions in exercise **3a** and repeat.

4a **1.16**))) Listen to the second part of the conversation again. What are the missing words?

A It's antonio@russorest.com.
R ¹_____, can you ²_____ that, please?
A Yes, Antonio – A-N-T-O-N-I-O – at russorest dot com.
R ³_____ do you ⁴_____ 'russorest'?
A R-U-double S-O-R-E-S-T
R OK. Great. Thanks. Now, the cost of the course is ...

MAKE YOUR OWN WEBSITE FOR BUSINESS OR FUN

BEGINNERS' COURSE – ALL WELCOME

INTERESTED?

Please send us a short description of yourself and your reason for attending the course.

Location: Eastfield Adult College
Start date: 12th January   **Time:** 6.00 – 7.30 p.m.

b Check your answers in the Language for speaking (2) box.

> **LANGUAGE FOR SPEAKING (2)** checking you understand
>
> *Sorry, can you repeat that, please?*
> *How do you spell that?*
> *How do you spell 'russorest'?*

c **1.17**))) Listen to the questions in exercise **4b** and repeat.

5a Match questions 1–7 to answers a–g.

1 What's your name?
2 Sorry, can you repeat your name?
3 What's your job?
4 What's your nationality?
5 What's your email address?
6 How do you spell 'joelkubi'?
7 Is your website for business or for fun?

a J-O-E-L-K-U-B-I.
b It's a website for my friends and family.
c joelkubi@mailbox.com.
d I'm Czech.
e Joel Kubicek.
f I'm a car mechanic.
g Yes, I'm Joel Kubicek.

b Work with a partner. Take turns to practise the questions and answers in exercise **5a**.

6 Work with a partner. Take turns to ask and answer personal information questions. Student A, turn to page 126. Student B, turn to page 132.

Reading & Writing   a personal profile

7   Work with a partner. Look at the advert in exercise **1** again. What details do you think they want?

8a Read Cristina's profile for the course and complete the form. Compare your answers with a partner.

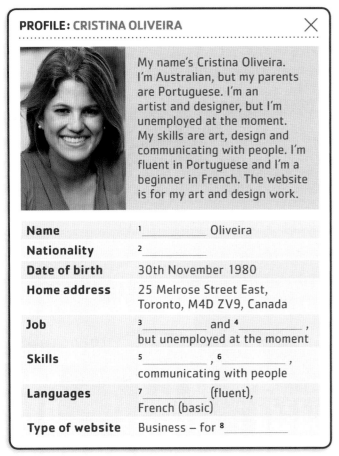

PROFILE: CRISTINA OLIVEIRA

My name's Cristina Oliveira. I'm Australian, but my parents are Portuguese. I'm an artist and designer, but I'm unemployed at the moment. My skills are art, design and communicating with people. I'm fluent in Portuguese and I'm a beginner in French. The website is for my art and design work.

Name	¹_____ Oliveira
Nationality	²_____
Date of birth	30th November 1980
Home address	25 Melrose Street East, Toronto, M4D ZV9, Canada
Job	³_____ and ⁴_____, but unemployed at the moment
Skills	⁵_____, ⁶_____, communicating with people
Languages	⁷_____ (fluent), French (basic)
Type of website	Business – for ⁸_____

b   Work with a partner. Answer the questions.
   1   What is Cristina's normal job? What is her situation now?
   2   Are Cristina's Portuguese and French
      a very good   **b** OK   **c** not very good?

9   Look at Cristina's profile and form again. Find examples of capital letters for 1–6.
   1   people's names   *Cristina Oliveira*
   2   beginning of a sentence
   3   towns and countries
   4   nationalities
   5   languages
   6   days of week or months

10 Work with a partner. Put nine capital letters in the correct places in this profile. Use exercise **9** and the Language for writing box to help you.

i am a student at columbia university. my saturday job is at a chinese supermarket called jing jing foods.

LANGUAGE FOR WRITING using capital letters

We use capital letters for:
people's names	*Petra Park*
companies	*Brown's Café*
universities	*Manchester University*
beginning of a sentence	*My brother is a doctor.*
towns and countries	*Buenos Aires, Argentina*
nationalities and languages	*British, Chinese, Spanish*
days of week and months	*Monday 14th July*
the pronoun 'I'	*Kasper and I are good friends.*

11a Work with a partner. Use Antonio's form to write a personal profile like Cristina's.

Name	Antonio Russo
Nationality	Italian
Date of birth	1st May 1985
Home address	210 Lakeview Road, Toronto, M4B 1B3
Job	Restaurant owner
Skills	Cooking, business management
Languages	English (fluent) and Italian (fluent)
Type of website	Business – for restaurant

b   Work with a different partner. Compare your profiles for Antonio.

12a **TASK** Write a similar profile of yourself. Use capital letters in the correct places.

b   Swap profiles with a partner. Check the capital letters.

1.5 Video

Brighton language exchange

1a Look at the photos. Which of these things do you see in them?

> beach conversation flag library pavilion pier
> reading student teacher

b Work with a partner. Look at the photos and the words in exercise **1a** again. What do you think the video is going to be about?

2 ▶ Watch the video and check your ideas. What skill/skills do you see students practising? How are they practising?

3 ▶ Watch the video again. Decide if the sentences are true (T) or false (F). Correct the false sentences.

1 Rebecca is a student and she comes from London.
2 The population of Brighton is 27,000.
3 Many people go to Brighton to learn English.
4 There are conversation exchanges once a week at the Jubilee Library.
5 In the conversation exchange you speak your own language for forty-five minutes.
6 The language exchange costs £45 to join.
7 After the language exchange, students go out together.
8 Brighton is famous for Brighton Pizza, Brighton Clock Tower and the Royal Pavilion.

4a Work in small groups. Think of the things you can do to improve your English. Make notes about each skill.

- Speaking
- Listening
- Reading
- Writing
- Pronunciation
- Grammar
- Vocabulary

b Compare your ideas with another group. Which ones would you like to try?

c Think about 4–5 things you want to improve. How are you going to do it?

I want to improve my listening. I am going to watch a DVD without subtitles every week.

d Compare your ideas with a partner.

A *I want to improve my English grammar.*
B *Me too, I'm going to buy a grammar book.*
A *I'm going to use a good website with grammar games on it.*

Review

1a Complete the conversation with the verb *to be* in the positive (+), negative (–) or question (?) form. Use contractions where possible.

A ¹_____ (?) you and your wife from England?

B No, we ²_____ (–). I ³_____ (+) from Edinburgh in Scotland and my wife ⁴_____ (+) Canadian.

A Canadian? ⁵_____ (?) she from Montreal? My sister's at university in Montreal.

B No, she's from Vancouver. What about you? You ⁶_____ (–) English. ⁷_____ (?) you Australian?

A No, I ⁸_____ (–). I'm from Wellington in New Zealand.

b **1.18**))) Listen and check your answers.

c Work with a partner. Use your own ideas and have a similar conversation.

2a Complete the questions with the correct form of the words in (brackets).

1 What's ____*your*____ name? (you)

2 Where are _____ from? (you)

3 What's _____ name? (he)

4 Is _____ from Mexico? (she)

5 Is this _____ book? (she)

6 What are _____ names? (they)

7 What's _____ teacher's name? (we)

b Work with a partner. Take turns to ask and answer the questions in exercise **2a** about you and other people in the class.

3a Read the text and add an apostrophe in the underlined words if it is necessary.

My <u>names</u> Memed. I'm from Izmir. <u>Its</u> a city in Turkey. I have two <u>sisters</u>. Their <u>names</u> are Sevil and Fatima. Sevil is 10 and <u>Fatimas</u> 14. My <u>brothers</u> name is Cem. <u>Hes</u> a doctor. His <u>wifes</u> name is Eda.

b Compare your answers with a partner.

4a **1.19**))) Listen and write the words in the correct column.

	Country	Nationality	Main language
1			
2			
3			
4			

b Complete the table with the missing words.

c Complete the text with words from the table.

Dubai is a very multicultural city in the ¹_____ . People come here to work from many different countries. Only 10% of people in Dubai are ²_____ : 90% of the city's population are from other countries. Some people come from the UK and the ³_____ , but many people are from Asia. India is home for most of Dubai's workers, but people come from ⁴_____ and the Philippines, too. The language of the United Arab Emirates is ⁵_____ , but because of its international population, lots of people use ⁶_____ .

d **1.20**))) Listen and check your answers.

5 **1.21**))) Listen to the definitions and write the family word.

1 ____*aunt*____   3 _____   5 _____

2 _____   4 _____   6 _____

6 Complete the table with the missing words.

Singular	Plural	Singular	Plural
nationality	¹_____	wife	⁴_____
²_____	languages	⁵_____	women
child	³_____	address	⁶_____

7a Make questions from the prompts.

1 you / name?   4 you / job?

2 you / spell that?   5 you / email address?

3 you / nationality?   6 sorry / you / repeat?

b Work with a partner. Ask and answer the questions.

My day

2.1 A day in the life of a scientist

GOALS ■ Talk about everyday actions ■ Use the present simple positive to talk about your day

Listening & Grammar present simple and adverbs of frequency

Penguins on the beach on Bird Island

Location of Bird Island

Seals on Bird Island

1 Work with a partner. Look at the photos and information about Bird Island and answer the questions.

1 Where is Bird Island?
2 What animals live there?

2 **2.1))))** Melanie Szabo is a scientist on Bird Island. Listen to her talking about her day in the summer and in the winter. Tick (✓) the activities she mentions.

1 study penguins
2 get up early
3 have breakfast
4 go out in a boat
5 visit different islands
6 take photos
7 have dinner
8 work in the lab
9 write emails
10 go to bed late
11 relax
12 read a book

3 **2.1))))** Listen again and complete the sentences with the correct verbs. Is Melanie talking only about today, or things she does every day?

1 In the summer, my days are long. I _____ early and _____ to the beach. I watch the penguins.
2 We _____ different islands and we _____ photos.
3 In the winter, we usually _____ more free time.

4a Work with a partner. Read the article about Melanie and her colleague, Sven. How are their jobs different?

SCIENTISTS ON BIRD ISLAND

Bird Island is an important scientific research centre. Every year lots of scientists visit the island, but Melanie Szabo, a professor of zoology, works there all year. Sven Olafsson, who is from Bergen in Norway, also works on the island. He studies seals and Melanie watches penguins. The penguins come to the beaches on the north of the island and Melanie often works there alone. Sven never works alone – he always works with the other scientists because the male seals are big and sometimes dangerous! Sven loves his job, but he works very hard and he hardly ever has free time. For Melanie, her favourite time is Saturday night. One of the scientists usually makes a big dinner for the group and they watch a movie together, relax or play games.

b Work with a partner. Would you like to work on Bird Island? Why/Why not?

5 Work with a partner. Read the sentences and complete the rules in the Grammar focus box.

1 We visit different islands and we take photos.
2 Sven loves his job, but he works very hard and he hardly ever has free time.
3 Melanie watches penguins.

GRAMMAR FOCUS present simple positive

- We use the present simple to talk about repeated actions and things that are always true.
- To make the present simple positive, we use:

I/You/¹_____/They + infinitive without to

²_____/She/It + infinitive without to + (e)s

- When a verb ends in -ch, -sh, -ss, -s, -z, -x, we add ³_____ to the third person he/she/it form.
- The third person he/she/it form of have is ⁴_____ .

→ Grammar Reference page 138

PRONUNCIATION third person -*(e)s*

- The third person -*s* is pronounced /s/ or /z/ with most verbs, e.g. *works, goes*.
- With verbs ending in -*ch*, -*sh*, -*ss*, -*s*, -*z* or -*x*, the third person *he/she/it* form is pronounced /ɪz/, e.g. *watches, washes*.

6a 2.2))) Listen to three sentences and repeat.
1 Melanie **watches** penguins. /ɪz/　3 Sven **loves** his job. /z/
2 Sven also **works** on the island. /s/

b 2.3))) Listen and circle the final sound you hear in verbs 1–6.
1 goes /z/ /ɪz/　3 cooks /s/ /ɪz/　5 makes /s/ /ɪz/
2 teaches /z/ /ɪz/　4 relaxes /s/ /ɪz/　6 plays /z/ /ɪz/

c 2.4))) Listen, check and repeat.

7a Read the Grammar focus box about adverbs of frequency.

GRAMMAR FOCUS adverbs of frequency

- Adverbs of frequency, e.g. *always, never, sometimes*, etc. tell us how often or how frequently something happens.
- In the present simple, adverbs of frequency come **after** the verb *to be*, but **before** all other verbs.
*In the winter, the weather **is always** very cold.*
*Melanie **often works** there alone all day.*

→ Grammar Reference page 138

b Work with a partner. Underline the adverbs of frequency in exercise **4a**. Write them in the correct place in the diagram.

¹*always*　3 _____　⁵*hardly ever*
　²_____　4 _____　6 _____
100%　　50%　　0%

8a Read the sentences about a scientist's week and complete the sentences with the correct form of the verbs in the box.

arrive　be　go (x2)　~~get up~~　have　relax　return　work

1 During the week, he _*gets up*_ early and he _____ at a volcano at seven o'clock. (always/usually)
2 His work _____ dangerous and he _____ alone. (sometimes/never)
3 He _____ to the research centre at about 1 o'clock. and he _____ lunch in the lab. (usually/always)
4 On Friday and Saturday nights he _____ at home. He _____ out with friends and he _____ to bed early. (usually/hardly ever/often)

b Read the sentences in exercise **8a** again and put the adverbs in (brackets) in the correct places.

c 2.5))) Listen and check your answers.

Vocabulary & Speaking daily activities

9a Work with a partner. Match illustrations 1–12 to the phrases in the box.

get up　go home　go to bed　go to work/college
have a shower　have lunch/dinner　listen to music
make breakfast　play video games　read a book
see friends　watch TV/a film

b 2.6))) Listen, check and repeat.

10a **TASK** Tell your partner five things about your day, using the phrases in exercise **9a** and adverbs of frequency. Give more information when you can.
I get up at about eight o'clock.
I (sometimes/always/never) have a shower …, etc.

b Work with a different partner. Tell them about your first partner's day.
Alexa gets up at eight o'clock. She always has a shower.

▶ VOX POPS VIDEO 2

2.2 Spending time

Listening & Vocabulary telling the time

1a Work with a partner. Do you think sentences 1–3 are true (T) or false (F)?

1 It takes about a year to learn to be an astronaut. T / F
2 Some astronauts stay in space for over a year at a time. T / F
3 Astronauts don't need perfect eyesight. T / F

b Turn to page 127 and check your answers.

2 **2.7**))) Sanaa Diya is a trainee astronaut at the European Astronaut Centre (EAC) in Cologne, Germany. Listen and answer the questions.

1 What does she think about the training?
2 What subjects does she learn?

3 **2.7**))) Listen again and match activities 1–6 in Sanaa's day to times a–f.

1 She gets up
2 She has breakfast in the canteen
3 She goes to morning classes
4 She stops for a break in the morning
5 Classes finish in the evening
6 She goes to sleep

a at quarter to eight.
b at ten to seven.
c at quarter to six.
d at five past ten.
e at quarter past eleven.
f at half past eight.

4a Work with a partner. Write the times under the clocks.

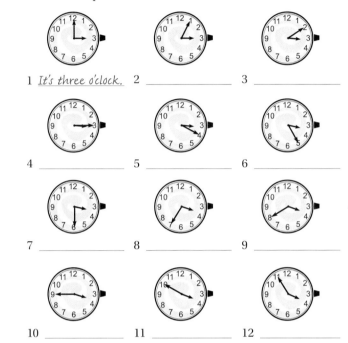

1 *It's three o'clock.* 2 _____ 3 _____

4 _____ 5 _____ 6 _____

7 _____ 8 _____ 9 _____

10 _____ 11 _____ 12 _____

b **2.8**))) Listen, check and repeat.

PRONUNCIATION saying the time

- When we say the time, we don't stress *past* or *to*, e.g.
  twenty-five past three, ten to seven.
- We don't pronounce the letter *l* in *half*, so we say /ha:f/.
- *Quarter* begins with a /k/ sound, so we say /kwɔ:tə/.

5a **2.9**))) Listen to the times. Circle the words you hear.

1 *quarter / half* past eight
2 quarter *to / past* three
3 ten *to / past* ten
4 *five / quarter* to six
5 twenty *to / past* three
6 *twenty / twenty-five* to four

b **2.9**))) Listen again and repeat.

6 Work with a partner. Talk about what time you do these things or what time they happen where you live.

- the sun rises in summer
- you get up
- the shops open
- your favourite TV programme starts
- you have lunch
- the shops close
- public transport stops

The sun rises at about half past six.
Shops like the baker's open early, at eight o'clock.

Reading & Grammar present simple negative

7 Work with a partner. What's different about life on earth and life in space? Use the ideas in the box.

> daytime and night-time   washing   sleeping

8a Read the article about Canadian astronaut Chris Hadfield and life in space. Check your ideas in exercise **7**.

_____A perfect day_____

When Chris Hadfield goes into space, he <u>doesn't have</u> a lot of free time. He works twelve hours a day and also does two hours' exercise. Life in space is very different to life on earth. Astronauts don't have showers like people on earth do – they wash with a cloth. They don't sleep in a bed – they sleep in special sleeping bags on the walls. It is difficult to know the time because in space the sun doesn't rise once a day – it rises once every 45 minutes. It's hard work, but most astronauts love being in space. Chris says it is amazing and he doesn't want to sleep. For him, every day in space is a perfect day!

b <u>Underline</u> the negative verb forms in exercise **8a**, e.g. *doesn't have*, and complete the rules in the Grammar focus box.

GRAMMAR FOCUS present simple negative

To make the present simple negative, we use:
I/You/We/They + *do not* (_____'_____) + infinitive without *to*
He/She/It + *does not* (_____'_____) + infinitive without *to*

→ Grammar Reference page 139

9a Change these sentences from positive to negative. Use contractions.

1 They have a lot of free time.
  They don't have a lot of free time.
2 I go to classes in the evening.
3 Chris has a shower in the morning.
4 Sanaa sleeps in a sleeping bag.
5 They speak to their families every day.
6 He works eight hours a day.

b 2.10))) Listen, check and repeat.

10a Work with a partner. Do you think these things usually happen or not in space?

A *I don't think astronauts get sick on their first trip into space.*
B *Really? I disagree. I think they usually get sick.*

1 get sick on their first trip into space
2 wear special clothes in the space station
3 change their clothes every day
4 exercise a lot
5 go on a spacewalk every day
6 sleep a lot

b 2.11))) Listen and check your ideas.

11a TASK Chris says every day in space is a perfect day for him. Describe a perfect day for you. Write down three things you do and three things you don't do.

On a perfect day, I don't go to work. I have breakfast in bed at about half past nine – fresh fruit, coffee and a croissant – and I get up at ten o'clock.

b Compare your sentences with a partner. Is their perfect day similar or different to yours?

c Work with a different partner. Tell them about your first partner's perfect day.

2.3 Vocabulary and skills development

Reading & Speaking — understanding conjunctions

1 Work in small groups. When do you think is the best time to do the things in the box? Why?

> go to sleep   have breakfast   have dinner   wake up

2a Read the sentences about sleep. Look at the words in **bold** and answer questions 1–4.
- I usually only sleep five **or** six hours a night, **but** I sleep well.
- I sleep for a long time, **but** I don't always feel good in the mornings.
- I am often worried about something **and** wake up in the night.
- I never get enough sleep **because** I am always busy.

1 Which word joins two similar ideas?
2 Which word do we use to show something different?
3 Which word answers the question *Why*?
4 Which word joins two possibilities?

b Read the information in the Unlock the code box about conjunctions. Check your answers to exercise **2a**.

> ### 🔒 UNLOCK THE CODE
> understanding conjunctions
>
> - Understanding conjunctions in sentences, e.g. *and*, *but*, *because*, and *or*, helps you understand a text.
> - We use:
>   ***and*** with <u>similar ideas</u>
>   ***or*** with two or more <u>choices</u> or possibilities
>   ***because*** to say <u>why</u> something happens
>   ***but*** to <u>contrast</u> two different pieces of information.

3a Match beginnings 1–4 to endings a–d. Use the conjunctions to help you.

1	I have lunch at one or	a	have breakfast.
2	I wake up and	b	it's difficult!
3	People eat because	c	they're hungry.
4	I try to wake up early, but	d	two in the afternoon.

b 2.12))) Listen, check and repeat.

4a Complete each sentence with a different conjunction.
1 Some scientists say to eat small meals often, _____ others say it is important to eat only three meals a day.
2 Some scientists believe it's a bad idea to drink tea _____ coffee late in the evening.
3 I go to bed early _____ I wake up early.
4 There is no perfect time to wake up _____ people are different.

b Work with a partner. Discuss the sentences in exercise **4a**.

5a Read the article and answer questions 1–5.
1 What can happen if we sleep or eat at the wrong time?
2 Is there a perfect time to sleep? Why/Why not?
3 When is the best time to sleep? Why is this often difficult to do?
4 When is the best time to eat?
5 '... *if you listen to your own body clock, you can live a healthier life.*' What does this mean?

b Work in small groups. Do you agree with the ideas in the article?

Know your body clock

Many of us get enough sleep and food, but still feel tired and hungry during the day. Perhaps this is because we sleep or eat at the wrong times.

There is no perfect time to sleep because everyone's body clock is different, but sleep expert Dr Michael Howell says the best sleep is six hours at night and two hours in the afternoon. The best time to have your afternoon sleep is six hours after you wake up, but this is not possible for most people because they are at work.

It is also useful to think about what time you eat. It is important to eat breakfast two hours after you wake up and dinner three hours before you go to sleep.

Perhaps the most important thing to remember is that if you listen to your own body clock, you can live a healthier life.

Vocabulary & Speaking   verb + preposition

6a Complete the two sentences with prepositions.

1 It is also useful to think _____ what time you eat.

2 ... if you listen _____ your own body clock, you can live a healthier life.

b Check your answers in the article in exercise **5a**.

c Read the information in the Vocabulary focus box about verbs and prepositions.

> **VOCABULARY FOCUS** verb + preposition
>
> - Some verbs have a preposition, e.g. *with, for, about, to,* after them. These verbs need an object after the preposition.
>   *I **listen to** music every day.*
>   *He never **agrees with** her.*
>   *Are you **looking for** your keys?*
> - We don't use a preposition when there is no object.
>   *Wait!* NOT *Wait for!*
>   *Listen!* NOT *Listen to!*

*the **International***

7a Work with a partner. Match beginnings 1–8 to answers a–h to make eight short conversations.

1 I watch the news on TV every morning.
2 It's a good idea.
3 Do you pay for tea and coffee at work?
4 Do people often wait for buses and trains in your city?
5 I'd like to talk to you before the meeting tomorrow.
6 Do we have a reply from them?
7 It's not nice to laugh at other people.
8 Do students often ask for a discount?

a No, they want more time to think about it.
b I listen to it on the radio.
c OK, are you free after lunch?
d I agree with you.
e No, they're free, but we buy sandwiches at lunchtime.
f I know, my grandmother always says that!
g Yes, but they need to show their student card.
h No, not often. They're usually on time.

b **2.13**))) Listen and check your answers.

c Work with a partner. Take turns to practise the conversations.

8a Work with a partner. Complete sentences 1–8 with a verb and preposition phrase from the box. Change the form of the verb if necessary.

> agree with   ask for   laugh at   listen to   pay for
> ~~talk to~~   think about   wait for

1 Tarik _talks to_ his family on the phone every day.
2 Kristofer never _____ funny films. He doesn't enjoy them.
3 My sister never _____ people who are late.
4 I usually _____ my friends but we sometimes have different ideas.
5 Gregorja _____ pop and classical music.
6 When he's alone, he _____ his friends and family.
7 We always _____ our shopping in cash.
8 Intira always _____ help when she doesn't understand something in class.

b **2.14**))) Listen and check your answers.

9a **TASK** Make the sentences in exercise **8a** true for you. Give more information by using conjunctions.
I don't talk to my family on the phone every day, but I talk to them every week.

b Compare your sentences with a partner. Tell the class two things that are similar and two things that are different.
We both talk to our families on the phone every day.

2.4 Speaking and writing

Listening & Speaking making suggestions and arrangements

1 Work in small groups. Discuss the questions.

1 What time do the shops and restaurants open and close where you live?

2 What do you think is a 24-hour city?

2a **2.15))** Karl Schmidt is from Germany and he is visiting Seoul for work. Bon Dae Kim, his Korean colleague, meets him at the airport. Listen and choose the correct answers.

1 Bon Dae Kim first invites Karl to go ...

   a shopping   b to a meeting   c to a restaurant

2 Bon Dae Kim first suggests they go at ...

   a midday   b midnight   c half past nine

3 Karl agrees to go at ...

   a midday   b half past nine c five o'clock

4 Bon Dae Kim and Karl agree to go shopping ...

   a after dinner   b at 5 a.m.   c at 5 p.m.

b Compare your answers with a partner.

c Match questions 1–5 from the conversation to answers a–e.

1 Are you free tonight?

2 Would you like to go for dinner at Jinju Jip?

3 What time do you want to eat?

4 Do you want to do some shopping while you're here?

5 Where shall we meet?

a Let's go at half past nine.

b I will pick you up from your hotel.

c Yes, that sounds nice.

d Yes, I'd love to.

e Yes, I am.

d **2.15))** Listen again and check your answers.

3 Work with a partner. Take turns to practise making suggestions and arrangements. Use the prompts and the Language for speaking box to help you.

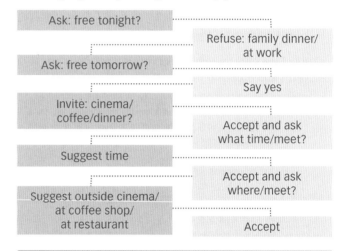

Ask: free tonight?

Ask: free tomorrow?

Invite: cinema/ coffee/dinner?

Suggest time

Suggest outside cinema/ at coffee shop/ at restaurant

Refuse: family dinner/ at work

Say yes

Accept and ask what time/meet?

Accept and ask where/meet?

Accept

LANGUAGE FOR SPEAKING
making suggestions and arrangements

Making suggestions and arrangements
Are you free (tonight)?
Would you like to (do) ...?
Do you want to (do) ...?
Let's (do) ...
What time do you want to (do) ...?
Where shall we (do) ...?

Accepting
Yes, I'd love to.
Yes, that sounds nice.

Refusing
I'm sorry, but I'm busy this evening.
Thanks, but I'm afraid I have plans tonight.

4 Work with a partner. Take turns to make suggestions and arrangements. Student A, turn to page 127. Student B, turn to page 132.

Reading & Writing describe where you live

5 Work with a partner. Do you prefer to live in the town or the country? Talk about the good and bad things about each. Use the ideas in the box to help you.

> buses/trains fresh air jobs noise prices
> things to do traffic

6a Read what three people say about where they live. Match a photo a–c to a description 1–3. Compare your answers with a partner.

1
> I love it here! It's a very big city ¹_____ you don't need a car – the buses and trains are very good. I often have lunch outside a café or a restaurant and watch people walk past. Of course the food ²_____ drink here is great but I sometimes have problems in the restaurants ³_____ I don't speak very good French! (**and/because/but**)

2
> It's a really beautiful place. In summer, there are lots of tourists, ⁴_____ in winter it's very quiet. I live in a small town: it doesn't have many shops, restaurants ⁵_____ museums, but for me that's not important. I love living near the sea ⁶_____ I can go swimming or walk along the beach when I want to. (**because/but/or**)

3
> We live in this city because our jobs are here. We don't always enjoy city life – it's sometimes noisy and dirty, ⁷_____ it's exciting. It's a 24-hour city: you can go out shopping ⁸_____ clubbing all night. My favourite place is the port. My office is there ⁹_____ I love watching the ships arrive from all over the world. (**or/and/but**)

b Work with a partner. Which place in exercise **6a** would you like to live in? Why?

7a Read the information in the Language for writing box.

> **LANGUAGE FOR WRITING** using conjunctions
> Use *and/but/or/because* to help the reader understand your ideas.
> *Sydney has a lot of parks **and** museums.*
> *It's a beautiful city, **but** it's very expensive.*
> *You can travel by bus **or** train.*
> *You need a car **because** the country is very big.*

b Complete the descriptions in exercise **6a** with the conjunctions in (brackets).

Lagos, Nigeria

Phuket, Thailand

Paris, France

8a Complete these sentences about where you live using your own ideas.
1 I like _____, **but** I don't like _____.
2 At the weekend, I usually _____ **or** I _____.
3 My two favourite things to eat are_____ **and** _____.
4 I like/don't like big cities **because** _____.

b Compare your sentences with a partner. What is similar and what is different?

9a **TASK** Work with a partner. Think about where you live or a place you both know well. Make a list of good and bad things about it.

b Write a paragraph about the place (60–80 words). Leave gaps for the conjunctions.

c Give your text to another pair to complete the sentences. Check their answers.

10 **TASK** Work in small groups. Read all your texts. Which places would you like to live in? Why/Why not?

2.5　Video

The Menna family

1　Work with a partner. Look at the people in the photos and think about …
   - what nationality they are
   - where they live
   - what they like eating
   - how old they are
   - what jobs they do
   - what they do at weekends

2　▶ Watch the video about the Menna family. Check your ideas in exercise **1**. What other information do you find out about the family?

3　▶ Watch the video again. Choose the correct option. Sometimes more than one answer is possible.

   a　Roberto works *for a television network / for Channel 9 / at home*.
   b　Gabriela goes to work at *5.30 / 6.30 / 7.30* a.m.
   c　Milagros and Julieta *go to school by bus / go to the same school / go to different schools*.
   d　The girls get up at *8 a.m. / 9 a.m. / 10 a.m.* on Saturdays.
   e　Gabriela drinks *chocolate milk / mate / coffee*.
   f　After breakfast the girls play *football / tennis / video games*.
   g　They go to the park *in the evening / in the afternoon / before lunch*.
   h　The family usually visits the girls' *aunt and uncle/ cousins / grandparents* on Sundays.
   i　They eat *salad / pasta / rice* with their barbecue.
   j　On Sundays they go to bed *early / late / at 11 p.m.*

4a　**TASK**　Work with a partner. You are going to do a class survey to find out whose weekend is the most different to yours. Write 6-8 questions to find out about other students' weekend routines.

   Do you work at the weekend?
   What time do you get up on Saturdays?

   b　Ask other students in the class about their weekend routines. Whose weekend is the most different to yours?

Review

1a Complete the sentences with the present simple positive form of the verbs in the box.

> go have like live study work

1 I _____ classical music.
2 After class, I _____ home by bus.
3 My friend _____ in a bank.
4 We _____ English on Mondays and Wednesdays.
5 In my country, people _____ their main holiday in August.
6 My classmate _____ in a flat in the city centre.

b Work with a partner. Make the sentences in exercise **1a** true for you. Give more information.
I don't like classical music. I like rock.

2a Look at the information and write sentences about people in the UK. Use words from the box.

> always never sometimes hardly ever usually often

They never have fish for breakfast.

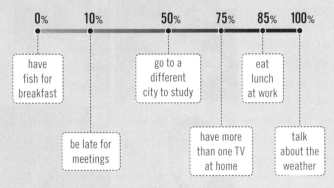

b 2.16))) Listen and check your answers.

c Change the adverbs of frequency to make the sentences true for where you live. Compare your sentences with a partner. How many sentences are the same?

3a Put the daily activities in the order people usually do them.

> go to bed go to work get up have a shower
> have dinner go home have lunch watch TV

b Work with a partner. Think of three more daily activities. Decide where they go in your order from exercise **3a**.

4 Work with a partner. Say what time you usually do the activities in exercise **3a**. Do you do things at the same time as your partner?
I usually get up at six o'clock, but at weekends …

5a Match beginnings 1–6 to endings a–f to make questions.
1 What radio station do you
2 Do you usually agree
3 Do you normally
4 Do you like waiting
5 Who's the first person
6 Do you pay

a for public transport?
b for things in shops in cash or by credit card?
c with everything your family/colleagues say?
d you talk to in the morning?
e listen to?
f ask for directions when you are lost?

b Work with a partner. Ask and answer the questions in exercise **5a**.

6a Complete the conversation with the words in the box.

> busy free like love let's plans shall want

A Are you ¹_____ after class today?
B I'm sorry, but I'm ²_____ this evening. But I don't have any ³_____ tomorrow.
A Would you ⁴_____ to go out for a pizza?
B Yes, I'd ⁵_____ to. What time ⁶_____ we meet?
A Eight o'clock at Gino's? Or do you ⁷_____ to meet at the station?
B Yes, ⁸_____ meet there at 7.45.
A OK, see you then!

b 2.17))) Listen and check your answers.

c Work with a partner. Use your own ideas and have a similar conversation.

25

3

The world of work

3.1 Jobs

GOALS ■ Talk about jobs ■ Ask yes/no questions

Vocabulary & Speaking jobs

1a Work with a partner. Match the jobs in the box to photos 1–12.

businessman/businesswoman   chef   cleaner   dentist   hairdresser
journalist   mechanic   musician   nurse   photographer   pilot   student

b 3.1))) Listen to people talking about the jobs in exercise 1a and check your answers.

c 3.2))) Listen and mark the stressed syllable in the words from exercise 1a.
●
businessman

d 3.2))) Listen again and repeat.

2 Work with a partner. Write jobs from exercise 1a and any others you know in the table. You can write a job in more than one group.

Work inside	Work outside

Well-paid	Badly-paid

Work with a computer	Work with their hands

3 Work in small groups. Use the ideas in exercise 2 and your own ideas to choose the three best jobs. Tell your partners your reasons.
I think the best job is a … because …

Grammar & Listening   *yes/no* questions

4   Read the advert and answer the questions with a partner.

1   What is the advert for?

2   What type of person will answer the advert?

Do you have an unusual job?

Are people **surprised** when
you tell them what you do?

Does your job
make you happy?

Is your job
very difficult?

Do you do something
very dangerous?

We want to make a television programme about
people with unusual jobs and we want to hear from
you. If you have an unusual job, please telephone
us on 0456 789789 and leave a message.

---

5   Underline the first word in all the questions in the advert and complete the questions in the Grammar focus box.

GRAMMAR FOCUS *yes/no* questions

- Questions with *be*
  Are you a pilot?   Yes, I **am**./No, I'**m not**.
  ¹___ your job very difficult?   Yes, it **is**./No, it **isn't**.
- Questions with other verbs
  ²___ your job make you happy?   Yes, it **does**./No, it **doesn't**.
  ³___ you have an unusual job?   Yes, I **do**./No, I **don't**.

→ **Grammar Reference** page 140

6a   Máté Fehér from Budapest, Hungary and Dana Schriffer from Santa Fé, USA have unusual jobs. Work with a partner. Look at the words and photos. What do you think their jobs are?

music   cinema   weather   fire

Máté

Dana

b   **3.3**))) Listen to Máté and Dana talking about their jobs and check your answers to exercise **6a**.

c   Work with a partner. Would you like to do Máté and Dana's jobs? Why/Why not?

7a   Complete the questions and answers about Máté and Dana.

1   _Does_ Máté _____ at the cinema?
   Yes, he _____ .

2   _____ he always _____ fast music?
   No, he _____ .

3   _____ Dana a police officer?
   No, she _____ .

4   _____ she _____ in a big office?
   No, she _____ .

5   _____ she _____ her job?
   Yes, she _____ .

6   _____ Dana and Máté _____ unusual jobs?
   Yes, they _____ .

b   **3.4**))) Listen and check your answers.

PRONUNCIATION   *do* and *does*

Do and *does* are not stressed in questions, but they are
stressed in short answers.
   ●   ●   ●   ●
Do they like their jobs? Yes, they do.

---

8   **3.5**))) Listen and repeat the questions and answers.

1   **A** Do they like their jobs?   **B** Yes, they do.

2   **A** Does he play the piano?   **B** Yes, he does.

3   **A** Does he sell tickets?   **B** No, he doesn't.

4   **A** Do you have a job?   **B** No, I don't.

9   Work with a partner. Take turns to ask and answer questions about Dana and Máté using the phrases in the box.

Dana	Máté
be a police officer	be a piano player
check the weather every day	play slow music
work from home	work at the theatre

A   *Is Máté a piano player?*

B   *Yes, he is.*

10a   **TASK** Work with a partner. Write 4–6 questions for a quiz called 'What's the best job for you?' Use the ideas in the box and your own ideas.

Are you an outdoor person?   *Do you walk a lot?*

a calm person   an outdoor person
enjoy helping people   get up early in the morning
like being busy   like children   like working alone
like working with computers   organized   walk a lot

b   Work with a different partner. Take turns to ask and answer your questions in exercise **10a**.

c   What is a good job for your partner in exercise **10b**? Tell the class and give reasons.

3.2 What do you do?

GOALS ☐ Talk about work ☐ Ask *Wh-* questions

Vocabulary & Speaking work

1 Work in small groups. Which of the things in the box do you think are most important in a job? Are any of them not important?

> hours   money   people you work with   place of work

2 Read the blog and answer the questions.
1 Who works in their house?
2 Who likes their job very much?
3 Who makes a lot of money?
4 Who doesn't like the clothes they wear at work?

WHO DOES WHAT IN MY FAMILY?

My name's Pierre and I'm 24 years old. I'm French and I live in Lyon. I'm a photographer and I **work from home** – I don't have a **boss** because I **work freelance**. My father is a mechanic and he **works in a factory**. He really enjoys his job because his **colleagues** are also his friends! My mother is a journalist and she **works for a fashion magazine**. She **works in a big office** in the centre of town and earns a very good **salary**. My brother really wants to work and **earn** money, but at the moment he is **unemployed**. My sister is a police officer and she's always tired because she **works long hours**. And she hates the uniform that police officers wear! My grandfather is **retired** now, but my grandmother **works part-time** as a cleaner. She works twenty hours a week.

3a Read the blog again and write the words and phrases in **bold** in the correct place in the diagrams.

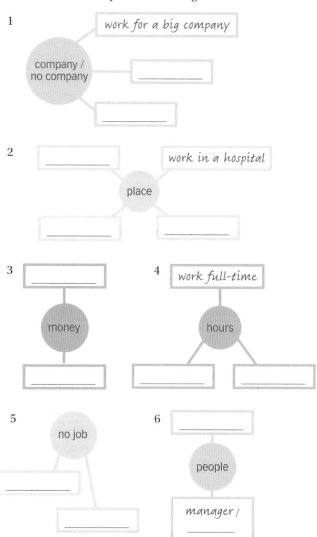

1
work for a big company
company / no company
_____
_____

2
_____
work in a hospital
place
_____
_____

3
_____
money
_____

4
work full-time
hours
_____ _____

5
no job
_____

6
_____
people
manager / _____

b 3.6))) Listen and check your answers.

c 3.6))) Listen again and repeat.

4 Work with a partner. Take turns to ask and answer questions about yourselves or someone you know using the phrases in the box.

> colleagues   earn   manager/boss   office   retired
> salary   unemployed   uniform   work freelance
> work for a big company   work from home
> work long hours   work part-time

A *Do you work in an office?*
B *No, I don't. I work outside.*

Reading & Grammar *Wh-* questions

5a Work with a partner. Look at the photo and the caption and answer the questions.

1 What are stand-up meetings?

2 Why do you think people have them?

Workers in a stand-up meeting

b Read the online article and check your answers. What do you think of stand-up meetings?

┌───┐
│ **FAQs STAND-UP MEETINGS** │
│ │
│ **1** _____ Like a normal meeting, a group │
│ of people from the same office come together and │
│ discuss work. But they don't sit down, they stand up! │
│ │
│ **2** _____ They happen in the offices of │
│ many companies around the world. They are very │
│ common in software companies. │
│ │
│ **3** _____ Because when people stand up, │
│ they don't feel comfortable, and they only talk about │
│ the important things. And it's not easy to play with your │
│ phone when you're standing up because your boss │
│ can see your hands! │
│ │
│ **4** _____ Everyone usually speaks, │
│ but sometimes there isn't enough time. │
│ │
│ **5** _____ Companies usually have │
│ stand-up meetings in the morning, at about 9.00 a.m. │
│ │
│ **6** _____ They are usually once a │
│ week, but some companies have them every day. │
│ │
│ **7** _____ People talk about three │
│ things: work from yesterday, plans for today, │
│ possible future problems. │
└───┘

6 Work with a partner. Write questions a–g next to the correct answers 1–7 in the article.

a When do the meetings happen?

b Where do these meetings happen?

c Who speaks at the meetings?

d What does everyone talk about?

e What is a stand-up meeting?

f How often do the meetings happen?

g Why do people stand up?

7 Complete the rules in the Grammar focus box with the correct word. Use the questions in exercise **6** to help you.

┌───┐
│ **GRAMMAR FOCUS** *Wh-* questions │
│ │
│ We use: │
│ 1 _____ to ask questions about things. │
│ 2 _____ to ask questions about people. │
│ 3 _____ to ask questions about times. │
│ 4 _____ to ask questions about places. │
│ 5 _____ to ask about reasons. │
│ 6 _____ to ask about frequency, e.g. *once a week, every day.* │
│ │
│ → Grammar Reference page 141 │
└───┘

8a Work with a partner. Choose the correct question word.

1 *When / Where / Who* do you live?

2 *Where / When / What* do you usually wear to work?

3 *Who / What / Why* do you want to learn English?

4 *What / What time / Who* do you start work or class?

5 *When / Who / What* do you take breaks?

6 *Why / Who / How often* do you live with?

7 *What / When / Why* do you do when you're bored?

8 *Who / What / How often* do you check your emails?

b **3.7** ⟫ Listen and check your answers.

PRONUNCIATION *Wh-* questions

Intonation usually falls ⤵ at the end of *Wh-* questions.

9 **3.8** ⟫ Listen and repeat the questions.

1 Where do you live?

2 What do you usually wear to work?

3 How often do you check your emails?

10 Work in small groups. Take turns to ask the questions from exercise **8a**. Remember to use falling intonation.

11a **TASK** Work with a partner. Ask questions to find out about your partner's family and their jobs. Make notes.

A *What does your brother do?*

B *He's a journalist.*

A *Where does he work?*, etc.

b Write three sentences about your partner's family and their jobs. Do not write what member of your partner's family they are.

Erika's _____ is a journalist and he works from home.

c Work in small groups. Take turns to read your sentences and guess who the people are.

I think Erika's brother is a journalist.

▶ VOX POPS VIDEO 3

3.3 Vocabulary and skills development

Listening & Speaking the schwa /ə/

1 Work with a partner. Look at the four photos of people at work. What jobs do they do? Do you think these jobs make them happy?

2a **3.9**)) Listen to the names of the jobs in exercise **1** and circle the unstressed syllables.

author   mechanic   pilot   teacher

b **3.9**)) Listen again and repeat.

3 **3.10**)) Read and listen to the information in the Unlock the code (1) box about the schwa /ə/ sound in words.

> 🔒 **UNLOCK THE CODE (1)**
> the schwa /ə/ sound in words
>
> Many words have an unstressed syllable that is usually pronounced with a **schwa** /ə/ sound. The sound is often (but not always) on the last syllable.
>
> farm**er**, wom**a**n, hairdress**er**, s**a**lary, **a**gree

4 **3.11**)) Listen to the words and circle the schwa /ə/ sound in each word.

address   after   again   answer   breakfast
clever   daughter   forget   internet   later

5 **3.12**)) Read and listen to the information in the Unlock the code (2) box about the schwa /ə/ sound in phrases.

> 🔒 **UNLOCK THE CODE (2)**
> the schwa /ə/ sound in phrases
>
> Many common words are often unstressed in phrases and pronounced with a schwa /ə/ sound, e.g. a, the, can, are, that, etc.
>
> **a** new book   auth**or and** me**c**hanic
> **to** be happy   **for** ten minutes
> lots **of** books   **at** home

6a **3.13**)) Listen to phrases from a radio programme about jobs and happiness. Complete each phrase with one or two words.

1 _____ recent report
2 one job _____ makes people very happy
3 there _____ three reasons
4 work _____ company
5 a lot _____ different people

b **3.13**)) Listen again and repeat.

7 **3.14**)) Work with a partner. Listen to the radio programme and answer the questions.

1 What are Matthew Crawford's two jobs?
2 Which people does he think are ...
  a happy in their jobs? Why?
  b unhappy in their jobs? Why?
3 Why do some people disagree?
4 In a recent report, what job makes people very happy?
5 Why are these people happy?

8 Work in small groups. Discuss the questions.

1 Do you agree with Matthew Crawford? Why/Why not?
2 What jobs do you think make people happy? Why?

b Work with a partner. Complete the table.

Verb	Noun
teach	a teacher
paint	1 _____
2 _____	a dancer
build	3 _____
4 _____	a singer
write	5 _____
6 _____	a beginner
run	7 _____
8 _____	a baker
play a DVD	9 _____
work	10 _____

11 Work with a partner. Use the verbs in the box to make nouns ending in -*er*. Complete each sentence with the correct noun.

~~bake~~ begin drive farm heat manage win write

1 My father is a _baker_ . We get free bread and cakes every day!
2 When I have a problem at work, I speak to my _____ .
3 My cousin is a famous _____ . Her books are very popular.
4 It's difficult for a _____ to understand very much in a new language.
5 I don't like being in the car with my brother. He's a really bad _____ .
6 My Uncle Andrew is a _____ . He keeps animals and grows vegetables.
7 The _____ of the competition receives £100.
8 It's a bit cold in here. Shall I go and get the _____ ?

Vocabulary & Writing   -*er* suffix

9 Look at the words in the box and answer the questions.
   1 What are the last two letters of each word?
   2 How are the two letters pronounced?

cleaner farmer hairdresser office worker

10a Read the information in the Vocabulary focus box.

VOCABULARY FOCUS -*er* suffix

• Sometimes we add -*er* to a verb to make a noun.
  -*er* can mean the person or the thing that does the action.
  *I teach. I'm a teach**er**.*
  *It plays MP3s. It's an MP3 play**er**.*
• For most verbs ending in -*e*, we just add -*r*.
  *I drive a bus. I'm a bus drive**r**.*
• For most verbs ending in a single vowel + a consonant, we double the consonant and add -*er*.
  *You win. You're the win**ner**.*

12a **TASK** Work with a partner. Write five definitions for words that end in -*er* from exercises **9–11**. Do not use the verb in your definition.

This person makes bread.
We use this thing to listen to music.

b Work with a different partner. Take turns to read your definitions and guess the word.

A *This person makes bread.*
B *A baker.*

3.4 Speaking and writing

GOALS ■ Make requests ■ Use opening and closing phrases in an email

Listening & Speaking making requests

1 Work with a partner. What requests do students and teachers make on the first day of a computer course? Make a list.

2 **3.15**))) Listen to a teacher talking to a class of students on the first day of a computer course. Are any of the requests the same as yours in exercise **1**?

3a Match requests 1–6 from the listening to answers a–f. Which answers are positive (+) and which are negative (–)?

1 Could I open the window?
2 Could you give your personal details to the administrator?
3 Could I send them by email later?
4 Can you repeat that, please?
5 Can we use the computers after class?
6 Can we leave our books and bags in the computer room?

a Sorry, but I don't have them with me today.
b Yes, of course. It's really hot in here.
c That's fine. Just tell the administrator before you leave.
d I'm afraid not. There are evening classes in that room from 6 p.m.
e Yes, of course, but you need a password.
f Sure. It's student451. That's S-T-U-D-E-N-T-451.

b **3.16**))) Listen and check your answers.

c Work with a partner. Take turns to practise the requests and answers in exercise **3a**.

4a **3.17**))) Listen to some sentences from the Language for speaking box. Notice that the intonation rises ⟋ at the end of *yes/no* questions, and falls ⟍ on the answers.

1 A *Can I sit here, please?*
  B *Of course you can.*
2 A *Could I leave early tomorrow?*
  B *I'm sorry, but that's not possible.*

b **3.17**))) Listen again and repeat.

5 Work with a partner. Complete the requests with verbs from the box.

~~bring~~	call	leave	lend	park	pay	tell	use

1 Can I ___bring___ a friend with me?
2 Could you _____ me at my office in the morning?
3 Can I _____ the phone?
4 Could you _____ me some money for the bus?
5 Can I _____ my coat here?
6 Can I _____ here for about an hour?
7 Could you _____ me the time?
8 Can I _____ for this later?

6 Work with a partner. Take turns to make and answer requests with the eight questions in exercise **5**. Use the Language for speaking box to help you.

LANGUAGE FOR SPEAKING making requests

Making requests
Can I/we sit here, please?
Could I/we start the meeting?
Can you pass me the salt?
Could you open the window, please?

Answering requests
(+) *Yes, of course.*   (–) *I'm afraid not.*
    Yes, that's fine.   *No, I'm sorry, but …*
    Sure.

NOTE: We use *Could I/Could you*, not *Can I/Can you*, when we want to sound more formal and polite.

7 **TASK** Work with a different partner. Look at the situations 1–3. Take turns to make and answer requests. Think of three requests for each situation.

1 first day staying with an English-speaking family
2 joining a library
3 staying in a hotel

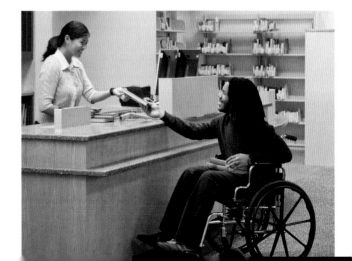

Reading & Writing opening and closing an email

8 Work with a partner. Match emails 1–3 to replies a–c.

1
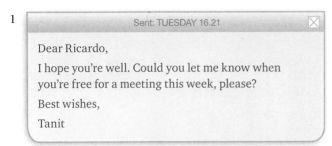

Sent: TUESDAY 16.21

Dear Ricardo,

I hope you're well. Could you let me know when you're free for a meeting this week, please?

Best wishes,

Tanit

2
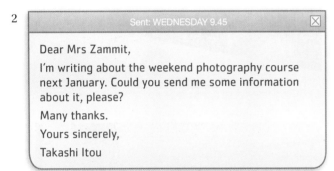

Sent: WEDNESDAY 9.45

Dear Mrs Zammit,

I'm writing about the weekend photography course next January. Could you send me some information about it, please?

Many thanks.

Yours sincerely,

Takashi Itou

3
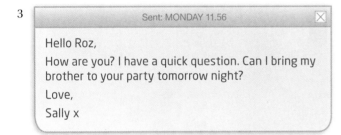

Sent: MONDAY 11.56

Hello Roz,

How are you? I have a quick question. Can I bring my brother to your party tomorrow night?

Love,

Sally x

a
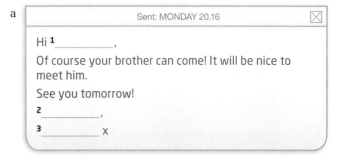

Sent: MONDAY 20.16

Hi **1**_____,

Of course your brother can come! It will be nice to meet him.

See you tomorrow!

2_____,

3_____ X

b
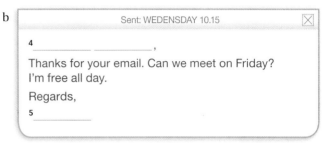

Sent: WEDENSDAY 10.15

4_____ _____,

Thanks for your email. Can we meet on Friday? I'm free all day.

Regards,

5_____

c
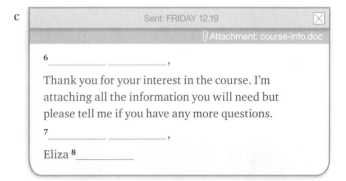

Sent: FRIDAY 12.19

Attachment: course-info.doc

6_____ _____,

Thank you for your interest in the course. I'm attaching all the information you will need but please tell me if you have any more questions.

7_____ _____,

Eliza **8**_____

9a Work with a partner. Look again at emails 1–3. How well do the people know each other?

b Complete the gaps in emails a–c with names and phrases. Use the Language for writing box to help you.

LANGUAGE FOR WRITING
opening and closing an email

FORMAL	*Dear Mr/Mrs/Ms/Miss* Gulzar, *Yours sincerely,*
	Dear Patricia, *Best wishes,/Regards,*
INFORMAL	*Hi/Hello* Johan, *All the best,/Love,*

10a TASK Look at requests 1–3. Choose one of them and write a short email. Decide how well you know the person you are writing to.

1 ask a colleague to go for lunch

2 ask a hotel about a car park

3 ask another student to join your study group

b Swap emails with a partner and write a reply.

c Return your email to your partner. Are the phrases for opening and closing the email correct?

3.5 Video

An Iranian doctor in the USA

1a Work with a partner. Think of three jobs where people help others. How do they help people?

b Look at the photos. Which of these things do you see in them?

> bed degree doctor hospital laptop medicine
> nurse patient phone pillow reception university

c Would you like to work as a doctor or a nurse? Why/Why not?

2 ▶ Watch the video. What do times and numbers 1–8 refer to?

1	1,000	5	7.30 a.m.
2	36,000	6	midday
3	2001	7	three times a day
4	6.30 a.m.	8	9 p.m.

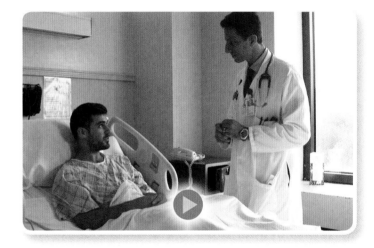

3 ▶ Watch the video again and complete the sentences.

a Arash Fazl is a _____ in neurology at Mount Sinai Hospital.

b He is from _____ but he lives in _____ now.

c He is a _____ doctor in his last year.

d He moved to the USA in 2001 because he wanted _____.

e Arash Fazl has a PhD from Boston _____.

f When he visits his patients, he discusses their illnesses and the _____ they need.

g At lunchtime he doesn't eat a lot because he _____.

h His days are always _____.

i Mount Sinai is _____ all over the world.

j He enjoys his job because every day he _____ and can really _____ their lives.

4a **TASK** You are going to have a discussion about jobs. Choose a job and make notes about how important this job is and how you help other people.

b Work in groups of 4–6 students. Imagine you are all travelling on a ship together. There is a problem, the boat is going down, and one of you must jump into the sea to save the others. Take turns to explain ...

- why you can't jump
- what will happen if you do not return
- why people in your town need you

Review

1a Complete phrases 1–6 with a word from the box.

> retired   office   uniform   meetings   student   hours

1 work in an _____   4 wear a _____
2 have a lot of _____   5 work long _____
3 be a _____   6 be _____

b Make questions with the phrases in exercise **1**.
Do you have a lot of meetings?

c Work with a partner. Take turns to ask and answer your questions in exercise **1b** and give more information.
A *Do you have a lot of meetings?*
B *Yes, I do. I have meetings every day.*

2a Match questions 1–6 to answers a–f.
1 Where do you work?
2 What time do you start work?
3 What do you wear at work?
4 Why do you enjoy your job?
5 Who do you speak to at work?
6 How often do you work from home?

a A uniform, so everyone knows what I do.
b I speak to my customers, of course!
c I work in a hospital.
d Every day! I only need my computer.
e We usually start at about 10 p.m.
f Because I go to a different country every month.

b Work with a partner. What jobs do you think the people in exercise **2a** do? Explain your guesses to your partner.
I think the person in 1 is a nurse because he works in a hospital.

3a Answer questions 1–7 using jobs from the box. There may be more than one possible answer.

> businessmen/businesswomen   chefs   cleaners   dentists
> hairdressers   journalists   mechanics   musicians   nurses
> pilots   photographers   students

Who …
1 earns a lot of money?   5 works in a factory?
2 works long hours?   6 has a lot of colleagues?
3 works from home?   7 works part-time?
4 has a boss?

I think cleaners work long hours.
I don't think nurses work long hours.

b Work in small groups. Talk about your answers to exercise **3a**. Do you all agree?

4a **3.18** Listen to six definitions and write the correct -er words.
1 *teacher*   3 _____   5 _____
2 _____   4 _____   6 _____

b Write three questions using the words from exercise **4a**.
What time do teachers finish work?

c Work with a partner. Take turns to ask and answer your questions in exercise **4b**.

5a Complete each gap with *I* or *you* to make requests.
1 Can _____ help me with the photocopier, please?
2 Could _____ leave early today, please?
3 Can _____ give me your number, please?
4 Could _____ write your name here, please?
5 Could _____ ask a question?
6 Can _____ use your phone for a moment, please?

b Work with a partner. Take turns to make the requests in exercise **5a** and answer them.

work freelance   earn   retired   meeting   photographer   chef   work long hours   businessman   unemployed   cleaner   nurse   pilot   journalist   musician   hairdresser   boss   student   work from home   dentist   office   uniform   colleagues   mechanic   salary   work part-time

4.1 Underground towns

Vocabulary & Reading | places in a town

1 Work with a partner. Look at the title of the article and the photos from a place called Coober Pedy. Do you think the sentences are true (T) or false (F)?

1 This place is in the USA.
2 People work underground.
3 People live in normal houses.
4 It's a popular place for tourists to visit.

2 Read the article about Coober Pedy. Check your answers to exercise **1**.

3 Work with a partner. Where can you do 1–7 in Coober Pedy? Use the words in **bold** from the article. You can use each word more than once.

1 eat   *restaurants*
2 buy things
3 stay
4 visit
5 go in your free time
6 find information about the town
7 travel to/from

4a Work with a partner. Match the words in the box to illustrations 1–6.

chemist   cinema   hairdresser's   hospital
library   theatre

b Work with a partner. What other places in a town do you know?

COOBER PEDY
THE UNDERGROUND TOWN

a room in a house in Coober Pedy   opal earrings

Coober Pedy is a very small town in Australia. It's very hot and it hardly ever rains. There's no water and there aren't many trees, but near Coober Pedy, there are opals under the ground – lots of them! Coober Pedy is the opal capital of the world.

A lot of the people in Coober Pedy work in the opal mines*. The mines are underground and the houses are underground too because it's cool down there. The houses are very comfortable but they don't have windows or gardens. There are underground **shops** and **restaurants**, and there's also an underground **swimming pool**. A lot of tourists come to Coober Pedy to visit the underground buildings – some of these buildings are more than 100 years old. There are four or five **hotels** and there's also a **campsite** where visitors can stay. There's a **museum** about the history of the town and a big **tourist information centre**. The **roads** to Coober Pedy are good and there's an **airport**, but there isn't a **railway station**.

■ **mines** very big holes in the ground where people work to get things like coal, gold or diamonds

PRONUNCIATION word stress

5a Work with a partner. Say the words aloud and (circle) the stressed syllable.

> airport campsite chemist hairdresser's hospital
> hotel library museum railway station restaurant
> swimming pool theatre

b 4.1))) Listen, check and repeat.

6a Choose three places you think are *very* important in a town, three places you think are *quite* important, and three places you think are *not* important.

b Work with a partner. Compare your choices and give reasons.

    A *Theatres aren't important for me because I never go there.*

    B *Really? For me, they're very important because I love seeing plays.*

Listening & Grammar *there is/there are*

7 4.2))) Amir and Farah Badawi from Malaysia are in a hotel in Coober Pedy. Listen to their conversation with the receptionist. Tick (✓) the places they talk about.

1	shop	5	tourist information centre
2	museum	6	theatre
3	cinema	7	restaurant
4	chemist	8	swimming pool

8a Work with a partner. Complete parts of the conversation in exercise **7** with the words in the box.

> there is are isn't aren't

  1 **A** _____ _____ a swimming pool?

      B No, I'm sorry, _____ _____. It doesn't rain a lot here, so _____ _____ many swimming pools.

  2 **A** _____ _____ any museums near the centre?

      B Yes, _____ _____. There's the opal mine museum.

  3 **A** _____ _____ a theatre in Coober Pedy?

      B No, _____ _____ any theatres here.

b 4.3))) Listen and check your answers.

c Work with a partner. Take turns to practise the parts of the conversation.

9 Read examples 1–6 and match them to the correct form in the Grammar focus box.

  1 There aren't any theatres here.

  2 There isn't a swimming pool at the hotel.

  3 There are some nice restaurants in the town centre.

  4 And is there a cinema near the hotel?

  5 Are there any underground buildings we can visit?

  6 There's an opal museum near the centre.

GRAMMAR FOCUS *there is/there are*

(+) *There's* + *a/an* + singular noun (_6_)
    There are + *some* + plural noun (__)

(–) *There isn't* + *a/an* + singular noun (__)
    There aren't + *any* + plural noun (__)

(?) *Is there* + *a/an* + singular noun? (__)
    Are there + *any* + plural noun? (__)

→ **Grammar Reference** page 142

10 Complete the text about another underground town, RÉSO, with the correct forms of *there is/are*. Use the symbols (+/–/?) to help you.

> The underground city of RÉSO is in Montreal in Canada. **1** _There are_ (+) 30 kilometres of tunnels. **2** _____ (+) also forty cinemas and 1,700 shops. **3** _____ (–) an underground campsite like in Coober Pedy, but **4** _____ (+) lots of hotels and 200 restaurants if you want to eat out. **5** _____ (–) any schools but **6** _____ (+) some universities. **7** _____ (?) an airport in RÉSO? No, **8** _____ (–), but **9** _____ (+) seven underground stations, two train stations and a bus station. Don't worry if you get lost – **10** _____ (+) always someone to help you because about half a million people use the city every day.

11 **TASK** Work with a partner. Take turns to ask and answer questions about Bruges in Belgium or Krakow in Poland. Student A, turn to page 127. Student B, turn to page 132.

4.2 Where I live

Vocabulary & Speaking

rooms, furniture and prepositions of place

1a Complete the information about yourself.

I live in a ... (*house/flat*).

I live with ...

In my house/flat, there is/are ... (*a kitchen, a living room, a bathroom, a dining room, three bedrooms, a toilet, an office*).

b Work with a partner. Tell them about where you live.

2 Match the prepositions in the box to the illustrations 1–8.

above   behind   between   in front of
next to   on   opposite   under

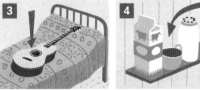
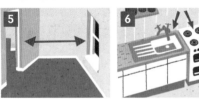
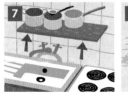

3 4.4))) Listen to Claire talking about her flat and answer the questions.

1 Where is the flat?

2 How many rooms are there?

4a Look at the illustrations and read Claire's description of her flat. Complete each gap with a different preposition from exercise **2**.

The flat's ¹_____ the 4th floor of a building ²_____ Delancey Street and Grand Street. The building is ³_____ a 24-hour garage and ⁴_____ an Indian restaurant, so there are always lots of cars and people in the street. The cars are quite noisy.

It's a studio flat with only one room. My bed is on a shelf ⁵_____ the kitchen. The toilet and shower are ⁶_____ the shelf. In the kitchen there's a sink, a fridge, and a cooker, but there isn't a dishwasher or a washing machine – I go to the launderette on Grand Street to wash clothes. ⁷_____ the window, there's a red carpet on the floor and there's an armchair and table with a television on it. From the window, I can see the East River. It's ⁸_____ the building.

b 4.5))) Listen and check your answers.

5 Look at Claire's description again and find words to match these definitions.

1 It's above the kitchen. Claire sleeps in it.

2 Claire sits on it to watch TV.

3 Claire washes things in the kitchen in it.

4 It's in the kitchen. It has food in it.

5 Claire goes to the launderette because she doesn't have this.

6 It's in the kitchen. Claire cooks food on it.

7 It's on the floor in front of the window.

8 It's under the shelf. Claire washes there.

6 Work with a partner. Ask questions and describe your studio flat to your partner to find seven differences. Student A, turn to page 127. Student B, turn to page 132.

Grammar & Speaking articles *a/an, the, –*

7a Look at the highlighted words and phrases in the text in exercise **4a** and complete the Grammar focus box with *a/an*, *the* or – (no article).

> **GRAMMAR FOCUS** articles *a/an*, *the* or no article
>
> Before nouns we can use *a/an* or *the* or no article (–).
>
> • The first time we describe one person/thing, we usually use
>   ¹_____ or ²_____. We use ³_____ before
>   consonant sounds, e.g. *red carpet*, *university* and ⁴_____
>   before vowel sounds, e.g. *Indian restaurant*, *hour*.
> • The first time we describe people or things using a plural
>   noun, we usually use ⁵_____.
> • We usually use ⁶_____ with singular or plural nouns, to
>   say 'you know which one(s) I mean':
>   • because we have already talked about it/them
>   • because there is only one, e.g. *4th floor*
> • We usually use ⁷_____ with the names of cities,
>   countries and streets (but: *the UK*, *the USA*).
>
> → Grammar Reference page 143

b Add more highlighted words and phrases from exercise **4a** for each rule.

8a Read what Claire says about the part of New York where she lives. Choose the correct option.

> It's very difficult to find ¹_____ (*a/an*) flat
> in ²_____ (*the/–*) New York. I'm very lucky. I like
> my flat because it's in ³_____ (*the/–*) centre of
> the city. There are ⁴_____ (*the/–*) shops and
> restaurants all around me. The Lower East Side
> isn't the best district in the city but my flat is near
> a theatre and it's also near ⁵_____ (*the/–*) East
> River and ⁶_____ (*the/a*) small park. One of the
> things I don't like about my flat is that there isn't
> ⁷_____ (*a/the*) lift. Also, unfortunately I'm not
> near ⁸_____ (*a/the*) underground station, but
> there's ⁹_____ (*a/the*) bus stop opposite
> ¹⁰_____ (*a/the*) door of my building.

b 4.6))) Listen and check your answers.

9a **4.7**))) Listen to sentences 1–3 from the text in exercise **8**. Notice the stressed words and the schwa /ə/ sound on *a/an* and *the* before nouns beginning with a consonant sound.

1 It's in the centre of the city.
       /ə/   /ə/

2 It's near a theatre.
           /ə/

3 It's difficult to find a flat.
                        /ə/

b **4.8**))) Listen to sentences 1–3. Underline the schwa /ə/ sounds.

1 I live in a flat.
2 My flat is on the 5th floor.
3 There's a supermarket opposite my house.

c **4.8**))) Listen again and repeat.

10a Make questions from the prompts.

1 live / house / flat ? *Do you live in a house or a flat?*
2 which / floor / live on ?
3 how many / rooms / there / in / house or flat ?
4 what / opposite / your house or flat ?
5 which / your / favourite room ?
6 why / like it ?

b Work with a partner. Take turns to ask and answer the questions in exercise **10a**.

11 **TASK** Work with a partner. Describe your favourite room.
There's an armchair next to my bed.

▶ VOX POPS VIDEO 4

4.3 Vocabulary and skills development

Reading & Speaking pronoun referencing

1 Work in small groups. Look at the photos and answer the questions.

1 How many things in the photos can you name?

2 Which desk do you prefer? Why?

2 Read the information in the Unlock the code box about pronoun referencing.

> ### 🔓 UNLOCK THE CODE
> pronoun referencing
>
> The first time we talk about a thing or person we usually use the noun. After that we often refer to it using a pronoun because we don't want to repeat the same noun.
>
> Where's my **pen**? I can't find *it*.
> *it* = **pen**
>
> **My grandparents** are French. *They* live in Paris.
> *They* = **my grandparents**

3 the word in each sentence that the highlighted word refers to.

1 My bedroom is very big, but I share it with my sister.

2 His things are all on the floor. He never tidies them.

3 We've got two big armchairs in the living room – they're really comfortable.

4 That's a beautiful picture. Where did you get it?

5 Our house is quite small, but I really like it.

6 **A** Are those your keys?
  B No, they're yours.

4 Read the website forum. Write the thing or person that the highlighted word refers to.

1 they (line 3) = _____

2 it (line 4) = _____

3 they (line 4) = _____

4 They (line 14) = _____

5 them (line 16) = _____

> ### Are you a tidy worker or a messy worker? What's on your desk? Write and tell us.
>
> Yesterday 15:23 ☑ ☒ ⤴
> Officegirl94: I'm a very messy person. My colleagues think my desk's really terrible; they can't believe all the things that are on it! Are you ready? Here they are: batteries, scissors, five or six magazines,   5 about ten pens and pencils, a clock, a bottle of water, an apple, a cup, books, envelopes and a cheese sandwich! Oh, and my computer.
>
> Today 11:35 ☑ ☒ ⤴
> Netguy: Wow Officegirl94! A cheese   10 sandwich on your desk? Ugh! For me, a messy place is difficult to work in. I need a big desk to work on. The only things on my desk are a computer and a printer. They're both new and expensive, so I like to keep 15 them very clean.

5 Read another reply from the website. Use the highlighted words to help you answer questions 1–7.

1 Which two rooms are never clean?
2 Who never does any cleaning?
3 Who doesn't want to come and see Mala?
4 What's not expensive?
5 Who's good fun?
6 What's on Mala's desk?
7 What does Mala keep in the cupboard with her computer?

> Today 11:35
>
> **Homeworker 77:** I'm Mala. I live in a shared house with four other students and it's always messy. I share a kitchen and bathroom. They're never clean because my housemates are very lazy. They never do any cleaning. My friends think the house is awful and they don't want to visit me. But it's a cheap place to live and I like my housemates – they're fun! My bedroom is different to the rest of the house. I work from home, so I keep everything tidy and organised in there. My desk's perfect – there's nothing on it! I only have one or two books on my desk when I'm working, but I put them in the cupboard with my laptop when I finish my work. I hate mess! Hmmm, maybe I do need to move house!

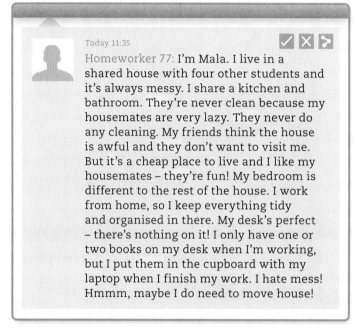

6 Work with a partner. Describe your office or flat/house. Don't repeat any nouns – use pronouns instead.

My kitchen's always messy. I only wash dishes when I need to use them.

Vocabulary & Speaking opposite adjectives

7 Work with a partner. Underline the adjectives in the two forum posts in exercise **4**.
I'm a very messy person.

8a Read the information in the Vocabulary focus box about opposite adjectives.

> **VOCABULARY FOCUS** opposite adjectives
>
> Many adjectives have opposites. Dictionaries often give you information about them. Learning words with their opposites increases your vocabulary, e.g.
> *messy/tidy   cheap/expensive   terrible/fantastic*

b Match adjectives 1–10 to their opposites a–j.

1 difficult   a short
2 big   b old
3 new   c bad
4 good   d light
5 clean   e modern
6 long   f small
7 heavy   g beautiful
8 quiet   h easy
9 ugly   i noisy
10 old-fashioned   j dirty

c 4.9))) Listen, check and repeat.

9 Work in small groups. Which adjectives in exercise **8b** can you use to talk about …

1 a bag?   3 a person?
2 a building?   4 a restaurant?

10a **TASK** Choose words from exercises **8a** and **8b** to complete the questions about your home and where you live.

1 Do you live in a big or a _____ flat/house?
2 Is it modern or _____?
3 Is your furniture mostly new or _____?
4 Is it usually tidy or _____?
5 Is your road quiet or _____?
6 Is it in a cheap or an _____ part of town?
7 Is your journey to work/college/your English lesson _____ or _____?

b Work in small groups. Take turns to ask and answer the questions. Ask for more information and use pronouns instead of nouns if possible.

A *My road's quite noisy.*
B *Why?*
A *It's very busy. There are a lot of buses and cars.*

4.4 Speaking and writing

Listening & Speaking
asking for and giving directions

1 Susan Melba is visiting the town of Ubud on the Indonesian island of Bali. Work with a partner and find the places from the box on the map.

bank	bookshop	chemist	internet café	market	palace
police station	post office	supermarket	Susan's hotel		

2 Work with a partner. Use the table and the map to help you make sentences about Ubud.

There's a (place)	next to/opposite/in front of/near/ behind the (place).
The (place) 's/is	between the (place) and the (place).
	on (street/road).

There's a police station near the supermarket.
The bookshop is on Ubud Main Road.

3 Match places and directions 1–10 to illustrations a–j.

1 on the right
2 take the first left
3 on the left
4 go straight on
5 take the second right
6 go past
7 turn left
8 on the corner
9 at the end of
10 turn right

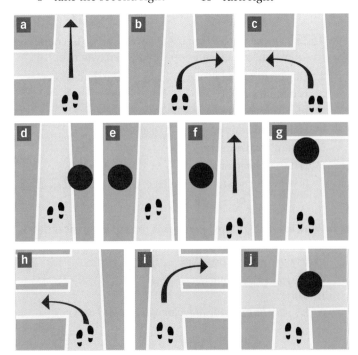

🏛 ◄ Palace	🛒 ◄ Supermarket	👮 ◄ Police Station
🍎 ◄ Market	@ ◄ Internet Café	✉ ◄ Post Office
📖 ◄ Bookshop	$ ◄ Bank	✚ ◄ Chemist

4a 4.10 ⟫ Susan asks Alan at reception for directions. Listen and tick (✓) the places in exercise **1** that she asks directions to.

b 4.10 ⟫ Listen to the conversation again. Use the words and phrases in the box to complete the gaps.

corner	end	Excuse	get	left	near	on	past
straight	where's						

1 _____ me, could you give me some directions, please?
2 Is there a chemist _____ here?
3 How do I _____ there?
4 Go out of the main door and turn left. Then go to the _____ of the road and turn left again.
5 Go _____ on for about five minutes.
   Go _____ the internet café and the bank, and then turn _____ into Raya Andong.
   It's _____ the left, next to the supermarket.
6 OK, thanks. Oh, and _____ the palace?
7 That's easy. It's at the end of this road on the _____ .

c Compare your answers with a partner.

5a Work with a partner. Put the words in the correct order.

1 Excuse / there / is / a bank / here / near / me, ?

2 me, / the library / where's / Excuse ?

3 to the post office / me, / how / Excuse / get / do I ?

4 past / Go / café / the .

5 the / It's / left / on .

6 into / right / Turn / Albert Street .

7 the / Take / right / second .

8 straight / Go / about / for / on / minutes / ten .

9 the end / Go / this / of / to / street .

10 on / It's / corner / the .

b **4.11**))) Listen, check and repeat.

6a You are in the police station in Ubud. Choose three places on the map.

b Work with a partner. Take turns to ask for and give directions. Use the Language for speaking box to help you.

A *Excuse me, is there a bookshop near here?*

B *Yes, go out of the door and turn left …*

LANGUAGE FOR SPEAKING
directions

Asking for directions
Excuse me, where's the …?
How do I get to the …?
Is there a … near here?

Giving directions
Turn left/right (into …).
Take the first/second/third left/right.
Go straight on/to the end of this street/past the …
It's on the left/on the right/on the corner/at the end of the road.

7 Take turns to ask for and give directions around Denpasar in Bali. Student A, turn to page 128. Student B, turn to page 133.

Reading & Writing imperatives

8 Susan has booked a tour to visit caves and temples in Bali. Read the tour organizer's email and answer the questions.

1 Where does the tour leave from?

2 What time does the tour bus leave?

3 What does she need to take with her?

Subject: Caves and temples tour

Hello everyone,

Welcome to Bali! Here are the instructions for tomorrow's tour. The tour bus leaves from in front of the Ubud Village Hotel in the city centre at 10 a.m. Please <u>arrive</u> by 9.30 a.m. <u>Bring</u> the booking form and your passport with you.

<u>Wear</u> comfortable shoes for the walk and <u>take</u> a hat or scarf to wear on your head when we go inside the temples. Please <u>don't take</u> photographs inside the temple. Finally, <u>don't forget</u> to bring some money to tip the bus driver.

See you all tomorrow!

Best wishes,

Kusuma

---

9 Look at all <u>underlined</u> verbs in the email and read the information in the Language for writing box.

LANGUAGE FOR WRITING imperatives

- We use the imperative to tell people what to do, and to give orders, instructions and directions.
- The imperative uses the infinitive without *to*, e.g. **Take** a hat.
- We make the negative with *don't/do not* + infinitive without *to*, e.g. **Don't forget** your passport.

10 Work with a partner. Complete the instructions for tourists in Bali with the correct form of the verbs in the box.

| bring drink learn leave not drink not use smile |

1 _____ a sunhat. It's very hot in Bali.

2 _____ when you speak to people.

3 _____ some words in the local language.

4 _____ your left hand to give or pass things.

5 _____ water from the tap. _____ water from bottles.

6 _____ your shoes at the door when you go into someone's house.

11a **TASK** Write a similar email to the one in exercise **8**. Turn to page 128 and read the instructions.

b Read your partner's email and answer the questions.

1 Does it include all the information you need?

2 Does your partner use imperatives correctly?

4.5　Video

Almas Tower

1　Work with a partner. Look at the photos. Which of these things can you see in them?

> basement　car park　diamond　facilities　glass　gold
> ground floor　jewellery　lake　pearl　shops　skyscraper
> tower　wonderful view

2　▶ Watch the video about the Almas Tower. Choose the correct option. Sometimes more than one answer is possible.

1　The Almas Tower is the tallest *business tower / hotel / shopping centre* in the Middle East.
2　The Almas Tower is *in the sea / on an island / in a lake*.
3　The Almas Tower is *one large tower / two towers joined together / four towers joined together*.
4　The outside of the Almas Tower is *metal / glass / plastic*.
5　Dubai's *pearl / gold / diamond* exchange is in the Almas Tower.
6　*Harley Davidson / Toyota / Ford* has its head office in the building.
7　The Almas Tower has *offices / restaurants / hairdressers*.
8　At the top of the tower there is a *car park / viewing area / five-star restaurant*.

3　▶ Watch the video again. What do the numbers refer to?

a　360 　　　　　d　48
b　68 　　　　　e　1,700
c　66

4a　TASK　Work in small groups. Your office/school is going to receive some English-speaking visitors. You are going to take them to a famous or unusual building in your town. Think about and prepare notes on …
- why the building is important (age, purpose, etc.)
- where the building is located
- what is inside the building (facilities, offices, etc.)
- why it is interesting to visitors
- how to get to the building

b　Share your ideas with the class and choose the best building.

Review

1a Complete the gaps in the interview about Neft Daşhlari in Azerbaijan with the correct form of *there is* or *there are*.

an oil platform

A What's special about Neft Daşhlari?
B It's a town on an oil platform in the Caspian Sea.
A A town in the sea? Is it very small?
B No, not really. ¹_____ 300 km of streets and 2,000 people. And ²_____ lots of things to do.
A Really? ³_____ any restaurants?
B Of course! ⁴_____ some nice restaurants and hotels, and ⁵_____ a cinema and a park, too.
A What about education? ⁶_____ a school?
B Yes, ⁷_____ a school but ⁸_____ a university.
A So can people visit the place?
B No, ⁹_____ any tourists. Only people who work on Neft Daşhlari can go there.

b **4.12**))) Listen and check your answers.

c Work with a partner. Practise the interview.

2a Choose the correct option in (brackets).

> I'm from ¹___(–/the) Madrid, ²___(a/the) capital of ³___(the/–) Spain. I live in ⁴___(a/the) flat in ⁵___(–/the) centre. It's ⁶___(the/a) nice area. There are restaurants and cafés, and there's ⁷___(a/an) art gallery. There's also ⁸___(an/–) underground station opposite my flat.

b Write a similar text about the place where you live.

c Work with a partner. Read each other's texts. What is similar and what is different?

3a **4.13**))) Listen to seven descriptions and write the names of the places.

b Write similar descriptions for three more places in a town and read them to a partner. Can they guess the places?

4 Which room in the house can you find these things in? Think of two more things for each room and compare with a partner.

> armchair   bed   dishwasher   shower

5a **4.14**))) Listen and write the opposite of each adjective.

b Use adjectives from the box to make sentences 1–5 true for you. Compare your answers with a partner.

> big   cheap   difficult   easy   expensive   fantastic
> modern   new   noisy   old   old-fashioned   quiet   small

1 I live in a _____ town.
2 It's _____ to find a flat in my town.
3 Where I live, public transport is _____ .
4 My house/flat is (very) _____ .
5 The furniture in my house/flat is _____ .

6a Look at the map. You are at the station. Complete the conversation and write the place in the gap.

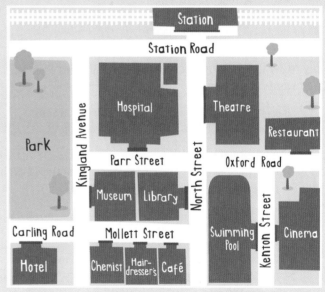

A Excuse me. Is there a _____ near here?
B Yes, there is. Turn right onto Station Road, then take the first left. That's Kingland Avenue. Go past Parr Street and the museum, and it's on the corner of Kingland Avenue and Mollett Street, opposite the hotel.

b Work with a partner. Look at the map again.

Student A
Ask for directions from the hotel to:
1 the swimming pool   3 the café
2 the theatre

Student B
Ask for directions from the station to:
1 the cinema   3 the hairdresser's
2 the restaurant

Clothes and shopping

5.1 Shopping

GOALS ■ Talk about shopping ■ Use *can* and *could* to talk about possibility and ability

Vocabulary & Speaking shopping

1 Work in small groups. Read what three people say about shopping. Which is most true for you? Give more information.

> I don't like shopping. It's boring.

> I love shopping and I go all the time.

> I only shop when I need something.

2a Work with a partner. Complete the sentences with the words in the box.

> baker's butcher's cash discount newsagent's
> online return sales shopping centre spend

1 I buy bread from the _____.
2 I _____ a lot of money at the weekends.
3 I buy magazines and newspapers from the _____.
4 I buy meat from the _____.
5 I do a lot of my shopping _____.
6 I get a _____ because I'm a student.
7 I go shopping to a _____. I prefer them to small shops.
8 When I buy something I don't like, I _____ it to the shop.
9 I stand outside and wait for the shops to open on the first day of the _____.
10 I pay for small things with _____.

b 5.1))) Listen and check your answers.

3a Add *never, sometimes, often, usually* and *always* to the sentences in exercise **2a** to make them true for you. Compare your answers with a partner.

b Work with a different partner. Tell them about you and your first partner.

We are similar because we both shop online.
We are different because I always pay cash, but Maria doesn't.

Listening & Grammar *can/can't/could/couldn't*

4a Work with a partner. Look at the photo of a shopping street in a British town in the 1970s. How do you think shopping was different in the 1970s?

b 5.2))) Listen to a woman talking about shopping in the town today and in the 1970s and check your ideas in exercise **4a**.

5 5.2))) Listen again and put the phrases into the correct columns in the table. Compare your answers with a partner.

- talk to people in shops
- shop online
- ask for information
- buy everything in one shop
- buy bread/meat/newspapers on the high street
- have a cup of coffee on the high street

	1970s	Now
Possible	*talk to people in shops*	*shop online*
Impossible		

6 Work with a partner. Look at sentences 1–4 from the listening and complete the rules in the Grammar focus box.

1 Today you can buy most things online.
2 The internet can't cut your hair.
3 In the 1970s, you could talk to people in the shops.
4 In the 1970s, you couldn't get a cup of coffee in the town centre.

GRAMMAR FOCUS *can/can't/could/couldn't*

- We use **1**_____ (positive) and **2**_____ (negative) to talk about ability and possibility <u>in the present</u>.
- We use **3**_____ (positive) and **4**_____ (negative) to talk about ability and possibility <u>in the past</u>.
- We use *can/can't/could/couldn't* with the **5**_____ form of the verb, without *to*.

→ Grammar Reference page 144

7a Work with a partner. Complete the questions in the Shopping Quiz with *can* or *could*.

Shopping then and now

1 _____ people buy things online in 1994?

2 In the 1990s, _____ rich people buy trips into space?

3 _____ you buy eggs from vending machines in Japan today?

4 _____ you buy a bottle of rainwater for $11 these days?

5 _____ you use euros in Norway and Sweden?

6 _____ people buy things from machines in 1890?

7 In the 1960s, _____ you buy petrol at supermarkets?

8 _____ you buy clothes online from all the big fashion companies?

■ **vending machines** machines from which you can buy snacks, drinks, etc.

b Answer questions 1–8 in the Shopping Quiz. Compare your answers with a partner.

PRONUNCIATION *can*

5.3))) In positive sentences and questions *can* is pronounced /kən/.
A *Can you use euros in Norway and Sweden?*
B *I think you can use euros in Sweden, but not in Norway.*
In short answers *can* is pronounced /kæn/.
Yes, you can.

8a **5.4**))) Listen to three students discussing a question from exercise **7a**.
A *Can you use euros in Norway and Sweden?*
B *Yes, you **can**.*
C *I think you **can** use them in Sweden, but not in Norway.*

b **5.4**))) Listen again and repeat.

9a Work in small groups. Take turns to ask and answer the questions in exercise **7a** and give reasons.
A *Could people buy things online in 1994?*
B *Yes, (maybe) they could.*
C *No, they couldn't because …*

b **5.5**))) Listen and check your answers. How many did you get correct? Which of the answers surprised you?

10 **TASK** Work with a partner. Talk about the ideas from the list using *can/can't/could/couldn't*.
A *Children could play outside in the past, but now they can't.*
B *Yes, they can!*

- children play outside
- book holidays online
- buy clothes in a supermarket
- buy things with a credit card
- children walk to school
- drink water from the tap
- drive in the town centre
- get cash from a cash machine abroad
- get cash when you buy something
- spend euros

5.2 What is he wearing?

Vocabulary & Speaking clothes and accessories

1a Work with a partner. Write down ten items of clothing.

b Compare your answers with another pair.

2 Read texts 1–4 and match them to illustrations a–d.

1 Vera is at a wedding. She is wearing a blue **dress**, gold **jewellery** and a **hat**. She is also wearing designer **shoes**.

2 Beatrice is wearing these clothes because she's outside and it's raining. She's wearing a **coat** and has a big **scarf** round her neck. She has a **hat** on her head and **gloves** on her hands and she's carrying an umbrella.

3 Anita and Paul are having a meeting with their boss. Paul is wearing a suit (**jacket** and **trousers** which go together) and a tie. Anita is wearing a skirt and **top** and her reading **glasses**.

4 Leila and Mike are relaxing at home because they aren't working today. Leila is wearing **jeans** and a **hoodie** and Mike is wearing **shorts** and a **T-shirt**. On his feet, he is wearing **socks** and **trainers**.

3 Work with a partner. Which things in **bold** in exercise **2** do people usually wear …

1 on their feet/hands?
2 outside only?
3 to do sport?
4 in cold weather?
5 in hot weather?
6 to a job interview?
7 to exercise?
8 to relax?

Grammar & Speaking present continuous

4a Work with a partner. Look at the sentences 1–3 and complete the information in the Grammar focus box.

1 Paul is wearing a suit.
2 Anita and Paul are having a meeting with their boss.
3 They aren't working today.

GRAMMAR FOCUS present continuous

We use the present continuous to talk about things happening at or around this moment.

(+)	I	'm/am	
	You/We/They	're/[1] _____	doing.
	He/She/It	's/[2] _____	
(−)	I	'm not/am not	
	You/We/They	[3] _____/are not	doing.
	He/She/It	isn't/is not	
(?)	What am	I	
	are	you/we/they	doing?
	[4] _____	he/she/it	

→ Grammar Reference page 145

b 5.6))) Listen to the sentences in exercise **4a** and repeat.

5 Work with a partner. Underline four more examples of the present continuous in the texts in exercise **2**.

6a TASK Write two positive and two negative sentences about other people in the classroom. Do not write their names.
He's wearing a yellow jacket.
She isn't wearing blue trousers.

b Work with a partner. Read out your sentences and guess who your partner is talking about.

Grammar & Listening

present continuous or present simple

7a Work with a partner. Look at the title of the podcast and try to match photos a–e to the words in the box.

serious　fun　strong　tidy　peaceful

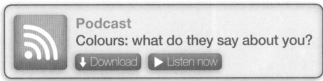

Podcast
Colours: what do they say about you?
↓ Download　▶ Listen now

b 5.7))) Listen and check your ideas.

8 5.7))) Listen again and complete the sentences in the table. Check your answers with a partner.

Favourite colour	What it says about you
black	You like to be the ¹_____ . It can make you look serious and ²_____ .
white	You enjoy a simple life and like things to be tidy and ³_____ .
blue	You are a peaceful person and you don't like ⁴_____ .
red	You are probably ⁵_____ person and you ⁶_____ hard at everything you do.
yellow	You love ⁷_____ and you are a lot of ⁸_____ .

9 Work with a partner. Read the examples in the Grammar focus box and answer the questions.

a　*You always try hard at everything you do.*
b　*I'm wearing white today.*
1　Which sentence talks about actions happening at or around this moment?
2　Which sentence describes actions that happen all the time or regularly?

→ **Grammar Reference** page 145

10 Work in small groups. Answer the questions.
1　What colours do you usually wear? What colours are you wearing at the moment?
2　Are there any colours you don't like for clothes? Why?
3　Do you agree with what the podcast says about your favourite colours?

11a Mike (M) calls Leila (L) when she's out shopping. Read the conversation and choose the correct verb form.

L　Hello?
M　Where are you?
L　I'm in a clothes shop. Why?
M　Because I need your help. What ¹ *do you do / are you doing*?
L　What ² *do I do / am I doing*? What ³ *do people usually do / are people usually doing* in clothes shops? I ⁴ *buy / 'm buying* clothes, of course.
M　Well, are you nearly finished? I ⁵ *try / 'm trying* to cook a meal for six people and the kids ⁶ *make / are making* a lot of noise and the dog ⁷ *runs / 's running* around and …
L　Why are the kids there? They ⁸ *go / are going* to tennis practice on Thursdays.
M　Not today because it ⁹ *rains / 's raining*. They ¹⁰ *never play / are never playing* in the rain.
L　OK, I ¹¹ *pay / 'm paying* now. I'll be back in an hour.
M　An hour? Why …

b 5.8))) Listen and check your answers.

12 **TASK** Work with a partner. Take turns to ask and answer questions to find the differences between two pictures. Student A, turn to page 128. Student B, turn to page 133.

▶ VOX POPS VIDEO 5

5.3 Vocabulary and skills development

GOALS ■ Understand similar vowel sounds ■ Use adjectives and adverbs

Listening & Speaking understanding similar vowel sounds

1 Work with a partner. Look at the photos. What do you think the 'virtual mirror' is?

2 **5.9**))) Listen to three pairs of words from a radio programme about the virtual mirror. Is the vowel sound in each pair the same (S) or different (D)?

1 _____ 2 _____ 3 _____

3 **5.10**))) Read and listen to the information in the Unlock the code box about similar vowel sounds.

🔓 **UNLOCK THE CODE**
understanding similar vowel sounds

• Vowel sounds can sound very similar to each other when you listen.

/æ/	/eɪ/	/e/
man	main	men
/ɒ/	/ʌ/	/əʊ/
not	nut	note
/e/	/ɪ/	/iː/
set	sit	seat

• Listening for the general meaning of the sentence can help you understand the correct word.

The ~~not~~/~~nut~~/note says 'Wait here'.

---

4 **5.11**))) Listen to six sentences and underline the correct word.

1 man / main / men
2 set / sit / seat
3 not / nut / note
4 mat / mate / met
5 red / rid / read
6 cot / cut / coat

5a **5.12**))) Listen to the words in the box and complete the lines.

hate	man	boat	shop	shut	cheap	eat	live
main	text	long	jeans	take	stand	press	sales
sells	tin	one	thing	page	not	note	coat

/æ/	*hat, …*		/əʊ/	*home, …*
/eɪ/	*play, …*		/e/	*set, …*
/ɒ/	*lot, …*		/ɪ/	*sit, …*
/ʌ/	*cut, …*		/iː/	*seat, …*

b **5.13**))) Listen, check and repeat.

6a **5.14**))) Listen to a radio programme about the virtual mirror. Tick (✓) the words from the box in exercise **5a** that you hear. Compare with a partner.

b **5.14**))) Listen again. Which five things in the list does the radio presenter do?

1 takes jeans to the changing rooms
2 presses a button to see all the jeans in the shop
3 presses a button to choose a pair of jeans
4 chooses ten pairs of jeans
5 sends a picture to Facebook
6 makes a note of the best jeans
7 pays for the jeans

c Compare your answers with a partner.

7 Work in small groups. Answer the questions.
1 Do you enjoy shopping for clothes? Why/Why not?
2 Do you think the virtual mirror is a good idea? Why/Why not?

Vocabulary & Speaking adjectives and adverbs

8a Work with a partner. Look at two sentences from the radio programme in exercise **6** and choose the correct options in 1 and 2.

… I leave **quickly**.   … I find the right jeans **easily**.

1   The **highlighted** words are adverbs. They describe …
    a an action   **b** a thing
2   We usually form adverbs with …
    a adjective + -ly   **b** verb + -ly

b Read the Vocabulary focus box about adjectives and adverbs, and check your answers.

> **VOCABULARY FOCUS** adjectives and adverbs
>
> • Adjectives describe people and things.
>   *He's a **quick** worker.*
>
> • Adverbs of manner tell us how something happens.
>   *He works quickly.*
>
> • Form:
>   1 Many adjectives can be changed into adverbs by using -ly/-ily, e.g. quick → **quickly**   easy → **easily**
>   2 Sometimes we do not add -ly/-ily to the adjective to make an adverb, e.g. hard → **hard**   late → **late**   fast → **fast**.
>   3 Some adverbs are irregular, e.g. good → **well**.

9 Are the words in **bold** in sentences 1–7 adjectives (adj) or adverbs (adv)?

1   He's a very **hard** worker. *adj*
2   She writes **well**.
3   This train often arrives **late**.
4   I like swimming, but I'm not a very **fast** swimmer.
5   Be **quick**! We're in a hurry.
6   Drive **safely**.
7   He speaks English **fluently**.

10 Work with a partner. Make adverbs from the adjectives and complete the table.

Adjectives	Adverbs
quiet	
careful	
clear	
dangerous	
good	
correct	
late	

11a Work with a partner. Complete the conversations using the adverbs from exercise **10**.

1   **A** How much money do you earn?
    B Not much, so I try to spend it _____ .
2   **A** What's the matter? Why do you look so scared?
    B Because you're driving _____ ! Be careful!
3   **A** Why are you talking so _____ ?
    B Shhhh! Because we're in the library!
4   **A** I always get up _____ at weekends.
    B Me too, at about 10 o'clock!
5   **A** I can't see the television _____ .
    B I think you need glasses.
6   **A** Maria answers every question _____ .
    B I know. She's the best student in the class.
7   **A** Did you do _____ in your exam?
    B I got an 'A'.

b 5.15))) Listen and check your answers. Take turns to practise the conversations with a partner.

12a **TASK** Work with a partner. Talk about things you, your family or your friends do …

| well   quickly   slowly   badly   carefully   quietly |

My husband drives carefully.

b Work with a different partner and compare.
    A *My boss always talks really quietly.*
    B *Really? My boss is very loud – she usually shouts at me!*

GOALS ■ **Buy things in a shop** ■ **Write an online product review**

Listening & Speaking   in a shop

1 Look at the photos. What kind of shops do they show? Label the things and people in the photos with words from the box.

> changing rooms   customer   shop assistant   till

2a **5.16**))) Listen to three conversations and match them to photos a–c.

b **5.16**))) Listen again. What is each customer buying?

3a Match questions 1–9 from the conversations to answers a–i.

1 Can I help you?
2 Do you need a bag?
3 Can I try this on, please?
4 Can I pay by card?
5 How much is this magazine?
6 Do you offer a student discount?
7 Would you like a receipt?
8 Do you sell batteries?
9 What time do you close?

a No, I'm afraid we only take cash.
b It's £4.99.
c Yes, we do. You get 20% off.
d At eight o'clock.
e No, thanks. I'm just looking.
f Yes, please. Just a small one.
g Yes, we do. What kind do you need?
h Of course. The changing rooms are over there.
i Yes, please. Just put it in the bag.

b **5.17**))) Listen and check your answers.

c Who says each line in exercise **3a**: the customer (C) or the shop assistant (SA)?

d Work with a partner. Practise the conversations in exercise **3a**.

4 **TASK** Work with a partner. You want to buy a small gift for someone. Take turns to be a customer and a shop assistant in a gift shop. Ask and answer questions about:
 • prices • discount • opening and closing times, etc.
Use the Language for speaking box to help you.

> **LANGUAGE FOR SPEAKING** in a shop
>
> *What time do you open/close (on Sundays)?*
> *Can I pay by card/have a receipt, please?*
> *Do you sell newspapers/offer a student discount?*
> *How much is this/are these shoes?*

Reading & Writing a product review

5 Work in small groups. Make a list of information you need to have before you decide to buy something (e.g. the price).

6a Read product reviews A and B and match them to photos 1 and 2. Would you like to buy either of these products? Why/Why not?

b Work with a partner. Look at the highlighted words and phrases in the reviews. Put them into the correct category.

   a cost 2

   b value for money

   c look

   d user-friendliness

   e delivery

   f writer's opinion/advice

7a Read the information in the Language for writing (1) box. Find a sentence in product review B with a list and underline it.

> ### LANGUAGE FOR WRITING (1) using commas in lists
>
> When three or more items are in a list, use commas before each item. Before the last item use *and*.
>
> *I ride it on the road, through fields, up hills* **and** *down mountains.*

b Work with a partner. Put the commas into sentences 1–3 and take out *and* where it is not necessary.

   1 My job is to open the shop and sell products and answer customers' questions.

   2 I use it for the internet and sending emails and doing homework and playing games.

   3 If you are looking for a machine that's fast and cheap and easy to use, then this is for you.

8 Read the information the Language for writing (2) box.

> ### LANGUAGE FOR WRITING (2) a product review
>
> When you write a product review, include information on price, look, quality, user-friendliness and delivery. Write what you think of the product, too.
> - It's *good/great/poor* value.
> - It's (not) worth *£100/the money*.
> - It's too *big/small/heavy/expensive*.
> - It looks *good/expensive/cheap*.
> - It's *easy/simple/hard/difficult* to use.
> - I (don't) recommend it.

1

2

★ ★ ★ ★ ★ 19 JUNE

A This is a great product and ¹ I recommend it to everyone. ² It's only £150 but ³ it looks expensive. I really like the fact that ⁴ it's light and very comfortable. I ride it on the road, through fields, up hills and down mountains, and it's no problem. In general, I think ⁵ it's great value. ⁶ It arrived very quickly too, on the day after I ordered it.

[RECOMMEND (35)]   [REPORT]

★ ☆ ☆ ☆ ☆ 14 JANUARY

B I'm sorry to say I'm very disappointed with this product. ⁷ It's big, awful and ⁸ very heavy, so I can't carry it. ⁹ It's also very difficult to use. So overall, ¹⁰ it's definitely not worth the money and it's very poor value. And ¹¹ it was nearly two weeks late. My advice is ¹² don't buy it.

[RECOMMEND (2)]   [REPORT]

9a **TASK** Work with a partner. Choose a product from the box to write a review about.

| phone computer/laptop clothes bike car |

   1 Decide if you want to write a good or bad review.

   2 Think about who you are writing it for and what information the reader needs to know about this type of product. Make a list of information you want to include.

b Write your product review. Use the Language for writing boxes to help you. Include a list and use commas.

c Work with a different pair and read each other's reviews. Would you like to buy the product they reviewed? Why/Why not?

5.5 Video

Camden Market

1 Work with a partner. Look at the photos. How do you think shopping in each place is different? Think about …
   - choice of products
   - shopping hours
   - prices
   - forms of payment
   - type of customer
   - quality

2 Complete sentences 1–6 with words from the box.

   fashion   high street   home-made   stall   stylish   vintage

   1 A … is a small shop or table in a street or market where people sell things.
   2 Something that is old, but high quality is called …
   3 A style that is popular.
   4 People make … products in their houses to sell.
   5 The … is the street where the most important shops, banks and businesses are.
   6 Something that is … attractive and of good quality.

3 ▶ Watch the video. Which items in the list did you see?

   double-decker bus   flag   hat   red letter box
   red telephone box   shoes   somebody swimming
   street café   sunglasses   umbrella

4 ▶ Watch the video again and choose the correct option.
   a Popular fashion in the UK is called *street fashion / high street fashion / popular clothes.*
   b People prefer shopping in Camden Market because they can find *cheaper clothes / clothes they can't find on the high street / the latest fashion.*
   c In the past Camden Lock sold *art and furniture / clothes / bread and cakes.*
   d All the speakers are wearing *something hand-made / white shoes / something black.*
   e At Camden Market you can also buy *international food / holidays / old cars.*

5a **TASK** Work in small groups. Your local tourism board wants to make a short video to promote shopping in your area. Think about places to go and make notes on …
   - different shopping locations
   - traditional/local/unusual products
   - price/quality

b Make a short presentation to the class and choose the three best ideas.

Review

1a Make questions with *can* and *could* to ask a partner about now and when they were a child.

Can you play a musical instrument?
Could you play a musical instrument when you were a child?

- drive a car?
- run for half an hour?
- stay up late?
- play a musical instrument?
- speak English?
- use credit cards in most shops?

b Work with a partner. Take turns to ask and answer your questions in exercise **1a**. Give more information.

A *Can you play a musical instrument?*
B *No, I can't.*
A *Could you play a musical instrument when you were a child?*
B *Yes, I could! I could play the piano.*

2a Complete sentences 1–6 with your own ideas. Use the present continuous.

1 Look at the people in the park! They …
2 Do you have a job interview today? You …
3 Don't turn off the TV. I …
4 Listen! The birds …
5 You can't go in that changing room. Someone …
6 He can't answer the phone. He …

b Compare your sentences with a partner. Choose your favourite three ideas and tell the class.

3a **5.18**)) Listen to parts from six conversations and match them to phrases a–f.

a the baker's
b a discount
c the sales
d return something to a shop
e the newsagent's
f a shopping centre

b Write six sentences about your shopping habits using the words in exercise **3a**.
I hardly ever buy bread from the baker's.

c Compare your sentences with a partner. What is similar about your shopping habits?

4a Circle the clothes item that is different from the others in 1–4.

1	hat	jeans	shorts	trousers
2	socks	jacket	trainers	shoes
3	top	T-shirt	jewellery	hoodie
4	coat	scarf	gloves	dress

b Compare your answers with a partner. How often do you wear the clothes in exercise **4a**?

5a Match illustrations a–f to sentences 1–6.

1 They're talking.
2 She's singing.
3 He's driving.
4 She's running.
5 They're dancing.
6 He's carrying the plates.

b Change the adjectives in the box into adverbs and use one with each sentence in exercise **5a**.

bad   careful   good   ~~quick~~   quiet   slow

She's running quickly.

c Write two true and two false sentences about you. Use the adverbs in exercise **5b** or your own ideas.

d Work in small groups. Take turns to read your sentences and guess which ones are false.

6a Write two questions you can ask in a shop for each prompt 1–4.

1 Can I …?
2 How much …?
3 Do you …?
4 What time do you …?

b Work with a partner. Ask and answer your questions in exercise **6a**.

7 Work with a partner. Take turns to be the customer and the shop assistant in the shop situations below.

1 A customer with a receipt wants to return a shirt because it's the wrong size. Ask for a smaller/bigger size or your money back.
2 A student wants to buy some cheap trainers by credit card. The shop assistant needs to know the colour and the size.

The past

6.1 Don't give up!

GOALS ▢ Use *was/were* to talk about the past   ▢ Use past time expressions

Reading & Grammar *was* and *were*

1   Work in small groups. Make a list of things a person needs to be successful in life. Do you all agree?

   a good education, ...

2   Work with a partner. Student A, read about Vera Wang. Student B, read about Akio Morita. Complete your column in the table.

	Vera Wang	Akio Morita
Born (when?)		
Early career		
Problems		
Famous for ... (what?)		

Successful people who failed at first

A Vera Wang was born in New York in 1949 and her parents were from China. When she was younger she was a very good ice skater and she wanted to skate in the Olympics. However, she was very unhappy when she wasn't in the US Olympic team in 1968 and she decided to become a fashion designer. She worked fifteen years for *Vogue* magazine, then another two years with Ralph Lauren. Today, she is a very successful designer. She has her own fashion label Vera Wang and sells dresses for $25,000!

B Akio Morita was born in 1921 and he was a businessman from the age of 25. He was the founder of Sony with his business partner and friend Masaru Ibuku. At first they weren't very successful. Their first product was an electric rice cooker and they only sold 100 of them because it always burnt the rice! Today, Sony is in the top 100 companies in the world.

Business Weekly

3   Tell your partner about the story you read and listen to your partner's story to complete the other column in the table in exercise **2**. Which story do you think is most interesting? Why?

4   Underline the examples of *was*, *were*, *wasn't* and *weren't* in the article in exercise **2** and complete the information in the Grammar focus box.

GRAMMAR FOCUS *was* and *were*

- ¹_____ and ²_____ are the past forms of *is* and *isn't*.
- ³_____ and ⁴_____ are the past forms of *are* and *aren't*.

   (+) She **was** a very good ice skater.
   Her parents **were** from China.

   (–) She **wasn't** in the US Olympic team.
   Morita and Ibuku **weren't** successful at first.

   (?) **Was** it expensive? Yes, it **was**./No, it **wasn't**.
   Were they born in China? Yes, they **were**./No, they **weren't**.

→ Grammar Reference page 146

5a Complete the article about a successful team using *was, were, wasn't* or *weren't*.

> **Cool Runnings**   ✕
>
> People ¹_____ surprised to see a bobsleigh team from Jamaica at the 1988 Winter Olympics in Canada. It ²_____ very easy for the team to practise in Jamaica before the Olympics because there ³_____ no ice and there ⁴_____ no bobsleighs for them to use. They ⁵_____ successful in their races, but they ⁶_____ very popular with the people watching because they tried so hard. There ⁷_____ a film telling their story in 1993 called *Cool Runnings* and it ⁸_____ a huge success, making $150,000,000 around the world.

b   **6.1**))) Listen and check your answers.

PRONUNCIATION the past of *to be*

6a **6.2**))) Listen to the questions and short answers. Are *was*, *were*, *wasn't* and *weren't* stressed in the questions or in the answers?

1 **A** *Was* there a bobsleigh team at the Olympics?
  B Yes, there *was*.
2 **A** *Was* it easy for them to practise?
  B No, it *wasn't*.
3 **A** *Were* there bobsleighs for them to use?
  B No, there *weren't*.
4 **A** *Were* they popular?
  B Yes, they *were*.

b **6.3**))) Listen again and repeat.

7a Make questions from the prompts using *was* or *were*.

1 you hungry / this morning ?
  Were you hungry this morning?
2 you / a good student at school ?
3 your partner / late for class today ?
4 your teacher / at work yesterday ?
5 your school friends / from the same town as you ?
6 you / at home / seven o'clock last night ?

b Work with a partner. Take turns to ask and answer the questions in exercise **7a**.

Vocabulary & Speaking time expressions

8a Work with a partner and do the History Firsts Quiz. Match questions 1–6 to answers a–f.

HISTORY
FIRSTS

When was/were the first …
1 football World Cup?   a In 1929.
2 Olympics?   b In the 19th century.
3 dishwasher?   c In 1927.
4 Sony Walkman?   d In 1930.
5 talking film?   e 2,800 years ago.
6 Oscars ceremony?   f In 1979.

b **6.3**))) Listen and check your answers.

9 Complete the table with the time expressions in the box.

three weeks   ~~night~~   the 18th century   year   six months
week   2001   summer   ~~a long time~~   ~~1999~~

in	last	ago
1999	night	a long time

10a Put the past time expressions in exercise **9** in the correct place on the timeline.

◄───────────────────────────────────►
a long time ago   last night

b Compare your answers with a partner.

11a **TASK** Complete the sentences by writing where you were at these times.

1 I ____was on the bus____ two hours ago.
2 I _____ at 3.30 yesterday afternoon.
3 I _____ last Tuesday.
4 I _____ last October.
5 I _____ five years ago.
6 I _____ last night.
7 I _____ in 2008.
8 I _____ last summer.

b Work with a partner. Take turns to guess about each other.

A *Were you on the bus two hours ago?*
B *Yes, I was. Were you at work at 3.30 yesterday afternoon?*
A *No, I wasn't. I was at home.*

▶ VOX POPS VIDEO 6

6.2 Stories

GOALS ■ Use regular verbs to talk about what happened in the past ■ Use common collocations

Listening & Grammar   past simple regular verbs

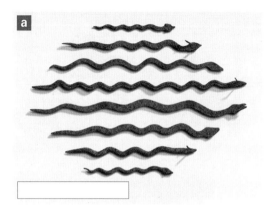

1a How many currencies do you know? Make a list, e.g. *dollars, pounds.*

b The four photos show different kinds of currencies from the past. Label them with words from the box.

> coins   metal snakes   ring   salt

2   **6.4**))) Listen to a programme called *The History of Money* and number the photos 1–4 in the order you hear them.

3   **6.4**))) Listen again and choose the correct option.
1 The *Romans / Chinese / Lobi / Egyptians* used jewellery as money.
2 The *Romans / Chinese / Lobi / Egyptians* copied a Turkish idea in the first century BCE.
3 The *Romans / Chinese / Lobi / Egyptians* earned something you can eat.
4 The *Romans / Chinese / Lobi / Egyptians* believed their money was lucky.

4a Are the sentences in exercise **3** about now or before now?

b Underline the verbs in the sentences in exercise **3** and complete the rules in the Grammar focus box.

GRAMMAR FOCUS   past simple regular verbs

Regular verbs can be changed into the past simple in three ways:
1 For most verbs, we add ¹_____ : *start → started*
2 For verbs that end in *-e*, we add ²_____ : *close → closed*
3 For verbs that end in consonant + *-y*, we delete *-y* and add ³_____ : *carry → carried*

→ Grammar Reference page 147

PRONUNCIATION   *-ed* ending in past simple verbs

5a   **6.5**))) There are three different ways to pronounce the *-ed* ending in past simple verbs. Listen to the examples and repeat.
/d/ : opened, returned, called
/t/ : finished, looked, thanked
/ɪd/ : started, collected, visited

b   **6.6**))) Listen and write the verbs in the box on the correct lines in exercise **5a**.

> copied   believed   liked   loved   moved   noticed   posted   prepared
> received   shouted   used   waited   wanted   worked

c   **6.7**))) Listen, check and repeat.

6   Work with a partner. Read and complete a story. Student A, turn to page 128. Student B, turn to page 133.

Vocabulary & Speaking   common regular verb collocations

7a Work with a partner. <u>Underline</u> the two correct options.

1	wait	for a long time / for a friend / for a bus stop
2	post	an email / a letter / a comment on a web page
3	enter	a race / a job / a competition
4	move	jobs / to the countryside / house
5	visit	the beach / a museum / a relative
6	shout	at your dog / at the weather / at someone
7	prepare	a party / a meal / for an exam
8	receive	a TV programme / an email / a phone call
9	call	a taxi / a bus / an old friend
10	use	a dictionary / a tablet / a newspaper

b 6.8))) Listen, check and repeat.

8a Match questions 1–10 to answers a–j.

When was the last time you …

1 moved house?
2 received an email?
3 prepared a meal?
4 posted a letter?
5 shouted at someone?
6 visited a relative?
7 called a taxi?
8 entered a competition?
9 used a dictionary
10 waited for a long time?

a A month ago. It was to my friend in Australia.
b Last summer. I travelled to Kenya to see my grandmother.
c When I was a child. I was in a swimming race.
d About a week ago. My son was very naughty.
e Yesterday. I was late for work.
f In 2010. From an apartment to a house.
g Last night. I cooked spaghetti for my housemate.
h Last week. I checked the meaning of *coin*.
i Two hours ago. My bus was very late.
j This morning. It was from my boss.

b 6.9))) Listen and check your answers.

c 6.10))) Listen to the questions again and repeat.

9a TASK Think about how to answer the questions in exercise **8a** so that they are true for you. Write a past time expression in each of the circles to answer the ten questions. Do not write the time expressions in order.

last night

b Work with a partner. Take turns to make guesses about the information in your partner's circles. Say if your partner was right or wrong and give more information.

A *I think you visited a relative last night.*
B *No! I visited a relative three days ago. I walked to my uncle's house.*
A *OK, I think you prepared a meal last night.*
B *Right! I cooked a meal for my family.*

6.3 Vocabulary and skills development

Listening & Speaking understanding present and past simple verbs

1 Circle the best option for you. Discuss the statements in small groups.

1 Art galleries are *interesting* / *boring*.

2 I *often* / *never* / *hardly ever* visit museums.

2 **6.11**))) Listen to two sentences about an art gallery. Which is present and which is past? How do you know?

3 **6.12**))) Read and listen to the information in the Unlock the code box about present and past simple verbs.

🔓 UNLOCK THE CODE
present and past simple verbs

Regular past simple verbs can sound very similar to their present simple forms.
I walk every day. → *I walked every day.*
They love it. → *They loved it.*
We want it. → *We wanted it.*

1 Regular past simple verbs end with three different sounds:
/t/: *walked* /d/: *loved* /ɪd/: *wanted*

2 Time expressions can help you decide if the verb is past or present.
*I moved house **in 2012**.* (past)
*I walk a lot **these days**.* (present)

4a **6.13**))) Listen and tick (✓) the word you hear in each pair 1–9. Compare your answers with a partner.

1 cook / cooked 6 listen / listened
2 carry / carried 7 chat / chatted
3 change / changed 8 dance / danced
4 help / helped 9 enjoy / enjoyed
5 wait / waited

b **6.13**))) Listen again and repeat.

5a **6.14**))) Listen to six sentences and decide if they are past or present. Write your answers on the lines.

1 *past* 4 _____
2 _____ 5 _____
3 _____ 6 _____

b Compare your answers with a partner.

6a Work with a partner. Look at the photos of a place called Inhotim and guess the answers to questions 1–3.

1 What was Inhotim before the 1990s?
2 What is it now?
3 Why is it important for the local area?

b **6.15**))) Listen to a programme about Inhotim and check your answers.

7a **6.15**))) Listen to the programme again. Are the verbs in the box in the present or past simple?

notice start live work look change decide
travel look include work visit

b Change the present simple verbs in **7a** to the past simple form.
*start**ed***

8 Work with a partner. Take turns to make present and past sentences about yourself, using the verbs and time expressions in the boxes. Your partner says if they are past or present.

A *I lived on a boat when I was a child.*
B *That's past.*

like listen live look love play study talk
travel visit wait want watch work

every day five years ago in 2006 last week
now these days when I was a child yesterday

Vocabulary & Listening adverbs of degree

9a Look at four sentences from the programme about Inhotim and read the Vocabulary focus box about adverbs of degree.

... Bernardo Paz decided to use the space for something **very** different.

... but as you get closer, you notice something **a bit** unusual.

Although it is **quite** far from the usual tourist spots of Brazil, ...

... it is **really** important for the local area ...

> **VOCABULARY FOCUS** adverbs of degree
>
> When we use adjectives to describe things, we often want to show how strongly we feel. To do this, we can use adverbs, e.g. *a bit, quite, very, really,* before the adjectives.
> *I'm **a bit** cold.*   *The exam was **quite** easy.*
> *He is **really** nice.*   *Russia is a **very** big country.*
> Note: We don't use *a bit* with positive adjectives.
> ~~I'm a bit happy.~~

b Write the words in **bold** in exercise **9a** on the line.
0%   ¹ <u>a bit</u>   ²____   ³____/⁴____   100%

10a **6.16**)) Listen to two people talking about their visits to Inhotim. Is speaker 1 or speaker 2 more positive about the different parts of their visit?

1 sculptures/art   3 food/restaurants
2 gardens   4 journey

b **6.16**)) Listen again. Write the language that helped you answer exercise **10a**.
very interesting

11 **6.17**)) Listen to four sentences from exercise **10a** and repeat them. Which adverbs have the strongest stress?

1 *... the sculptures were very interesting.*
2 *The gardens were quite nice, too.*
3 *I thought the sculptures in the park were a bit boring ...*
4 *... the journey to the park was really long ...*

12 Work with a partner. Discuss the ideas using the adjectives and a suitable adverb of degree.

1 Modern art/boring/interesting.
   A *Modern art is really boring.*
   B *No, it isn't! It's very interesting.*
2 Clothes in this country/expensive/cheap.
3 The classroom/hot/cold today.
4 Trains and buses/fast/slow in this country.
5 Cars/dangerous/safe.

13a **TASK** Plan a story about a place you visited, or an event you went to in the last two years. Use questions 1–7 to help you and include 2–3 adverbs of degree.

1 When was it?
2 Where did you go?
3 Who were you with?
4 How was the weather?
5 Were there a lot of people there?
6 What did you do there?
7 How was it?

b Work in small groups. Take turns to tell your stories. Write down the adverbs of degree and adjectives each person uses.

6.4 Speaking and writing

GOALS ■ Tell a story ■ Show interest ■ Write a tweet or text message

Speaking & Listening showing interest as a listener

1 Work with a partner. Look at the photos and the words. Guess the story and put the pictures in the correct order 1–6.

2 **6.18**))) Listen to Oscar telling the story and check your ideas. Why did he miss his Business Management class dinner?

3 **6.18**))) Listen to the conversation again. Tick (✓) the expressions the listener uses. How do these expressions 'help' the conversation?

That's terrible!	*Poor you!*
Oh no!	*Really?*
What a nightmare!	*That's great!*
That's brilliant!	*That's interesting!*
That's awful!	

4a Work with a partner. Decide which of the expressions in exercise 3 are for responding to …
 a good news **b** bad news **c** interesting news

 b Read the information in the Language for speaking box and check your answers.

LANGUAGE FOR SPEAKING
showing interest

Responding to good news
That's brilliant!   *That's amazing!*
That's great!

Responding to bad news
That's terrible!   *Oh no!*
That's awful!   *Poor you!*
What a nightmare!

Responding to interesting news
Really?   *That's interesting!*

5a **6.19**))) Listen to the expressions in the Language for speaking box. Notice how the voice goes up or down.

 b **6.19**))) Listen again and repeat.

6 Work with a partner. Take turns to tell each other some news and respond to it. Student A, turn to page 129. Student B, turn to page 134.

1 **a** *miss*

b *start*

c *find*

d *call*

e *home*

f *late*

Reading & Writing   write a tweet or text message

7   Work in small groups. Answer the questions.

1   Do you use any social media sites? (Facebook, Twitter, etc.) What do you use them for?

2   How much time do you spend on these sites?

3   Do you think they are useful? Why/Why not?

8a   Read the three tweets below. Which one …

1   gives the writer's opinion?

2   asks for information?

3   tells a short story?

1   Anyone know where I can dance salsa? Really want to learn!
← Reply ★Favourite ?Info

2   Just walked into boss's office and she was asleep! So funny!
← Reply ★Favourite ?Info

3   Watching *Gladiator*. Love it!
← Reply ★Favourite ?Info

b   Match replies a–c to tweets 1–3.

a
← Reply ★Favourite ?Info

Really?! Saw it years ago and hated it. Boring!

b
← Reply ★Favourite ?Info
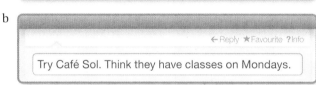
Try Café Sol. Think they have classes on Mondays.

c
← Reply ★Favourite ?Info
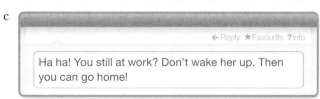
Ha ha! You still at work? Don't wake her up. Then you can go home!

9   Work with a partner. Look at the first tweet again and answer the questions. Check your answers in the Language for writing box.

1   Where can you put the words *does* and *I* in the tweet to make full sentences?

2   Why do you think the two words are not included in the tweet?

LANGUAGE FOR WRITING   tweets and texts

We often leave words out when we write quickly and informally, e.g. in text messages or on Twitter.

These words can be:

1   auxiliary verbs, e.g. *do, does, is, are*.
~~Does~~ *anyone know where I can dance salsa?*

2   subject pronouns, e.g. *I, you, it*.
~~I~~ *really want to learn!*

3   subject and the verb *to be*.
~~It was~~ *so funny!*

10   Find examples of missing words in the replies in exercise **8b**.
I
⎰*Saw it years ago …*

11   Look at four more tweets. They all contain words they don't need. Cross out the unnecessary words. Compare your answers with a partner.

1   **Mary** @MJSmart
I tried explaining Twitter to my dad. It wasn't easy!
← Reply ★Favourite ?Info

2   **Chris** @ChrisWong
Francis! Do you want to go out tonight?
← Reply ★Favourite ?Info

3   **Steven** @SteveC1985
Is anyone watching the programme on Channel 6? Does anyone understand it?!
← Reply ★Favourite ?Info

4   **Tim** @TimG
I just missed the bus again! It's the third time this week!
← Reply ★Favourite ?Info

12a   **TASK**   Write a tweet about something interesting.

b   Pass your tweet around the class and write replies to the tweets you receive from your classmates. Which tweet has the best replies?

6.5 Video

Istanbul

1 Look at the photos of Istanbul. Which of these things can you see in them?

> ancient buildings   buses   busy market   dome
> fishermen   gardens   herbs   modern buildings
> mosque   public transport   residents   ships and ferries
> souvenirs   spices   strait   tourists

2 Work with a partner. Look at the photos again and discuss the questions.

- Do you think Istanbul is a good place to live?
- Do you think life in Istanbul is the same or different to where you live? Why?
- Would you like to live in Istanbul?

3 ▶ Watch the video about Istanbul. Write a short summary including the most important facts about the city. Think about …

- how old the city is
- why the city was important/famous in the past
- why the city is important/famous now
- busy modern life
- East and West.

4 ▶ Watch the video again. Decide if the sentences are true (T) or false (F). Correct the false sentences.

a   Istanbul is the second largest city in Turkey.
b   In ancient times the city was first called Constantinople.
c   The city's name changed to Istanbul in 1833.
d   Today the Hagia Sophia is a mosque.
e   The strait that divides Istanbul is called the Bosphorous.
f   Only local people use the ferries on the Bosphorous.
g   Istanbul is famous for its fresh seafood.
h   The Grand Bazaar was first built in the 18th century.
i   There are sixteen streets in the market.
j   The market doesn't sell any food.
k   The city is the same now as it was in ancient times.

5a **TASK** Work with a partner. You went to Istanbul last week for a business trip/weekend visit/study trip. Make notes on …

- where you stayed
- what you did/saw
- what you ate
- what souvenirs you brought home
- if you recommend the visit

b Write an email to a colleague/friend telling them about your visit.

Review

1a Complete the questions with *was* or *were*.

1 How old _____ the speaker when it happened?

2 _____ it on a Monday?

3 _____ the lights on when he walked into the living room?

4 _____ his friends at the party?

5 _____ there a cake?

6 Where _____ the presents?

b **6.20**))) Listen to someone telling a story and answer the questions in exercise **1a**. Compare with a partner.

2a Imagine today is Wednesday 19th February 2015 and it is 1.20 p.m. Write a past time expression next to each item 1–6 to say when they were.

1 Tuesday 18th February 2015 *yesterday*

2 2014

3 Wednesday 12th February 2015

4 2010

5 1.15 p.m.

6 12.50 p.m.

b Write four dates and times from the past, e.g. your last birthday, first driving lesson, time you got up today, etc.

c Work with a partner. Take turns to say your dates and times from exercise **2b**. Your partner tries to guess what happened then.

A *1st September 2012*

B *Your son started school.*

3 Complete the article with the present simple or past simple forms of the verbs in (brackets).

The painter Vincent Van Gogh was born in 1853 and he **1**____ (die) in 1890. He **2**____ (be) a farmer and then a teacher before he **3**____ (decide) to become an artist when he was nearly 30. These days people **4**____ (love) his paintings and **5**____ (pay) a lot of money for them. Unfortunately nobody **6**____ (want) to buy his paintings when he was alive and he **7**____ (be) poor and unhappy. He **8**____ (paint) one of his most famous paintings – *Van Gogh's chair* – in 1888. Today it **9**____ (be) in the National Gallery in London and every year, art lovers from around the world **10**____ (travel) hundreds of miles to see it.

4a Match the verbs and noun phrases to make common collocations.

1 move   a competition

2 receive an   b at someone

3 prepare a   c letter

4 post a   d a relative

5 shout   e house

6 visit   f for a long time

7 enter a   g email

8 wait   h meal

b Work in small groups. Tell each other about the last time you did the things in exercise **4a**.

5a Make sentences 1–8 positive or negative so they are true for you. Add an adverb of degree from the box to give more detail about the positive sentences.

| very   quite   really   a bit |

1 I was *a bit* _____ tired last night.

2 I was *n't* _____ late for class today.

3 I was _____ early for class today.

4 I was _____ busy last week.

5 I was _____ naughty when I was a child.

6 I was _____ hungry an hour ago.

7 I was _____ young in 2010.

8 I was _____ happy on my birthday last year.

b Work in small groups. Take turns to read your sentences to each other and give more information.

I was a bit tired last night because I had a busy day at work.

I wasn't late for class today because I got up early.

6a **6.21**))) Listen to three sentences and choose an expression from the box to respond to each sentence.

| That's terrible!   Really?   That's brilliant! |
| Poor you!   What a nightmare!   That's amazing! |
| Oh no!   That's great!   That's awful! |

b Write sentences giving good news, bad news and surprising news.

c Work in small groups. Take turns to tell each other your news. Respond to each piece of news with an expression from exercise **6a**.

7 Health and fitness

7.1 My health, my business

GOALS ■ Use collocations for a healthy lifestyle ■ Use past simple irregular verbs

Vocabulary & Speaking
a healthy lifestyle

1 Work with a partner. Read the saying and answer the questions.

Healthy body, healthy mind.

1 What does the saying mean?
2 Do you agree? Why/Why not?

2a Work with a partner. Use the verbs in the box to complete the phrases for a healthy lifestyle.

> do (x2) drink eat go ride sleep
> take walk

1 _____ lots of fruit and vegetables
2 _____ the stairs, not the lift
3 _____ to work
4 _____ a bicycle
5 _____ eight glasses of water a day
6 _____ an hour of exercise each day
7 _____ seven to eight hours a night
8 _____ to the gym or an evening class
9 _____ physical jobs around the house

b **7.1**))) Listen and check your answers.

c Work in small groups. Discuss the questions.
1 Which actions in exercise **2a** are exercise and which are not?
2 Which things do you do?
3 What else is important for a healthy lifestyle?

Reading & Grammar past simple irregular verbs

3 Work with a partner and look at the menu. Do you think it is a good idea to show the calories? Why/Why not?

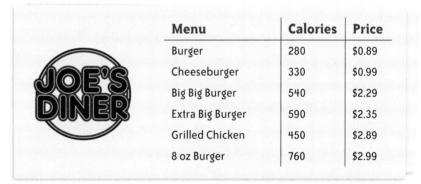

Menu	Calories	Price
Burger	280	$0.89
Cheeseburger	330	$0.99
Big Big Burger	540	$2.29
Extra Big Burger	590	$2.35
Grilled Chicken	450	$2.89
8 oz Burger	760	$2.99

4a Work with a partner. Look at the photo and title of the article. What do you think the mayor did?

the healthy mayor

In 2002 New York City chose a new mayor, Michael Bloomberg. Bloomberg wanted the people of New York to be healthy. In his opinion, they did the wrong things: they ate the wrong food, they smoked, they drove everywhere, and they did little or no exercise.

So Bloomberg tried to change their habits. Before he was mayor, restaurant menus only gave the price of the food. But after 2007 restaurants wrote the number of calories in their food on the menu. He banned smoking in public places. He also tried to reduce the size of sweet drinks, like Coca Cola (but the Supreme Court stopped him).

Bloomberg had other messages for New Yorkers, too: do more exercise, leave your car at home, walk or ride a bicycle, and take the stairs when you can. He told them he always took the stairs, not the lift.

Some people thought Bloomberg was wrong. People's health is their business. But is it?

■ **banned** said something was not allowed ■ **reduce** make something smaller

b Read the magazine article and check your answers.

5 Work with a partner. Read the article again and find …

　1 four things New Yorkers did that were bad for their health.

　2 two things Bloomberg changed.

　3 one thing he tried to change.

　4 Bloomberg's ideas for doing more exercise.

6 Work in small groups. What do you think about Mayor Bloomberg's ideas? Was he right? Why/Why not?

7 Work with a partner. Look at the **highlighted** past simple verbs in the sentences. Which verb is regular?

> In 2002 New Yorkers chose a new mayor, Michael Bloomberg. Bloomberg wanted the people of New York to be healthy.

8a Read the Grammar focus box about past simple irregular verbs.

> **GRAMMAR FOCUS** past simple irregular verbs
>
> Past simple irregular verbs are not formed by adding -*ed*. They all take different forms, e.g.
> *choose* → *chose*　*sit* → *sat*　*put* → *put*
>
> → **Grammar Reference** page 148

b Find past simple irregular verbs in the article and complete the table.

Present	Past
come	*came*
make	*made*
do	
eat	
drive	
give	
write	
have	
tell	
take	
think	

c **7.2** ⟫ Listen, check and repeat.

PRONUNCIATION past simple irregular verbs

9a **7.3** ⟫ Listen to the pronunciation of the groups of three past simple verbs. Are the vowel sounds in each group the same (S) or different (D)?

　1 thought / bought / taught

　2 got / chose / wrote

　3 sat / went / had

　4 came / made / ate

　5 flew / took / put

　6 met / said / slept

b **7.3** ⟫ Listen again and repeat.

10a Put the verbs in (brackets) in the past simple to complete the Student health survey results.

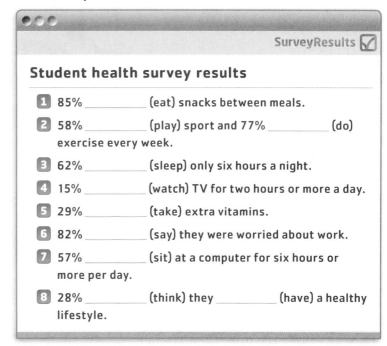

Student health survey results

1 85% _____ (eat) snacks between meals.

2 58% _____ (play) sport and 77% _____ (do) exercise every week.

3 62% _____ (sleep) only six hours a night.

4 15% _____ (watch) TV for two hours or more a day.

5 29% _____ (take) extra vitamins.

6 82% _____ (say) they were worried about work.

7 57% _____ (sit) at a computer for six hours or more per day.

8 28% _____ (think) they _____ (have) a healthy lifestyle.

b Compare your answers with a partner. Which facts surprised you?

11a **TASK** Think of a time in the past, e.g. when you were a child. Use the ideas in the survey and make a list of your healthy and unhealthy habits.

When I was about ten years old, I ate a lot of sweets.

b Work in small groups. Compare your habits.

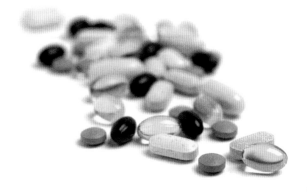

7.2 Sporting heroes

Vocabulary & Speaking
sports and fitness

1a Work with a partner. Write the activity under the correct illustration.

> cycle   do athletics   do judo   do yoga
> go fishing   go to the gym   jog/run
> play basketball   play football   play tennis
> ski   swim

b **7.4**))) Listen, check and repeat.

2 Work with a partner. Talk about sports or activities that are popular where you live. *People jog and play tennis in my local park.*

3a Tick (✓) the three best reasons to do sport.

1   to keep fit
2   to meet friends
3   to have fun
4   to win
5   to lose weight
6   to learn something new

b Compare your answers with a partner.

4 Work with a partner. Answer the questions.

1   What sports and activities do you do?
2   How often do you do them?
3   Why do you do them?

A *I play basketball and I do athletics.*
B *How often do you play basketball?*
A *Every Wednesday and Saturday evening.*
B *Why do you like it?*
A *I meet my friends and we have lots of fun.*

1 _____   2 _____   3 _____

4 _____   5 _____   6 _____

7 _____   8 _____   9 _____

10 _____   11 _____   12 _____

Listening & Grammar past simple negative

5 Work with a partner. Do you think famous sports people can be heroes? Why/Why not?

6 Work with a partner. Look at the photo of Fauja Singh and answer the questions.

1 How old do you think he is?
2 What sport do you think he does?
3 Why do you think he likes that sport?

7a **7.5**)) Listen and check your ideas. Do you think Fauja is a sporting hero? Why/Why not?

b **7.5**)) Listen again. Tick (✓) the true sentences and cross (✗) the false sentences. Compare your answers with a partner.

1 Fauja ran marathons when he was young.
2 He didn't walk before the age of five.
3 He had a lot of problems on his family's farm.
4 His happy life continued after he had a family.
5 He left India.
6 He stopped after his first marathon.

8 Complete the rule in the Grammar focus box.

> **GRAMMAR FOCUS** past simple negative
>
> To make the past simple negative we use:
>
> Subject + did not/ _____ + infinitive without to
> He **didn't walk** before the age of five.
>
> → Grammar Reference page 149

PRONUNCIATION past simple negative

9a **7.6**)) Listen and notice the stress.

He didn't walk ...   He didn't feel sad ...

b Work with a partner. Correct the false sentences in exercise **7b**. Use the correct stress.

A *Fauja ran marathons when he was young.*
B *False. Fauja didn't run marathons when he was young.*

c **7.7**)) Listen, check and repeat.

10a Work with a partner. Put the verbs in (brackets) into the positive or negative form to make the facts about Usain Bolt true.

USAIN BOLT JAMAICAN 100 & 200M RUNNER

1 When he was a young boy, Usain Bolt _____ (do) athletics all the time.

2 In 2008, when he won the Olympic 100m final, he _____ (slow) down at the end and he _____ (break) the world record.

3 When he won the 100m final at the 2012 London Olympic Games, two billion people watched him on TV. American TV _____ (show) the race when it happened.

4 There was a thunderstorm during the 100m World Championship final in 2013. Lightning _____ (hit) him.

b **7.8**)) Listen and check your answers. Did anything surprise you? Tell your partner.

11a **TASK** Write two true and two false sentences about sports or other activities you did in the past. Use the verbs in the box and other verbs you know.

> be do go have play run swim win

I won a chess competition when I was ten.

b Work in small groups. Take turns to read your sentences to each other. Say if you think each one is true (T) or false (F). Give more information.

A *I played basketball for my university.*
B *True?*
C *Hmm ... I think it's false.*
A *Yes, it's false. I didn't play basketball for my university. I'm only 1.6m tall!*

 VOX POPS VIDEO 7

7.3 Vocabulary and skills development

Reading & Speaking — time sequencers

1 Work with a partner. Read instructions a–e for staying fit and healthy. Which order do you think the instructions could be in?

   a Make a timetable.
   b Repeat the exercise twice a day.
   c Choose an activity you enjoy.
   d Set a goal for yourself.
   e Find a friend to exercise with you.

2a Read the information in the Unlock the code box about time sequencers.

> ### 🔓 UNLOCK THE CODE
> #### time sequencers
>
> Writers often use time sequencers to show the order in which something happens, e.g. *first*, *next*, *then*. If you understand these phrases, it is easier to understand what comes next in the text.

b When we talk about something that happened, which time expressions do we use to describe …

   1 the beginning? _____
   2 the middle? _____ _____ _____
   3 the end? _____ _____

> After that, …   Finally, …   First/Firstly, …   Lastly, …
> Next, …   Then, …

c Use the time sequencers in exercise 2b to make the order clearer in exercise 1.
   First, …

3a Work with a partner. Answer the questions.
   1 Do you think you take enough exercise?
   2 How many steps do you think you take every day?
   3 Do you ever check your own health? If so, how? If not, why not?

b Work with a partner. Look at the title of a TV programme review. How do you think technology can make you healthier?

c Read the review and check your ideas.

---

5 • THE REVIEW • TV

Technology
to make you healthier

The programme was about apps and gadgets that check our health and daily exercise. In the programme, three female office workers used this new technology for three weeks. What did they do and did it work?

Firstly, university scientist Blaine Price lent the women a gadget to count their steps, and a specially-programmed smartphone to check their sleep.

After that, the women went back to their normal lives and used the gadget to check their exercise. At the end of each day, the scientist sent them an email with the number of their steps. At the beginning they only took 5,000 steps, but the target was 10,000 a day.

Next, they checked their sleep. Every night, they put the smartphone on their bed when they went to sleep. The next morning, they looked at the phone and saw the number of hours they slept, and how deeply.

Finally, the three women and Blaine met again to talk about their progress. All the women said they were healthier and fitter, and one said she ran when she watched TV. They all lost weight, and they all understood better why and when they slept well.

So the programme showed that new gadgets and technology can help us change our routine and get healthier!

4a Put sentences a–d about the story in the correct order without looking at the review. Compare your answers with a partner.

a   The women talked about how healthy and fit they were.

b   The women lived normal lives.

c   The women used their phones to check their sleep.

d   The scientist gave the women some equipment.

b Work with a partner. Describe each stage of the story in your own words using the time sequencers from exercise **2b**.

5 Work with a partner. Answer the questions.

1   What do you think of the idea of checking your exercise and your sleep with a gadget or phone?

2   Do you think that technology can change your routine?

3   Is it a good idea to check your health and routines every day? Why / Why not?

Vocabulary & Speaking   easily confused words

6 Match the words in **bold** in each pair of sentences to the correct meaning.

1   I need to buy some food and I don't have any money. Can you **lend** me £10? I'll pay you back tomorrow.

2   I forgot my pen, so I **borrowed** one from my classmate.

a   take something from somebody for a short time (and then give it back later) _____

b   give something to somebody for a short time (and then get it back later) _____

3   Why don't you **come** to my house for dinner tomorrow?

4   Did you **go** to the swimming pool yesterday?

a   move from another place to here _____

b   move from here to another place _____

5   She **told** me her name.

6   He **said** that he was hungry.

a   give information by speaking or writing _____

b   give information to somebody by speaking or writing _____

7   He **looked** at his watch and said, 'It's late!'

8   The police **watched** the house for two days.

a   look at something for a long time to see what happens or because you like doing it _____

b   look at something for a short time _____

9   Can you **bring** me my glasses?

10   It's cold. **Take** a coat with you.

a   move something/somebody from another place to here _____

b   move something/somebody from here to another place _____

7a Read the Vocabulary focus box about easily confused words.

> **VOCABULARY FOCUS** easily confused words
>
> There are some common pairs of words in English that are easily confused. These are often:
>
> 1   words to do with movement or actions between people, e.g. *come/go*, *bring/take*, *lend/borrow*.
>
> 2   words describing similar actions but with different grammar or collocation, e.g. *say/tell*, *look/watch*.

b Complete the sentences with the correct form of a word in **bold** in exercise **6**.

1   Can you ___*lend*___ me your car for the weekend?

2   They _____ basketball on TV last night.

3   _____ here! I want to speak to you.

4   My colleague _____ me about a new restaurant in town.

5   Can you _____ this book to the library for me?

6   'I'm lost,' he _____ .

7   When Jacek _____ at his phone during the meeting, I got very angry.

8   I didn't have a pen, so I _____ one from my friend.

9   When you come to the party, can you _____ something to drink?

10   Let's _____ to the beach tomorrow.

c   **7.9**))) Listen and check your answers.

8a   **TASK**   Four of questions 1–5 use the wrong verbs. Correct the wrong ones.

1   How often do you go to the gym and do exercises?

2   Do you look at films in English without reading the subtitles?

3   Do you prefer playing or looking at sport?

4   Do you usually say your neighbours that you want to have a party?

5   Would you prefer to lend money from a bank or from a member of your family? Why?

b Work in small groups. Take turns to ask and answer the questions in exercise **8a**. Add follow-up questions.

A *How often do you go to the gym?*

B *Not very often.*

A *What kind of exercises do you do?*

7.4 Speaking and writing

Listening & Speaking opinions, agreeing and disagreeing

1a Work with a partner. Discuss the questions.
   1 Do you, your friends or your family play video games?
   2 What video games do you know?
   3 What's good and bad about video games?

b Compare your answers with another pair.

2 **7.10**))) Listen to the introduction to a radio programme about children and video games. Answer the questions with your partner.
   1 What do people usually think about video games?
   2 What did the research show?
   3 What did the children do in gym class?
   4 How did the children feel about this?

3a **7.11**))) Listen to two people talking on the radio programme. What do they think are the good and bad things about video games?

b Work with a partner. Use the words in the box to complete the sentences from the listening in exercise **3a**.

> agree but don't for of opinion right that think what

   1 _____ do you think _____ this idea?
   2 I _____ it's great.
   3 I _____ know about _____ .
   4 Yes, _____ they didn't use games like that at the school.
   5 Well, _____ me, it depends on the game.
   6 You're _____ .
   7 What's your _____ ?
   8 Yes, I _____ with that.

c **7.12**))) Listen, check and repeat.

4 Work with a partner. Which phrases from exercise **3b** ...
   1 ask for an opinion? _____ _____
   2 give an opinion? _____ _____
   3 show the speaker agrees? _____ _____
   4 show the speaker disagrees? _____ _____

5 Work with a partner. What do you think about using video games at school? Use the phrases in exercise **3b**.

6 Work with a partner. Read the statement and think of 3–4 ideas to complete each column of the table.

> ' *Companies and colleagues should help their employees and students to be fit and healthy.* '

Arguments for	Arguments against

7 Work with another pair. Discuss your arguments from exercise **6**. Use the Language for speaking box to help you.

LANGUAGE FOR SPEAKING
asking for/giving opinions, agreeing/disagreeing

Asking for opinions	Agreeing
What do you think (of …)?	*You're right.*
What's your opinion (of …)?	*I agree (with that).*
Giving opinions	**Disagreeing**
I think …	*Yes, but …*
For me, …	*I don't know about that.*

Reading & Writing   post a website comment

8a Read the online article about a video game experiment. Describe the experiment to your partner.

TECHNOLOGY   ✕

New research shows that video gamers don't live in the real world.

Researchers gave two groups of people a simple test. The first group played a lot of video games before the experiment. The people in the second group didn't play video games. Then, both groups took paper clips out of a bucket of ice-cold water. The first group took more paper clips. They didn't feel the cold because their brain thought that they were still in the video game world. The other group felt the cold because they weren't in a virtual world.

---

b Work with a partner. Answer the questions.

1 What does the writer say that the experiment shows?

2 Do you agree? Why/Why not?

9 Work with a partner. Read four comments from the website. Who agrees with the research? Who disagrees?

● ● ●

Like | Share | Comment

FT, Scotland
I agree, but I knew this before this research. People don't talk to each other anymore. They work with computers and they also relax with computers.
Like | Share | Reply

Firos, Lebanon
That's right. I think we live in another world. We look at computer screens for eight hours a day at work, then watch TV for four hours in the evening, too. We are also always on our phones.
Like | Share | Reply

Haruki, Japan
I'm afraid I don't really agree with this research. What's the problem? People relax in different ways. Some people read books. Others play video games.
Like | Share | Reply

Jeff, Canada
That's true, Haruki. For me, video games are a hobby. I think people know the difference between a game and the real world.
Like | Share | Reply

---

10 Underline the phrases the people in exercise **9** use to agree and disagree. Compare your answers with a partner.

11a Read the information in the Language for writing box.

LANGUAGE FOR WRITING
adding more information

- We can use *too* and *also* to add more information.
- *Also* goes before the main verb, but after the verb *be*.
  *… and they **also** relax with computers.*
  *We are **also** always on our phones.*
- *Too* goes at the end of a sentence.
  *… watch TV for four hours in the evening, **too**.*

---

b Work with a partner. Rewrite the sentences using *too* and *also*.

1 He played for his local team and he played for his national team.

2 She goes swimming every day and she goes to the gym twice a week.

3 He likes watching football on TV and he likes playing it.

4 My cousin is a black belt in judo and she's a black belt in karate.

12a **TASK** Write a comment about the article in exercise **8a**. Agree or disagree and use *too* or *also* to give more information.

b Work in small groups. Read each other's comments. Do you agree?

13a **TASK** Look at the ideas on page 129. Choose one and write a comment. Agree or disagree and use *too* or *also* to give more information.

b Work in small groups. Read comments from other students and write replies.

7.5 Video

Health and fitness in New York

1 Work with a partner. What do you know about New York? Think about …
  - where it is
  - population
  - transport
  - places to visit
  - food

2 Look at the photos of people in New York. Which activities …

  a are healthy?

  b are unhealthy?

  c do you do?

  d would you like to do?

3 ▶ Watch the video. Match beginnings 1–8 to endings a–h to complete the sentences.

  1 The most famous part of New York is
  2 Fifty million tourists visit New York
  3 People didn't cycle much
  4 Before 2002, most people travelled to work by
  5 The High Line was an
  6 Now the High Line is a
  7 You can rent a bike for ten dollars
  8 Restaurant menus include

  a before 2002.
  b information about calories in your meal.
  c place to jog, walk or relax.
  d every year.
  e old railway line.
  f a day with the Citibikes scheme.
  g Manhattan.
  h subway or car.

4 ▶ Watch the video again and make notes about what they said for topics 1–5.

  1 public transport
  2 the Mayor of New York
  3 taking exercise
  4 parks
  5 restaurants and food

5a **TASK** Work in small groups. Your employer, university or local government wants to make a short video advert to help local residents live more healthily. Think of four ideas and say why you think they will help people to have a healthy lifestyle.

  b Present your ideas to the class and choose the best four.

Review

1a Match beginnings 1–6 to endings a–f to make questions.

1 Do you eat a lot of
2 Do you do
3 Do you often ride
4 Can you walk
5 How many hours
6 Do you

a do a lot of physical jobs around the house?
b do you sleep every night?
c any exercise?
d fruit and vegetables every day?
e a bicycle?
f to local shops from your house, or do you drive?

b Work with a partner. Ask and answer the questions in exercise **1a** and give more information.

2a Put the verbs in (brackets) in the past simple positive or negative. Use the symbols (+/–) to help you.
Yesterday …

1 I ___didn't drive___ (drive/–).
   I _____came_____ (come/+) to work on foot.
2 I _____ (cook/–) chips or fried food.
   I _____ (make/+) a healthy salad for lunch.
3 I _____ (go/+) to the gym.
   I _____ (watch/–) TV.
4 I _____ (go/+) to bed early.
   I _____ (have/+) eight hours' sleep last night.
5 I _____ (have/+) an apple for dessert.
   I _____ (eat/–) ice cream or cake.
6 I _____ (take/+) the stairs.
   I _____ (use/–) the lift.

b Make the sentences in exercise **2a** true for you. Compare your answers with a partner.

3a Circle the correct verb to complete the questions.

1 Do you *go / come* to sporting events? Which sports?
2 Which of these things do you *borrow / lend* to your friends: books, clothes, money?
3 Do you *say / tell* your family or best friend everything?
4 Do you think it's OK to *look at / watch* your phone during class?
5 Which three things do you always *bring / take* to class?

b Work with a partner. Ask and answer the questions in exercise **3a**, and give reasons for your answers.

4a Read the text about popular sports in Argentina and complete the gaps with the words from the box.

| jog   ski   basketball   go to the gym   football   tennis |

The most popular sport in Argentina is **1**_____ .
People like playing it, going to games and watching it on TV. The Argentinian team won the World Cup in 1978 and 1986, and came second in 2014.

2_____ is also very popular especially after Argentina won the semi finals against the NBA players in 2004, and then took the Olympic gold home.

3_____ was a sport for rich people in the past, but now lots of people play it. The best Argentinian player, Juan Martín del Potro is world number 8.

Winter sports are also very popular in Argentina, people often **4**_____ in the Andes Mountains. And of course lots of people **5**_____ in local parks or **6**_____ to keep fit!

b **7.13**))) Listen and check your answers.

c Work with a partner. Which sports are popular where you live?

5a Read the conversation. Are the people *agreeing, disagreeing, asking for* or *giving an opinion*?

A What's your opinion of people taking their children out in the evening? **1**_____

B Well, I think it's fine. I don't have a problem with it.
   2_____

C I don't know about that. For me, it's not OK when the children have school the next day. **3**_____

A And what do you think of taking children to restaurants? **4**_____

B Um, I think it's OK if they're not too noisy.
   5_____

C Yes, I agree with that, but children can be very noisy!
   6_____

b Work with a partner. Ask for and give your opinion about …

1 the amount of money famous sportspeople make
2 people driving slowly but carefully
3 people talking in the cinema

8 Travel and transport

8.1 I went to ...

GOALS ■ Talk about holidays ■ Ask questions using the past simple

Vocabulary & Speaking talking about holidays

1a What kind of holidays do you like? Tick (✓) the options that are true for you.

- staying in your own country
- going to another country
- going on a city break
- staying in the countryside
- going on a beach holiday
- going with a group of friends
- going with family
- going on your own

b Compare your answers with a partner.

2a Complete texts 1–3 about different holidays with the words in the boxes.

1 | the beach   an apartment
swimming

> **BLOG | ABOUT | CONTACT**
>
> **The beach lover**
> I love lazy holidays.
> I normally rent **1**_____
> by the sea with my family.
> We lie on **2**_____ most
> of the day and go **3**_____
> in the sea. For me, the
> most important thing to do
> on holidays is to relax and
> have fun.

2 | museums   lost   a tour   the town
art galleries

> **THE CITY BREAKER**
>
> For me, holidays are about culture
> and I enjoy visiting all the **4**_____
> and **5**_____. Sometimes I go on
> **6**_____ with a guide because
> it's a great way to learn about a
> place and its history. I also like going
> out on my own and looking around
> **7**_____ without a map. I always
> get **8**_____, but I think it's the
> best way to find interesting places.

3 | sightseeing   local people   trek   cheap hotels

> BLOG   ABOUT   CONTACT
>
> THE BACK PACKERS
> We stay in **9**_____ and guest
> houses, and travel by public transport,
> so we can meet **10**_____. We don't
> go **11**_____. We prefer to **12**_____
> in the mountains and visit places that
> tourists don't often see.

3a Work with a partner. Match beginnings 1–6 to endings a–f to make questions about holidays.

1 Do you like lying
2 Do you visit
3 Do you usually take a map or
4 Do you like going on
5 Do you prefer to stay
6 Do you ever stay in

a a tour of places you visit?
b do you get lost?
c in a hotel or rent an apartment?
d on the beach?
e expensive hotels?
f art galleries and museums?

b **8.2**))) Listen, check and repeat.

c Ask and answer the questions with your partner. Give more information.

A *Do you like lying on the beach?*
B *Yes, I do. I like reading a book, but I enjoy playing beach volleyball, too.*

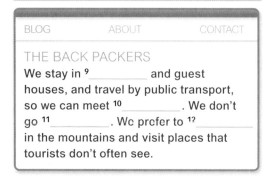

b **8.1**))) Listen and check your answers.

c Work with a partner. Which person is most like you? Why?

Grammar & Listening past simple questions

4 Work with a partner. Look at the map and photos of Guatemala. Answer the questions.

1 What do you know about Guatemala?

2 What can you do and see there?

ruined temple in the Mayan city of Tikal

Lake Atitlán

5a **8.3**))) Listen to Tom talking to his friend Katie about his trip to Guatemala. Tick (✓) the things he mentions.

- ruined temples
- Pacaya volcano
- trekking
- Lake Atitlán
- Antigua
- a Mayan city
- the mountains
- lying on the beach

b Match Katie's questions 1–6 to Tom's answers a–f.

1 Why did you go there?

2 Whereabouts in Guatemala did you go?

3 What did you do and see?

4 How long did you stay?

5 Did you stay in hotels?

6 Did you go on your own?

a About six weeks.

b Yes, I did, but I met lots of local people.

c I visited the whole country.

d No, mostly guest houses.

e I went on lots of tours and I went trekking.

f Because it's a really interesting country.

Antigua, the historic capital of Guatemala

c **8.4**))) Listen and check your answers.

6 Work with a partner. Read the Grammar focus box and complete the rules.

GRAMMAR FOCUS past simple questions and short answers

Questions with a question word

Question word + ¹_____ + subject + infinitive without *to*?
*What **did** you do and see?*

Yes/No questions

²_____ + ³_____ + infinitive without *to*?
***Did** you stay in hotels?*

With *yes/no* questions, we usually use short answers with the auxiliary *did* or *didn't*.
***Did** you go on your own? Yes, I **did**./No, I **didn't**.*

→ Grammar Reference page 150

7a Work with a partner. Put the words in the correct order to make questions.

1 did / on your / Where / go / last holiday / you ?
Where did you go on your last holiday?

2 go with / a friend / you / Did ?

3 you / did / do / What ?

4 you / Did / a good time / have ?

5 How / did / long / you / stay ?

6 did / Where / you / stay ?

7 Did / the food / like / you ?

b **8.5**))) Listen and check your answers.

PRONUNCIATION *did* in past simple questions

8.6))) In past simple questions, *did* + pronoun subject is usually unstressed.

We pronounce *did you* /dɪdʒə/, and *did he* /dɪdi/.

8 **8.7**))) Listen and notice the stressed and weak sounds.

1 How long did you stay?
/dɪdʒə/

2 Did you like the food?
/dɪdʒə/

3 Did he stay in hotels?
/dɪdi/

9a **TASK** Work with a partner. Take turns to ask and answer the questions in exercise **7a** about your last holiday.

b How different were your holidays?

▶ VOX POPS VIDEO 8

8.2 Journeys

Vocabulary & Listening transport

1 Work with a partner. What kinds of transport can you see in the photos? What other ways can we travel from place to place?

2a 8.8))) Listen to five people talking about their journeys to work. Match speakers 1–5 to photos a–e.

b 8.8))) Listen again and complete the diagrams with the words in the box. Compare with a partner.

car bike train foot taxi bus underground

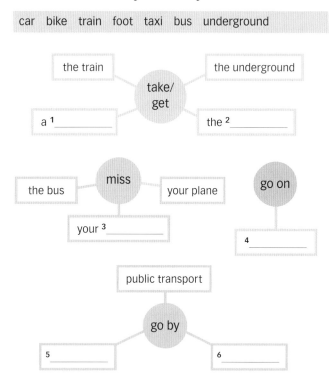

the train • the underground

take/ get

a ¹_____ • the ²_____

miss

the bus • your plane

your ³_____

go on

4 _____

public transport

go by

5 _____ • 6 _____

c 8.9))) Listen and check your answers.

3a Make sentences that are true for you. Use the phrases in *italics* or your own ideas.

1 It's *easy/difficult* for me to go to *class/work/college* by *public transport/underground/bus*.
2 I *often/sometimes/never* take *taxis/buses/trains*.
3 I *like/don't like* taking the *underground/bus/train* in big cities.
4 Yesterday I went by *one/two/more than two* kind(s) of transport.
5 I *often/sometimes/never* miss *buses/trains/planes*.
6 My favourite kind of transport is *on foot/by bike/by car/ by train* because …

b Work in small groups. Read your sentences to each other. Ask and answer questions to find out more.

A *I sometimes take taxis.*
B *Do you? When?*
A *In bad weather, but they're very expensive.*

Reading & Grammar *should, shouldn't, have to, don't have to*

4 Work with a partner. Look at photos 1–4. What do you think are the good and bad things about each kind of transport? Use the ideas in the box to help you.

> quick/slow dangerous/safe comfortable price weather

Photo 1 could be dangerous because …

5a Read the article and write the kind of transport under the correct photo. Compare your answers with a partner.

Getting around in Hanoi

Hanoi is a busy city of over six million people – what's the best way to get around?

CYCLO
Cyclos are a fun way to get around and they're good for the environment. You should have a map of the city, so you can show the driver where you want to go. Also, you shouldn't start your journey before you agree the price with the driver.

XE OM
A *xe om* is a motorbike taxi. The word *xe* means motorbike and *om* means hold. You should hold the driver, so you don't fall off! Your *xe om* driver has to give you a helmet and you have to wear it. It's against the law to travel without one.

TAXI
Air-conditioned taxis are a comfortable way to travel because it's usually so hot outside. But you shouldn't take a taxi when you need to get somewhere quickly. There's a lot of traffic in Hanoi and taxis don't go fast!

ON FOOT
You don't have to pay to see Hanoi – walking is free! We think it's the best way to see the street life of the city.

b Work with a partner. Which of your ideas in exercise 4 does the article talk about?

6 Look at the highlighted sentences in the article and match phrases 1–4 in the Grammar focus box to the correct meanings a–d.

GRAMMAR FOCUS
should, shouldn't, have to, don't have to

1	should	a	It's necessary.
2	shouldn't	b	It's the wrong thing to do, it is a bad idea.
3	have to	c	It's the right thing to do, it is a good idea.
4	don't have to	d	It's not necessary.

→ Grammar Reference page 151

1 _____

2 _____

3 _____

4 _____

PRONUNCIATION sentence stress

7a 8.10 Listen and notice the stressed words.

1 You should have a map …
2 You shouldn't take a taxi …
3 You have to wear it.
4 You don't have to pay …

b 8.10 Listen again and repeat.

8a Work with a partner. Use your own ideas to complete the sentences with *have to, don't have to, should* or *shouldn't*.

1 You _____ drink a lot of coffee on long plane journeys.
2 You _____ drive on the left side of the road in Japan.
3 You _____ wear a seat belt for the whole journey on a plane.
4 You _____ wear a helmet when riding a bike.
5 You _____ get up and walk around on long train journeys.

b Compare your ideas with another pair.

9a **TASK** Work with a partner. Write a list of 'rules' for public transport using *should, shouldn't, have to* or *don't have to*. Use the ideas in the box to help you.

> music food give your seat have a ticket feet bags
> wear seat belt stand in a queue at bus stop

You shouldn't put your feet on the seat on public transport.

b Compare your answers with another pair.

8.3 Vocabulary and skills development

Vocabulary & Speaking expressions with *get, take,* and *have*

1 Work with a partner. Take turns to ask and answer questions 1–10. Ask follow-up questions.

1 How many **emails** do you **get** a day?
2 Where do you usually **have lunch**?
3 Do you **take** many **photos** when you are on holiday?
4 Is it better in life to **have fun** or make money?
5 How often do you **get a taxi** to go somewhere?
6 How many **text messages** do you **get** a day?
7 Who do you usually **have dinner** with?
8 How often do you **take a bus**?
9 Do people in your country **have a** short **sleep** in the middle of the day?
10 Does it **take a long time** to do your homework?

A *How many emails do you get a day?*
B *About ten.*
A *Who are they usually from?*
B *Colleagues and sometimes friends. What about you?*
A *Oh, I get about 20 emails a day from work colleagues.*

2 Read the information in the Vocabulary focus box about expressions with *get, take* and *have*.

VOCABULARY FOCUS
expressions with *get, take* and *have*

- Some verbs, e.g. *get, take,* and *have* are often followed by a noun to make common expressions.
  ***get** a text message,* **take** *photos,* **have** *a shower.*
- It is useful to learn the whole expressions.

3 Put the nouns in the box in the correct column in the table. Add any other examples you know.

a bus   a good time   a long time   a shower   a sleep
a taxi   a text message   dinner   emails   fun   lunch
photos   something to eat

get	take	have

4 Complete sentences 1–8 with the correct form of the verbs *get, take* or *have*.

1 My brother always _____ a shower in the morning.
2 I sometimes _____ a sleep after lunch.
3 Grażyna and Łucja never _____ more than 50 emails a day.
4 Réka _____ a good time last weekend.
5 It doesn't _____ a long time to do this exercise.
6 Tanawat always _____ the bus to work.
7 I _____ a taxi this morning because I was late.
8 Alejandro usually _____ lots of photos when he visits his family.

5 Work with a partner. Have a conversation about your daily routines, using the expressions in exercise **3**. Who used the most expressions?

I have a shower and then I have something to eat …

Listening & Speaking present simple and past simple questions

6a **8.11**))) Listen to six questions. Are they in the present simple or the past simple? Write *present* or *past*.

1 _____   3 _____   5 _____
2 _____   4 _____   6 _____

b **8.12**))) Read and listen to the information in the Unlock the code box about understanding present simple and past simple questions.

> 🔓 **UNLOCK THE CODE**
> present simple and past simple questions
>
> - It is sometimes difficult to decide if a question is in the present simple or the past simple because of the weak sound of *do you, does he* and *did you*.
>   ***Do you*** /dʒə/ *live in London?*
>   ***Does he*** /ˈdʌzi/ *live in London?*
>   ***Did you*** /ˈdɪdʒə/ *live in London?*
> - Sometimes a time expression can help you decide if the question is present or past.
>   ***Do*** *you get the bus* **every day**?
>   ***Did*** *you get the bus* **last night**?
> - Remember that some time expressions can be used for the present and the past.
>   ***Do you/Did you*** *go to work on Saturdays?*

c **8.13**))) Listen to six questions and write them down. Compare your answers with a partner.

7a **8.14**))) Listen to a conversation between Hannah and George about Moscow and answer the questions.

1 Why are Hannah and George talking about Moscow?
2 What does Hannah think of the transport there?
3 What is an unusual way of travelling in this city?

b **8.14**))) Listen again. Are the questions in the conversation in the present simple or past simple? Write present or past next to prompts 1–6.

1 have to work? _____
2 how long/live there? _____
3 speak the language? _____
4 like the city? _____
5 what/think of the transport system? _____
6 local people use the buses? _____

c **8.15**))) Listen and check your answers.

8a **TASK** Write down two present simple and two past simple questions to ask your partner.
What languages do you speak?

b Work with a partner. Take turns to ask and answer your questions.

8.4 Speaking and writing

GOALS ■ Ask for information at the train station ■ Write an email about your perfect holiday

Listening & Speaking at the train station

1 Work with a partner. Think of the last time you went on a long journey. Take turns to ask and answer questions. Use the prompts in the box.

Where/go?	What kind of transport/take?
When/go?	How long/journey?
Why/go?	Enjoy the journey? Why/Why not?

indian RAILWAYS

- more than 8,000 stations across the country
- 25 million passengers travel on 11,000 trains every day
- about a million employees
- Howrah Station in Kolkata is the oldest and biggest station: 600 trains arrive and depart from 26 platforms every day.

2a Work with a partner. Marcel is at the ticket office in Howrah station. Match questions 1–7 to answers a–g.

1 Hello. Can I help you?
2 When would you like to travel?
3 When's the next train?
4 How long does it take?
5 And how much is a sleeper ticket?
6 Would you like a single or a return?
7 Which platform does it leave from?

a Later today or tomorrow.
b Just a single, please.
c About 17 hours. It arrives at 11.25 a.m. tomorrow.
d Yes, please. I need to get to New Delhi.
e Platform 7.
f That's 775 rupees.
g The next one leaves at 18.40.

b 8.16))) Listen to the conversation between Marcel and the ticket seller, and check your answers.

c 8.17))) Listen to the questions and repeat.

3a Work with a partner. Which questions does Marcel ask and which questions does the ticket seller ask? Mark the questions in exercise **2a** 'M' or 'T'.

b Read the Language for speaking box and check your answers.

LANGUAGE FOR SPEAKING at the train station

Ticket seller
Can I help you?
When would you like to go/leave/travel/come back/return?
Would you like a single or return?

Passenger
When's the next train/bus (to …)?
How much does it/a (first class) single/a (second class) return/ a sleeper cost?
How long does it take?
Which platform does it leave/go from?

c Work with a partner. Take turns to ask and answer the questions in exercise **2a**.

4 Work with a partner. Take turns to be a passenger and a ticket seller. Student A, turn to page 129. Student B, turn to page 134.

Reading & Writing email: a perfect holiday

5 Work with a partner. Read the emails Marcel sent from India to his friend Narong. Use phrases a–d to complete his emails.

  a **so** I'm taking lots of photos
  b **because** it took a very long time to get here – almost two days on the train
  c **so** I got lost
  d **because** there's just so much to do and see

Sent: THURSDAY 14.19 ⊠

Hi Narong,

Thanks for your email. India is amazing! I'm in Delhi at the moment. Today I looked around the old part of the city and went on a tour of the National Museum. Everywhere is really colourful and interesting, **1** _____ ! I decided to stay here for another week **2** _____ .

Bye for now.

Marcel

Sent: WEDNESDAY 12.45 ⊠

Dear Narong,

I arrived in Kerala a couple of days ago. I was tired after the journey **3** _____ . I went sightseeing around Kochi yesterday, but I forgot my map **4** _____ ! I took a taxi back to the hotel and it was very expensive, but I saw lots of interesting places.

Hope you're OK and see you soon.

Marcel

6a Read the information in the Language for writing box about linkers.

> **LANGUAGE FOR WRITING**
> linkers – *so* and *because*
>
> • *Because* tells us why something happens or happened.
>   *I was tired after the journey **because** it took a very long time to get here.*
> • *So* tells us the result of the first idea.
>   *It took a very long time to get here, **so** I was tired after the journey.*

  b Work with a partner. Complete the second sentence so it means the same as the first sentence. Use *so* or *because*.

  1 Everywhere is really colourful and interesting, so I'm taking lots of photos.
     I'm taking _____ .
  2 I decided to stay here for another week because there's just so much to do and see.
     There's _____ .
  3 I forgot my map, so I got lost.
     I got _____ .
  4 The weather was bad, so we stayed in the hotel.
     We stayed _____ .
  5 We love swimming, so we went to the beach.
     We went _____ .
  6 We ate at a local restaurant every night because the food was really good.
     The food _____ .

7a Imagine you are on a perfect holiday. Think about questions 1–10.

  1 What kind of holiday is it?   7 Who are you with?
  2 Where are you?   8 What do you do during
  3 When did you arrive?   the day/in the evening?
  4 How did you travel?   9 What did you do on the
  5 Where are you staying?   first day/yesterday?
  6 How long are you staying?   10 What do you like best
                                     about the place where?

  b Work with a partner. Take turns to ask and answer the questions in exercise **7a**.

8a **TASK** Write an email to a friend about your perfect holiday using your answers in exercise **7**. Remember to use *so* and *because*.

  b Give your email to another student and read their email. Answer questions 1–3.
  1 Do you want to go on their holiday? Why/Why not?
  2 Do they use *so* and *because* correctly?
  3 How do they start and finish their email?

8.5 Video

Adventure holidays

1a Work with a partner. What is an adventure holiday? How is it different from other holidays? Think of some examples.

b Work with a partner. Look at the photos of Sarah's adventure holiday and try to answer the questions.
- Where did she go?
- What did she do?
- What did she find difficult?

2 ▶ Watch the video about Sarah's adventure holiday and check your ideas in exercise **1b**.

3a Complete the notes about Sarah's holiday.
1 Sarah prefers _____ holidays.
2 Sarah went to South America on a _____ trip.
3 She travelled around South America for _____ months.
4 Sarah wanted to go to Patagonia in Chile because it's _____ .
5 Her favourite thing about the journey was _____ .
6 She thinks that the people of Chile are _____ .
7 Cycling on the Carretera Austral wasn't easy because _____ .
8 The bike was quite heavy, it weighed _____ kilograms.
9 Sarah also used other forms of transport, for example, _____ .

b ▶ Watch the video again and check your answers.

4a **TASK** Work in groups. Imagine you are Sarah and you are writing a blog of your journey through Patagonia. Choose from one of these options and write your day's blog entry.
- Your first day cycling as you leave Ushuaia.
- A difficult/good day on the road.
- Your last day cycling on the Carretera Austral.

b Work with a partner. Read your partner's blog entry and think of three questions to ask them for more details about their day.

How did you speak to the people?

Review

1a Read the answers about a holiday. Complete the questions from the prompts.

1   **A** Where / go? _Where did you go?_
    B I went to Corfu.

2   **A** What / do? _____
    B I went to the beach.

3   **A** How long / stay? _____
    B Ten days.

4   **A** When / go? _____
    B We went in August.

5   **A** Travel / alone? _____
    B No. I went with my parents.

6   **A** Stay / hotel? _____
    B No. We stayed in an apartment.

b Work with a partner. Ask and answer the questions in exercise **1a** about your last holiday. Give more information.

2a Put the words in the correct order to give advice for visitors to Auckland, New Zealand.

1   leave / have to / don't / a tip / You / in restaurants .
2   your umbrella / You / forget / shouldn't .
3   don't / have a visa / Australians / to visit / have to .
4   at night / You / Myers Park / go / shouldn't / to .
5   a student visa / for more than three months / to study / have to / You / get .
6   visit / the islands in the Hauraki Gulf / should / You .

b **8.18**)) Listen and check your answers.

c Write some advice for visitors to your country using *should*, *shouldn't*, *have to* and *don't have to*. Compare your answers with a partner.

3 Look at the words in the box and find ...

1   two types of holiday
2   two places to stay
3   five things you can do on holiday
4   two types of people

apartment	backpacker	beach holiday	beach lover
city break	go on a tour	go sightseeing	go trekking
hotel	lie on the beach	visit museums	

4 Work with a partner. Talk about how you travel in each of these situations.

How do you ...

1   come to your English class?   4   do the shopping?
2   go to work/college?   5   go out at night?
3   go on holiday?   6   see family/friends?

5a Complete questions 1–6 with *get*, *take* or *have*. There may be more than one possible answer.

1   How many times a week do you _____ a bus?
2   How many emails do you _____ on a normal day?
3   Do you _____ a shower before or after breakfast?
4   Does it _____ a long time to travel from your home to the town/city centre?
5   What do you do to _____ fun with your friends?
6   Do you usually _____ a sleep on a long journey?

b Work with a partner. Take turns to ask and answer the questions in exercise **5a**.

6a Complete the conversation at a bus station.
   A Hello. Can I ¹_____ you?
   B Yes, please. When's the next bus ²_____ Manchester?
   A There's one at 4.00 p.m.
   B How ³_____ does it cost?
   A Do you want a single or ⁴_____ ticket?
   B A return, please.
   A And when would you like to come ⁵_____ ?
   B Next Sunday.
   A OK, that's £32, please.
   B How ⁶_____ does it take?
   A Two hours 45 minutes. Here's your ticket.
   B Where does it ⁷_____ from?
   A Bay six. It's just over there.

b **8.19**)) Listen and check your answers.

c Have a similar conversation with your partner. Use your own ideas about places, times and prices.

9 Cooking and eating

9.1 Food and drink

GOALS ■ Talk about food and drink ■ Use countable/uncountable nouns with *some/any*

Vocabulary & Speaking food and drink

1a Work with a partner. Match the words in the box to numbers 1–16 in the photo.

> a bottle of lemonade   a pear   beef   bread   chicken
> honey   jam   lemons   mushrooms   noodles   olives
> pasta   rice   salad   sweetcorn   yoghurt

b 9.1))) Listen, check and repeat.

2a Write answers to questions 1–6. Use words from exercise **1a**.
Which things are …

1	meat? *beef*	4	sweet?
2	vegetables?	5	healthy?
3	fruit?	6	unhealthy?

b Work with a partner. Compare your answers.

Grammar & Listening countable and uncountable nouns

3a Read the Grammar focus box about countable and uncountable nouns.

> **GRAMMAR FOCUS**
> countable and uncountable nouns
>
> • There are two types of noun in English:
>   1 Nouns we can count (countable nouns)
>   e.g. *lemons, pears*
>   2 Nouns we can't count (uncountable nouns)
>   e.g. *rice, beef*
> • For singular countable nouns we use *a/an*.
>   *Do you have **a** lemon?   I'd like **a** pear.*
> • For uncountable nouns and plural countable nouns
>   we don't use *a* or *an*.
>   *I have yoghurt for breakfast.   I like mushrooms.*
>
> → Grammar Reference page 152

b Work with a partner. Put the words from exercise **1a** into the correct columns in the table.

Singular countable nouns	Plural countable nouns	Uncountable nouns
	lemons	

4a Work with a partner. Talk about the food and drink in exercise **1a** and other food and drink that you know.
• I like/don't like …
• I had … for breakfast/lunch/dinner yesterday/this morning.
• I often have … for lunch/dinner.

b Tell the class three things that are true for both of you.
We both had fruit and yoghurt for breakfast this morning.

pizza stall

Chinese stall

5 Work in small groups. Look at the photos of two street food stalls in Camden Market in London. Which of the two stalls would you like to eat at? Why?

6 **9.2**))) Lars and Carla are at Camden Market. Listen to them ordering some food. Which stall in exercise **5** do they go to and what do they order?

7a Work with a partner. Match beginnings 1–6 to endings a–f to make sentences from the conversation in exercise **6**.

1 It comes with	a there any bread?
2 Is	b have some rice.
3 We don't	c you like any drinks?
4 We	d some noodles.
5 Would	e any bottles of lemonade.
6 We don't have	f have any bread.

b **9.3**))) Listen and check your answers.

8 Work with a partner. Look at sentences 1–6 in exercise **7a** and complete the rules in the Grammar focus box about *some* and *any*.

GRAMMAR FOCUS *some/any*

- We use ¹_____ and ²_____ with uncountable nouns and plural countable nouns.
- We use:
  1 ³_____ in positive sentences.
  2 ⁴_____ in negative sentences.
  3 ⁵_____ in questions.
- Note: when we ask for something, we use ⁶_____.
  *Can I have **some** noodles?*

→ Grammar Reference page 152

9a Read the conversation between a customer (C) and a shop assistant (S). Circle the correct options.

S Hello. Can I help you?
C Hi. Yes, please. Do you have ¹ *some/any* beef?
S Yes, we have ² *some/any* nice steaks here. We also have ³ *some/a* small beef cubes.
C OK. Can I have ⁴ *some/any* beef cubes? About a kilo, please. And I'd also like ⁵ *a/some* small steak.
S Just one?
C Yes, just one. Thanks. Also, do you have ⁶ *a/any* yoghurt?
S No, I'm afraid we don't.
C What about rice? Do you have ⁷ *some/any* rice?
S Yes, we have ⁸ *some/any* bags of rice, but we also do rice salad.
C No, I'll just have ⁹ *a/some* bag of rice, please.
S OK. Anything else?
C Yes, do you have ¹⁰ *some/any* lemons?
S No, we don't sell ¹¹ *a/any* fruit or vegetables, I'm afraid.
C OK. That's everything, then, thanks.

> ■ **cube** shape like a box with six square sides

b **9.4**))) Listen and check your answers.

PRONUNCIATION sentence stress

In sentences we use weak sounds in *some* and *any*.

10a **9.5**))) Listen and notice the stressed and weak sounds.

1 Do you have any meat?   2 We have some beef.
   /dʒə/   /ənɪ/   /səm/

b **9.6**))) Listen and repeat.
1 I'd like some beef, please.
2 Do you have any mushrooms?
3 Can I have some sweetcorn?
4 We don't have any sweetcorn.

11 Work with a partner. Find the differences in two photos. Student A, turn to page 129. Student B, turn to page 134.

9.2 In the kitchen

Reading & Grammar quantifiers

1 Work in small groups. Answer the questions.
   1 How often do you cook?
   2 Who does the most cooking in your home?

2a Work with a partner. Look at the title of the magazine article. Why do you think cooking more often is good for our health?

b Read the article and check your ideas.

The secret to good health: cook more!

How much time do people spend cooking today compared to the past? The answer is: not much time at all. For example, the average American family today spends just 27 minutes a day preparing meals. In the 1960s, it was nearly an hour a day. And how many young people know how to cook? Well, there aren't many, according to a survey in the UK. 49% of 18–24 year olds don't know how many minutes it takes to boil an egg! But is this change in cooking habits a problem?

Jean-Michel Cohen, a French doctor, thinks we have quite a lot of health problems today because not many people cook enough. He says that when we buy ready-made meals or takeaway food, we don't really think about what we're eating. This means we often eat a lot of food – more than we need. But when we buy the ingredients, e.g. vegetables, meat, fish, and then fry, bake or boil them, we think more carefully about what we are eating. And when we think about the ingredients, we usually eat healthy meals and we eat well.

So, perhaps the answer to some of the health problems is not 'eat less' – it's 'cook more'!

Life & Style | Food

3a Read the article again and complete the notes.
   Cooking in the past:
   ¹ *People spent a long time preparing meals.*
   Cooking now: ² _____.
   When we buy ready-made meals or takeaways,
   we ³ _____ and
   ⁴ _____. When we cook,
   we ⁵ _____ and
   ⁶ _____.

b Compare your answers with a partner. Do you agree with Dr Cohen? Why/Why not?

4 Read sentences 1–6 from the article and complete the rules in the Grammar focus box with *much/many/a lot of*.
   1 We have quite a lot of health problems today ...
   2 How many young people know how to cook?
   3 Well, there aren't many, according to a survey in the UK.
   4 This means we often eat a lot of food.
   5 How much time do people spend cooking today?
   6 The answer is: not much time at all.

GRAMMAR FOCUS quantifiers

- **Countable nouns**
  We use ¹_____ in positive sentences. We use ²_____ in questions and negative sentences.
- **Uncountable nouns**
  We use ³_____ in positive sentences. We use ⁴_____ in negative sentences and questions.

  ⁵_____   quite a lot of   some   not ⁶_____ /
                                          not ⁷_____   none

→ Grammar Reference page 153

5a Circle the correct option in each question and the answer that is true for you.
   1 How *much / many* time do you spend in the kitchen?
     None / Not much / Some / A lot.
   2 How *much / many* meat do you eat?
     None / Not many / Some / A lot.
   3 How *much / many* cookbooks do you have?
     None / Not many / Some / A lot.
   4 How *much / many* tea and coffee do you drink?
     None / Not much / Some / A lot.
   5 How *much / many* money do you spend on food?
     None / Not much / Some / A lot.

b Work in small groups. Take turns to ask and answer the questions. Give more information in your answers.
   A *How much time do you spend in the kitchen?*
   B *Not much. My husband cooks all our meals.*

Vocabulary & Listening in the kitchen

6a **9.7**)) Listen to three people talking about their kitchens. Match the speakers to photos a–c.

Brigit _____   Laila _____   Joe _____

b Compare your answers with a partner.

7a Work with a partner. Label photos a–c with the words in the box.

bowls food-processor fork frying pan kettle
knife microwave oven plates spoon saucepan

b **9.8**)) Listen and check your answers.

8a Work with a partner. Complete the sentences with the cooking verbs in the box.

bake boil chop fry mix roast

1 You _____ water in a kettle to make tea.
2 For breakfast I often _____ eggs, mushrooms and tomatoes together in a big frying pan.
3 To _____ meat, you need a very hot oven.
4 _____ the water and flour together in a bowl with a spoon.
5 Not many people _____ their own bread or cakes at home these days.
6 You need to use a sharp knife to _____ the onions.

b **9.9**)) Listen and check your answers.

9a Work with a partner. How do you cook different food? Write sentences using the words in exercises **7a** and **8a**.
You can boil potatoes in a saucepan.

b Compare your sentences with another pair.

10a TASK Work with a partner. You want to cook mushroom soup for four people. Look at the list of ingredients and guess how much/many of each ingredient you need.

potatoes water milk mushrooms carrots butter

A *How many potatoes do you think we need?*
B *A lot, I think we need about ten.*

b Work with a partner. Take turns to ask and answer questions to check your answers to exercise **10a** and complete the recipe. Student A, turn to page 129. Student B, turn to page 134.

▶ VOX POPS VIDEO 9

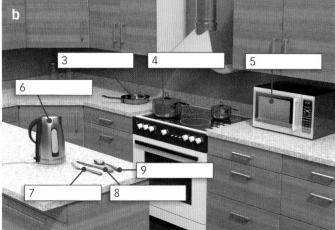

9.3 Vocabulary and skills development

GOALS ■ Understand numbers ■ Say numbers

Listening & Speaking understanding numbers

1 Work with a partner. Label the places a–h on the map using the words in the box.

> Indonesia Jakarta Java Malaysia Papua New Guinea
> Singapore Surabaya The Philippines

2a **9.10**))) Listen to six sentences about Singapore and Papua New Guinea. Tick (✓) the numbers you hear.

1	116	160	3	¼	¾	5	19.4	19.6
2	10%	20%	4	1965	1865	6	¾	¼

b Compare your answers with a partner.

3a **9.11**))) Listen and read the information in the Unlock the code box about numbers.

> 🔓 **UNLOCK THE CODE**
> numbers
>
> • Some numbers can sound very similar. Notice the different stress.
>   ●●   ●●   ●●   ●●
>   30 students   13 students   90%   19%
> • For large numbers we say:
>   100 – a hundred/one hundred
>   200 – two hundred (NOT ~~two hundreds~~)
>   3,420 – three thousand, four hundred and twenty
>   4,000,000 – four million
> • For years we say:
>   1998 – nineteen ninety-eight
>   2018 – two thousand and eighteen/twenty eighteen

b Work with a partner. Write down five numbers each. Take turns to read each other's numbers out.

4a **9.12**))) Listen to the first part of a lecture about Indonesia and complete the text with the numbers you hear.

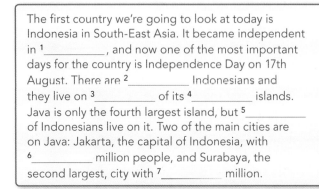

> The first country we're going to look at today is Indonesia in South-East Asia. It became independent in ¹_____, and now one of the most important days for the country is Independence Day on 17th August. There are ²_____ Indonesians and they live on ³_____ of its ⁴_____ islands. Java is only the fourth largest island, but ⁵_____ of Indonesians live on it. Two of the main cities are on Java: Jakarta, the capital of Indonesia, with ⁶_____ million people, and Surabaya, the second largest, city with ⁷_____ million.

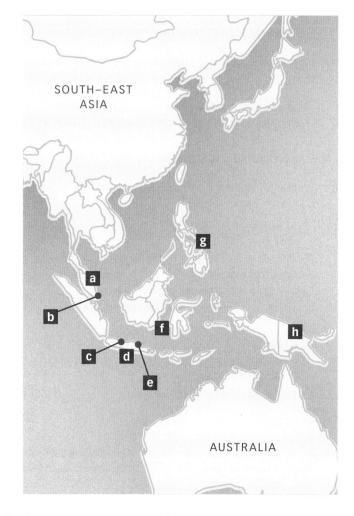

SOUTH–EAST ASIA

AUSTRALIA

b Compare your answers with a partner.

c **9.12**))) Listen again and check your answers.

5 **9.13**))) Listen to the second part of the lecture and complete the table with the correct numbers.

Size from east to west	
Indonesians working on farms	
Climate – minimum temperature	
Climate – maximum temperature	
Rain a year	
Maximum rain in mountain areas	
Rice imports	

Vocabulary Development say numbers

6a Work with a partner. What are the dates and numbers for your country/countries?

Number of people	
Largest city	
Minimum temperature	
Maximum temperature	
An important day	

b Compare your answers with another pair.

7a **9.14** 》 Read and listen to the information in the Vocabulary focus box.

VOCABULARY FOCUS saying numbers

Fractions
¼ – a quarter   ¾ – three-quarters
⅓ – a third   ⅔ – two-thirds
½ – a half   ⅖ – two-fifths

Percentages
15% – fifteen per cent
4.7% – four point seven per cent

Decimals
2.89 – two point eight nine
0.3 – nought point three

Temperatures
22°C – twenty-two degrees Celsius
-7°C – minus seven

Dates
01/09 – the first of September
26/03 – the twenty-sixth of March

b Match numbers 1–8 to the way we say them a–h.

1	7.35	a	sixteen point one degrees
2	03/10/16	b	eighty-two point four per cent
3	⅘	c	seven point three five
4	16.1°C	d	the third of October twenty sixteen
5	82.4%	e	minus fourteen
6	12/05/86	f	four-fifths
7	-14°C	g	one and three-quarters
8	1 ¾	h	the twelfth of May nineteen eighty-six

c **9.15** 》 Listen, check and repeat.

8 Work with a partner. Take turns to practise saying the numbers.

1	7.4%	5	0.23
2	2 ⅔	6	20/02/15
3	21/07/92	7	100°C
4	-11.7°C	8	1 ¼

9a Work with a partner. Look at the information 1–7 and guess the numbers.

1 the lowest temperature recorded on Earth
2 the date man first landed on the moon
3 the amount of chocolate Belgium produces a year
4 the number of times an adult laughs a day
5 the number of times a child laughs a day
6 the percentage of people using Facebook at work
7 the number of years people spend eating in their lifetime

b Turn to page 133 and check your answers.

10 Work with a partner. Take turns to ask and answer questions about the two countries. Student A, turn to page 130. Student B, turn to page 134.

9.4 Speaking and writing

GOALS ■ Ask about and recommend a place to eat ■ Order food in a restaurant

Reading & Writing asking about and recommending a place to eat

1 Work with a partner. Answer questions 1–3.

1 When did you last eat out?

2 Where did you go and who did you go with?

3 Was it good? Why/Why not?

2a Read the email from Stefano to his friend Vera. Why is he writing to her?

Sent: THURSDAY 14.19 ☒

Hi Vera,

How are you? Everything's good with me. I'm going to Edinburgh this weekend with Molly for her 25th birthday. I know you finished university there last year and I hope you can help me with something. We're looking for a restaurant to have dinner on Saturday night. What's your favourite restaurant? Do you know anywhere that's quite cheap and has good food? Also, where's a good place to sit outside and eat? And with a nice view of the castle? Are the restaurants in Edinburgh busy on Saturdays? Do I need to book a table?

Thanks for your help!

Stefano
---

b Work with a partner. Tick (✓) the things that Stefano wants to know about a place to eat in Edinburgh.

1 directions to get there?
2 Vera's favourite place?
3 the prices?
4 nice food?
5 opening times?
6 possible to sit outside?
7 the waiters?
8 the view?
9 busy or not?
10 need to book?

3 Work with a partner. Read Vera's reply and underline her answers to Stefano's questions. Does she tell him to go to her favourite restaurant?

Sent: THURSDAY 19.30 ☒

Hi Stefano,

Great to hear from you and I'm glad you're well. My favourite place is the Castle Terrace because the food is amazing, but it's quite expensive. There's also a place called Kayla's Kitchen with good, cheap food. You can't eat outside there – it's not often very warm in Scotland – but it has wonderful views of the city from the rooftop restaurant. The waiters are really friendly too, so I think you should go there.

OK, have a brilliant time and let me know how your trip goes!

Vera

P.S. You should book a table on the Saturday night because it's very popular.

4a Work with a partner. Put the words in the right order to make questions and answers about a place to eat.

1 restaurant / We're / a / for / looking / Thai .
2 the roof / outside / on / can / sit / You .
3 lunch / favourite / your / What's / café / for ?
4 to / need / Do / online / I / book ?
5 a / place / Where's / have / cake / to / good / some ?
6 a / menu / It / wonderful / has .
7 and book / call them / You / need to / don't .
8 know / you / a garden / has / Do / anywhere that ?
9 with a / called the Riverside / There's / place / nice view / a .
10 French food / is / place / Café Blanc / My favourite / it sells / because .

b 9.16 ⟫ Listen and check your answers.

5a Write an email to another student in the class. Choose a situation 1–3 and ask them to recommend a restaurant. Use the Language for writing box to help you.

1 You and your friends/family are tourists and want to have lunch in a restaurant with a view.

2 You're a group of students and want to have lunch in a cheap restaurant.

3 You're with some colleagues and want to have dinner in a smart restaurant.

> **LANGUAGE FOR WRITING**
> asking about and recommending a place to eat
>
> **Asking about a place to eat:**
> *I'm/We're looking for …*
> *What's your favourite …?*
> *Do you know anywhere that …?*
> *Where's a good place to …?*
> *Do I/we need to …?*
>
> **Recommending a place to eat:**
> *My favourite place is … because …*
> *There's a place called … with …*
> *You can/can't sit outside.*
> *It has wonderful …*
> *You should/don't have to …*
> *I think you should go there.*
> *It's very popular.*

b Work with a partner. Read your partner's email and write a reply.

c Read the reply from your partner. Would you like to eat in this restaurant?

Speaking & Listening   in a restaurant

6 **9.17**))) Stefano and Molly are at Kayla's Kitchen in Edinburgh. Listen to their conversation with the waiter. What do they order? Tell your partner.

7a Work with a partner. Complete the questions from the listening in exercise **6** with *Can/Could I/we* or *Would you like*.

1   _Would you like_ to order?
2 _____ have the grilled chicken, please?
3 _____ any side dishes with that?
4 _____ have some roast potatoes?
5 _____ something to drink?
6 _____ pay by credit card?

b **9.18**))) Listen, check and repeat.

8a Work with a partner. Complete six more restaurant questions with *Can/Could I/we* or *Would you like*.

1 _____ see the menu, please?   4 _____ order, please?
2 _____ have some bread, please?   5 _____ some dessert?
3 _____ another cup of coffee?   6 _____ a starter?

b Which questions from exercises **7a** and **8a** does the waiter (W) ask? Which does the customer (C) ask? Compare your answers with a partner.
Would you like to order? W

9 **TASK** Work with a partner. Take turns to be the waiter and the customer. Use the prompts and the Language for speaking box to help you.

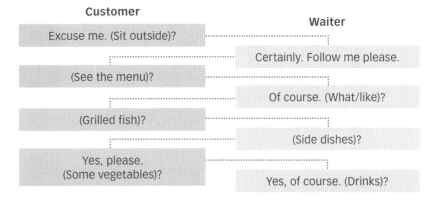

Customer
Excuse me. (Sit outside)?

Waiter
Certainly. Follow me please.

(See the menu)?

Of course. (What/like)?

(Grilled fish)?

(Side dishes)?

Yes, please.
(Some vegetables)?

Yes, of course. (Drinks)?

> **LANGUAGE FOR SPEAKING** in a restaurant
>
> **Waiter**
> *Would you like …   a starter/some dessert/more drinks?*
>   *any side dishes with that?*
>   *something to drink?*
>   *to order now?*
>
> **Customer**
> *Can/Could I/we …   see the menu/order?*
>   *have the grilled chicken/some more bread?*
>   *pay now/by credit card, please?*
>   *sit outside/by the window?*

10 Work with a partner. Take turns to order from a menu. Turn to page 130.

9.5 Video

Making a pizza

1 Look at the photos. Which of these things do you see in them?

> aubergine base basil cheese courgette dough
> flour ingredients recipe restaurant topping yeast

2 Work with a partner. Describe the photos using the words in exercise **1**. What is your favourite pizza topping?

3 ▶ Watch the video and choose the correct option.
1 La Cucina is in *London / Rome / Oxford*.
2 Pizza originally comes from *Chicago / Naples / Milan*.
3 La Cucina chefs follow a *modern / traditional* recipe.
4 Mozzarella comes from the *south / north / west* of Italy.
5 Pizza stays in the oven until it is a *golden brown / yellow / red* colour.
6 Cucina's chefs recommend you eat pizza *on its own / with a healthy salad / with chips*.

4a Complete the sentences with words from the box.

> cheese chicken mushrooms olive oil onions (x2)
> peppers salt tomato toppings water yeast

1 Pizza dough is made with wheat flour, _____ , _____ and _____ .
2 The tomato sauce on top of a pizza is made with _____ , _____ , tomatoes and salt.
3 Pizza Margherita has _____ , basil and mozzarella.
4 Pizza Romano has _____ .
5 Pizza al Funghi has _____ and garlic.
6 Pizza alle Verdure has _____ , _____ , aubergine and courgette.
7 For the 'your choice pizza' you can choose your own _____ and cheese.

b ▶ Watch the video again and check your answers.

5a **TASK** Work in small groups. Describe a traditional/your favourite dish. Use these ideas to help you make notes.
- ingredients
- how you make it
- why you like it

b Present your ideas to the class. Choose the top three dishes and make a class menu.

Review

1a Make sentences to describe the photo. Use *There* and a phrase in the box.

is a	is an	is some	are some	isn't any	aren't any

1 rice *There is some rice.*   5 mushrooms
2 bottle of lemonade   6 salad
3 apple   7 meat
4 pears   8 jam

b Work with a partner. Do they have the items in exercise **1a** in their kitchen?
  A *Do you have any rice in your kitchen?*
  B *Yes, I do. And you?*
  A *No, I never have any rice. I don't like it.*

2a Make questions using *How much* or *How many*.
  1 _____ types of tomato are there in the world?
  2 _____ calories are there in a lemon?
  3 _____ sugar is there in a cup of 2% fat milk?
  4 _____ food did the average American eat in 2011?
  5 _____ cups of coffee do Italians drink each year?

b Work with a partner. Compare your questions in exercise **2a** and try to answer them using the phrases in the box.

a lot	quite a lot	some	not much/many	none

  A *How many types of tomato are there in the world?*
  B *I think there are quite a lot. Maybe one thousand?*

c **9.19**)) Listen and check your answers.

3a Anoush is having a dinner party. Look at photos 1–5 and write sentences to describe what he is doing.

1 *He's boiling some potatoes.*

b Work with a partner. How do you cook different types of food and what do you use to cook them?
  I use a saucepan to boil potatoes.

4a How do we say the numbers 1–4?
  1 21°C   3 45.5%
  2 ⅔   4 2,478,000

b **9.20**)) Listen and check your answers.

c Write down a number for each category. Show your partner and ask them to say the number.
  1 a percentage _____   4 a date _____
  2 a fraction _____   5 a temperature _____
  3 a decimal _____   6 a large number _____

5a Put the words in the right order.
  1 have / potatoes / Could / please / some / I / roast ?
  2 don't / No / we .
  3 you / with / dish / that / side / like / Would / a ?
  4 like / order / Would / to / you ?
  5 any / you / juice / have / Do / apple ?
  6 the / I / fish / Could / please / have / baked ?
  7 bottle / please / just / of / OK / water / a .
  8 to / you / something / drink / like / And / would ?

b Put the sentences in exercise **5a** in the correct order to make a conversation between a waiter and a customer.

c **9.21**)) Listen and check your answers.

d Work with a partner. Practise the conversation.

10 The world around us

10.1 The weather

GOALS ■ Describe the weather ■ Use comparative adjectives

Vocabulary & Listening the weather

1 Work with a partner. Answer the questions.

1 Do you like the weather where you live? Why/Why not?
2 How would you like it to be different?
3 Which countries have the best weather in your opinion?

2 **10.1**))) Work with a partner. Listen to three people talking about the weather. Which recording 1–3 is …

a part of a news report?
b the weather forecast for Lisbon, Portugal?
c someone talking about the weather on their holiday?

3a Work with a partner. Complete the weather descriptions with the words in the box.

cloudy   dry   foggy   freezing   icy   lightning   rain
snow   storms   sunny   thunder   warm   wet   windy

b **10.1**))) Listen again and check your answers.

4a Work with a partner. Complete the table with some of the weather words in exercise **3a**.

Noun	Verb	Adjective
1_____	to snow	snowy
2_____	to rain	rainy
sun	to shine	3_____
wind	to blow	4_____
ice	to freeze	5_____ / 6_____
fog		7_____

b **10.2**))) Listen and check your answers.

5 Work in small groups. Describe …

1 the weather yesterday and today.
2 the weather in your country in the different seasons of the year.

Lisbon: It's ¹_____ this morning but ²_____ , and we don't expect any ³_____ . By the afternoon, it's going to be ⁴_____ and ⁵_____ , but not really hot.

Malaysia: We went in the ⁶_____ season, so we had some ⁷_____ . The first night we arrived, it was really ⁸_____ and there was a big storm with very loud ⁹_____ and ¹⁰_____ .

Chicago: It's ¹¹_____ here today. There was a lot of ¹²_____ last night and the roads are very ¹³_____ . It's cold and ¹⁴_____ now and there is more snow to come later today.

Grammar & Speaking comparatives

6 Work with a partner. Describe the photos.

7 Work with a partner. Read the profile and match the country to options a, b or c. What information helped you decide?
  a Saudi Arabia   **b** Austria   **c** Mali

COUNTRY PROFILE

Most of the country has a hot climate. It's colder and wetter by the sea than in the middle of the country, where it's hotter and drier. In the summer, the temperature's usually about 45°C and sometimes it even reaches 54°C. The temperatures at night are more comfortable than in the day, and on summer evenings, people go out onto their roofs to sleep.

The country's more famous for its hot temperatures than cold weather, so you might be surprised to know that sometimes it snows here. It doesn't happen very often and only during winter in the high parts of the country. Some people like snowboarding so much that they do it on the sand, even in the summer!

8a Look at the **highlighted** phrases and sentences in the profile and complete the rules in the Grammar focus box.

GRAMMAR FOCUS comparative adjectives

* We use comparative adjectives to compare two things, people, groups, etc.
* To make the comparative form of an adjective:
  1 We add _____ to most one-syllable adjectives.
    high → higher   cool → cooler
  2 We double the consonant and add _____ to most one-syllable adjectives ending in single vowel + consonant.
    wet → wetter   hot → hotter
  3 We delete _____ and add_____ to most one-syllable and two-syllable adjectives ending in y.
    windy → windier   dry → drier
  4 We use the word _____ before most adjectives with two or more syllables that don't end in -y.
    famous → more famous   comfortable → more comfortable
  5 Some comparatives are irregular.
    good → better   bad → worse   much, many → more   little → less

→ Grammar Reference page 154

b Make the comparative form of the adjectives.
  smaller   big   rainy   dangerous
  sunny   fat   boring   cheap

PRONUNCIATION *than* in comparative sentences

10.3)) When we make a comparative sentence, we say *than* with a weak sound /ðən/.
*The nights are colder **than** the days.*
*Is spring wetter **than** summer?*

9a **10.4**)) Listen to the questions and repeat.
  1 Is Dublin drier than Paris?
  2 Is Sydney bigger than Cairo?

b Work with a partner. Take turns to ask and answer the questions in exercise 9a.
  A *Is Dublin drier than Paris?*
  B *Yes, it isn't./No, it isn't. Paris is drier./ I'm not sure.*

c **10.5**)) Listen and check your answers.

10a Write comparative questions using the prompts and the adjectives in (brackets).
  1 Indian/African elephants? (heavy)
  2 Tokyo/Singapore? (expensive)
  3 giraffes/humans? (fast)
  4 Canada/the USA? (small)
  5 the North Pole/the South Pole? (cold)

b Work with a partner. Take turns to ask and answer the questions in exercise **10a**.

c **10.6**)) Listen and check your ideas.

11a **TASK** Work with a partner. Which is better – life in the city or life in the country? Complete the table with your ideas.

City	Country
more interesting	quieter

b Compare your ideas with another pair. What do most people prefer?

10.2 Natural wonders

GOALS ■ Describe nature and geography ■ Use superlative adjectives

Vocabulary & Speaking nature and geography

1a Work with a partner. Look at photos a–f and match a natural wonder to a name in the box. Which countries are they in?

> Lake Baikal Phuket Mount Kilimanjaro
> the Gobi Desert Victoria Falls the Amazon

b **10.7**))) Listen and check your answers.

2a Work with a partner. Complete sentences 1–6 from the listening in exercise **1a** with the words in the box.

> beaches coast desert islands lake mountain
> rainforest river waterfall

1 It's the highest _____ in Africa, but it's not difficult to climb.
2 It's a very big _____ on the Zambezi _____ .
3 It's the biggest and deepest _____ in the world.
4 The Amazon Jungle is the biggest area of _____ in the world.
5 The Andaman Sea has some very beautiful tropical _____ , with white sandy _____ , near the west _____ of Thailand.
6 It's a cold _____ because it's so far north and it sometimes snows there.

b **10.7**))) Listen again and check your answers.

3 Work with a partner. Talk about any natural wonders in your country or other countries you know.

4a Work with a partner. Match beginnings 1–3 to endings a–c.

1 Lake Baikal is in   a the <u>west</u> coast of Thailand.
2 The Gobi Desert is in   b the <u>south</u> of Siberia.
3 Phuket island is near   c <u>north-west</u> China and Mongolia.

b **10.8**))) Listen and check your answers.

c Complete the points of the compass with the words in the box.

> north west east south

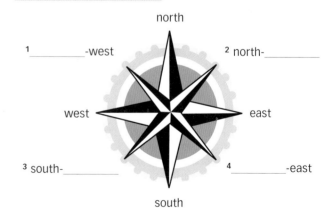

north

1 _____-west   2 north-_____

west   east

3 south-_____   4 _____-east

south

d Turn to page 130 and check your answers.

5 Work with a partner. Take turns to describe and complete a map. Student A, turn to page 130. Student B, turn to page 135.

Grammar & Speaking superlatives

6a Work with a partner. Complete the three texts about natural wonders with the numbers in the box.

| 87 | 25 | 1,600 | 3 | 20 | 5,895 | 12 |

Travel tips   ✕

Lake Baikal
Lake Baikal in Siberia is the **biggest**, **deepest**, and **oldest** lake in the world. It's more than ¹_____ metres deep and more than ²_____ million years old. It has almost ³_____ per cent of the world's fresh water, and thousands of different kinds of plants and animals live there.

Kilimanjaro
Mount Kilimanjaro, in Tanzania, is one of the **largest** volcanoes in the world. It's ⁴_____ metres tall – the **highest** mountain in Africa. It's sometimes called the 'Roof of Africa'. It's also one of the **easiest** mountains in the world to climb, even for tourists. The **oldest** person ever to climb to the top was a Frenchman, Valtee Daniel, who was ⁵_____ years old.

Al Hasa
An oasis is an area of water in a desert, and Al-Hasa is the **largest** oasis in Saudi Arabia. It covers over ⁶_____ km² and gives water to over ⁷_____ million trees and a million people, even at the **hottest** times of the year. Many Saudis believe Al-Hasa is the **most beautiful** and **best** area to visit in the country.

---

b **10.9**))) Listen and check your answers.

7a Read the Grammar focus box about superlative adjectives.

GRAMMAR FOCUS superlative adjectives

- We use the superlative form to compare a person or thing to the whole group it belongs to. We usually use *the* before superlatives.
  *Everest is the **tallest** mountain in the world.*
  *The Empire State Building is one of the **most famous** sights in New York.*

- To make the superlative form of an adjective, we add:
  1 *-est* to the end of a one-syllable adjective, e.g.
     *tall → tall**est***
  2 *-iest* to the end of a two-syllable adjective which ends in *-y*, e.g. *cloudy → cloud**iest***
  3 *most* before longer adjectives, e.g. ***most** dangerous*.
  4 Some superlatives are irregular
     *good → **best**   much, many → **most***
     *bad → **worst**   little → **least***

→ Grammar Reference page 155

b Complete the table with the superlative form of the adjectives. Check your answers in the texts in exercise **6a**.

	Adjective	Superlative form
short adjectives	big	*biggest*
	deep	
	old	
	large	
	hot	
adjectives ending in -*y*	easy	
longer adjectives	beautiful	
irregular adjectives	good	

PRONUNCIATION *the … -est* in sentences

10.10))) We say *the* in superlatives with a weak sound /ðə/ when the following adjective starts with a consonant. We say the ending *-est* with a schwa sound /əst/.

8 **10.11**))) Listen to three people talking about the longest rivers in the world and repeat.
   A *Which river's the longest in the world?*
   B *I think the Nile's the longest.*
   C *Maybe, but I think the Amazon is longer than the Mississippi.*

9a Work with a partner. Have similar conversations to the one in exercise **8**, using the adjective in (brackets).
   1 airports: Dubai, Los Angeles, Beijing (busy)
   2 islands: Sumatra, Madagascar, Greenland (big)
   3 monuments: the Colosseum (Rome), the Great Pyramid of Giza (Egypt), the Parthenon (Greece) (old)

b **10.12**))) Listen and check your answers.

10a **TASK** Work with a partner. Complete the phrases with the superlative form of the adjective in (brackets).
   1 (near) ____*The nearest*____ bank is …
   2 (cheap) _____ place to eat is …
   3 (good) _____ place to go shopping is …
   4 (old) _____ part of the town is …
   5 (interesting) _____ art gallery/ museum is …
   6 (busy) _____ street is …

b Work in small groups. Finish the sentences about where you are now. Agree or disagree and give more information.
   A *The nearest bank is about ten minutes on foot from here.*
   B *No, the bank on Palm Street is closer.*
   A *Oh yes, I forgot about that one!*

▶ VOX POPS VIDEO 10

10.3 Vocabulary and skills development

GOALS ■ Understand comparison ■ Use adjective + noun collocations

Reading & Speaking understanding comparison

1 Work with a partner. How many places can you think of for each category?

1 very cold places *the North Pole, ...*
2 very hot and dry places
3 places with dangerous animals
4 very wet places

2a Read the Unlock the code box about comparison.

> **🔒 UNLOCK THE CODE**
> comparison
>
> Comparative and superlative forms, and words like *the same/similar/different/more/less*, help you understand comparison in a text.
>
> *The Arctic is cold, but the Antarctic is **colder**.*
> (= colder than the Arctic)
> *Lions are fast animals on land, but cheetahs are **the fastest**.*
> (= the fastest animals on land)
> *A large area of North Africa is desert, but Central Africa is **different**.* (= not desert)
> *Adults pay $20 for a ticket to the national park, but students pay **less**.* (= pay less than adults)

b Work with a partner. Circle the comparison word(s) and underline the two things that the sentence compares.

1 The Burj Khalifa in Dubai is one of the tallest buildings in the world, but Everest is much taller.
2 We went on a tour of a mountain and a lake. They were both beautiful, but I enjoyed the lake more.
3 We don't really have winter. The weather in July is hot, and February is similar.
4 The south of the island was wet, but the north was wetter.
5 We get a lot of wind in the summer, and the autumn is the same.

3 Work with a partner. Read the sentences and answer the questions.

1 You can survive for only three days with no water, but longer with no food.
Longer than what? _with no water_

2 There were fifty runners in the first group and the same number in the second.
The second what? _____

3 In 2009, a Japanese man, Masahito Yoshida, aged 28, started walking 40,000 kilometres around the world. When he finished, he was four and a half years older.
Older than what? _____

4 We took some food on the journey, but after three days, we needed more.
More what? _____

5 In 2007, Martin Strel swam the 5,268 kilometres up the Amazon. Before the swim he was about 113 kilos and after he was a lot lighter.
Lighter than what? _____

4 Work with a partner. Read the magazine article and decide if sentences 1–6 are true (T) or false (F). Correct the false sentences.

1 Mauro thinks the *Marathon des Sables* is more difficult than the other two races.
2 The Sahara is bigger than all other deserts.
3 50 degrees is the highest temperature in the Sahara.
4 Mauro was at the front of the race before the storm.
5 After the storm, Mauro was in last place.
6 He decided not to run the *Marathon des Sables* again.

Man v Desert

People do some crazy things! Mauro Prosperi believes the three biggest races in the world are the *Marathon des Sables* in Africa, the race across the South Pole, and the marathon through the jungle in Brazil, but he believes the *Marathon des Sables* is the most difficult. It's a six- or seven-day race that goes through the Sahara Desert in Morocco, and it's about 240 km long. Deserts are dangerous places and the Sahara is the second largest in the world. High temperatures are usual: 50 degrees and sometimes hotter, and the runners have to carry their food and equipment. Mauro, a police officer from Rome, started the race, but he didn't complete it. There was a very bad storm and strong winds blew sand into the air, so he couldn't see. Before the storm, Mauro was one of the fastest runners, but after it, he couldn't find the other runners. The others were all in front of him. Nine days later, a local Tuareg family found him in Algeria – he was almost dead. But Mauro wasn't finished with the desert. He returned to the Sahara a few years later and he finished the *Marathon des Sables*.

5 Work with a partner. Answer the questions.

1 Do you think Mauro was 'crazy' to run in this race?
2 What's the most difficult sporting event you know?
3 Why do people do events like these?
4 What other stories do you know about people in very dangerous situations like Mauro?

Vocabulary & Speaking adjective + noun collocations

6a Answer the questions about the article in exercise **4**.
1 Are the highlighted words nouns, verbs or adjectives?
2 Are the highlighted words nouns, verbs or adjectives?

b Read the information in the Vocabulary focus box and check your answers.

> **VOCABULARY FOCUS**
> adjective + noun collocations
>
> - The collocations in the text are adjective + noun collocations or words that go together.
> - Sometimes we use opposite adjectives with the same noun.
>   high temperatures ✓   low temperatures ✓
> - Sometimes there is not a clear opposite.
>   a bad storm ✓   a good storm ✗
>   strong winds ✓   weak winds ✗   light winds ✓

7a Work with a partner. Match adjectives 1–4 to nouns a–d.
1 hard   a weather
2 strong   b friend
3 close   c worker
4 mild   d accent

b Complete sentences 1–4 with the correct form of a collocation from exercise **7a**.
1 Yuko has three _____.
2 In our company most people are _____.
3 People don't understand him because he has a _____.
4 In winter there is usually _____ and the temperatures are never below freezing.

8a Make opposite adjective + noun collocations using the correct form of the adjectives in the box.

> deep   high   heavy   low   strong

1 Is there usually ~~light~~ *heavy* traffic on your way to this class?
2 Did you have a low score in your last test?
3 Do you like weak coffee?
4 Which jobs usually have the highest salaries?
5 Are you a light sleeper?

b **10.13**))) Listen and check your answers.

9 **TASK** Work in small groups. Ask and answer the questions in exercise **8a** and give more information.
A *Is there usually heavy or light traffic on your way to class?*
B *Sometimes it's very heavy. It was bad today and I was late.*

101

10.4 Speaking and writing

Speaking & Listening reasons and preferences

1 Work with a partner. Are you an indoor person or an outdoor person? Give reasons and examples.
I think I'm an indoor/outdoor person because I like …

2 Work with a partner. Teach each other the names of some things you use for camping and outdoor activities. Student A, turn to page 130. Student B, turn to page 135.

3 Ted, Alex and Zoe are going on a survival weekend. Read the information from their group leader. What do they need to do to pass the course?

SURVIVAL COURSE LEVEL 2

⊙ **Where:** you are going to walk 10 km from the main camp to your survival camp in the rainforest next to the river.

▯ **Food and drink:** there is fresh water at the camp, and you can take any food you want or find your own.

⊙ **Time:** to pass the course, you need to survive for three days and two nights, and find your way back to the main camp.

△ **Equipment:** you have to carry everything you need. You can take your own clothes, things for washing, a tent and sleeping bag each, plus five more items per group.

4 **10.14**)) Listen to Ted, Alex and Zoe choosing five items to take. Which items in exercise **2** do they choose?

5a Work with a partner. Complete sentences 1–4 with the phrases in the box.

> a better idea   because (x2)   I'd prefer
> we should   most important

1 We need to decide on the five _____ things to take …
2 I think _____ take one stove instead of three _____ we don't need one each.
3 Taking a stove is _____ than making a fire …
4 _____ to take the GPS instead of the map and compass _____ then we can have the first-aid kit.

b **10.14**)) Listen again and check your answers.

6a Work with a partner. Put the words in order to make expressions about preferences.
1 a GPS / than / is better / I think a compass
2 in a hotel / I'd / to stay / prefer
3 thing to take / The most / is food / important
4 we should / only one / take / I think / torch
5 important / Taking / a first-aid kit is / than taking a knife / more
6 to have / I'd prefer / my own tent

b **10.15**)) Listen, check and repeat.

c Take turns to say the sentences in exercise **6a** and add extra information using *because*.
I think a compass is better than a GPS because it doesn't need batteries.

7a Work with a partner. You are going on a survival weekend. Choose five things you want to take and put them in order (1= the most important). Use the Language for speaking box to help you.

LANGUAGE FOR SPEAKING giving preferences

The most important/useful/best thing(s) is/are …
X is/are more important/useful than Y …
I think we should (do) …   *because …*
I'd prefer to (do) …
X is a better idea than Y …

b Work with another pair. Explain what you want to take and why. Listen to the other pair's ideas and decide on a final list.

Writing & Reading   describe places

8a Work with a partner. Look at the photos from a tourism website review for Zambia. What can you see and do there?

b Read the review and check your ideas.

HOME   TRAVEL   ACCOMODATION   ADVENTURES   CONTACT US

COME TO ZAMBIA!

We have over seventeen amazing waterfalls (including Victoria Falls, the world's largest waterfall), five big lakes and a lot of rivers. Lake Tanganyika is the second deepest natural lake in the world. You can fish, go swimming or even canoe on it.

Zambia also has some of the best national parks in the world – you can see elephants and lions as well as many other animals and birds.

Temperatures in Zambia are more comfortable than in many tropical areas because of the height of the country. There are three seasons: cool and dry from May to August, hot and dry from September to November, and warm and wet from December to April.

9a Read the review again. How many paragraphs does the review have? What is each paragraph about?

b Work with a partner. Complete the diagram about Zambia.

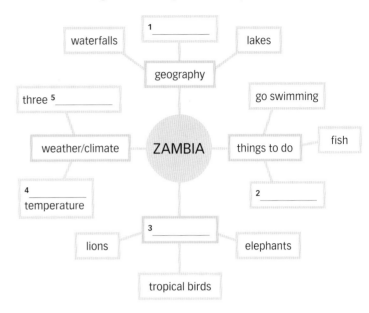

waterfalls — 1 _____ — lakes — geography

three 5 _____

weather/climate — ZAMBIA — things to do

go swimming

fish

4 temperature

2 _____

3 _____

lions — elephants

tropical birds

10a Work with a partner. Read the review about Zambia again. Underline the adjectives, comparatives and superlatives.

b Read the information in the Language for writing box. Why do we use adjectives in writing? Tell your partner.

LANGUAGE FOR WRITING
adjectives, comparatives and superlatives

- Adjectives, comparatives and superlatives make your writing more interesting.
  *There are some **beautiful** waterfalls in the north.*
  *Temperatures in Zambia are **more comfortable** than in many tropical areas.*
  *Tanzania has some of **the best** national parks in the world.*

- Other ways to use superlative phrases include:
  the biggest …
  the second/third biggest … | in the world/in Asia/
  one of the biggest … | in the country, etc.
  some of the biggest …

11a Work with a partner. Use the notes on page 131 to make a diagram about Australia like the one in exercise **9b**. Add your own information to it.

b Write three or four paragraphs about Australia for a tourism website review. Include adjectives in your review.
   Australia is the sixth largest country in the world …

12 Work with another partner. Compare their review with yours.

10.5 Video

The Grand Canyon

1a Look at the photos of the Grand Canyon. Which of these things do you see in them?

> building canyon cliff forest helicopter landscape
> map rafting river rock tourists wildlife

b Work with a partner. What do you think you can see and do in the Grand Canyon?

2 ▶ Watch the video and check your ideas in exercise **1**. What other things did the speaker mention?

3a ▶ Watch the video again and (circle) the correct option.

> The Grand Canyon is the **1** *south-west / south-east* of the United States. Each year over **2** *fourteen / four* million visitors come here. Most visitors usually **3** *walk / drive* to the Canyon's South Rim and enjoy the famous **4** *buildings / views* from Lipan Point. They can learn about the canyon's history, geography and **5** *wildlife / rivers* at the Grand Canyon Visitor Centre. **6** *Not many / A lot of* tourists travel into the canyon where there's lots to see. The bottom of the canyon is **7** *warmer / cooler* than the top, so the landscape here is very different. The Colorado River, which runs through the canyon, is **8** *still changing the canyon today / 200 feet wide*. Because there is no pollution in the Grand Canyon, it has some of the **9** *cleanest / driest* air in the country. The Grand Canyon isn't the longest canyon in the world, but it is one of the **10** *deepest / most spectacular*.

b Work with a partner. What would you like best about visiting the Grand Canyon?

4a **TASK** Work in small groups. According to several websites, these are the top seven natural wonders of the world:

- Grand Canyon
- Great Barrier Reef
- Rio de Janeiro harbour
- Mount Everest
- Aurora Borealis
- Parícutin volcano
- Victoria Falls

What do you know about these natural wonders? Why do you think they are in this list?

b Think about your own country, or a country you know well. Think of five places of natural wonder and make notes on each one. Put them in order with the most interesting first.

c Work with another group and take turns to present your ideas. Which places presented by the other group would you like to visit? Make a final list of five places from everyone's suggestions.

Review

1a Make comparative sentences.

1 Cairo / hot / Bangkok. *Cairo is hotter than Bangkok.*
2 Canberra / foggy / London.
3 The pollution in New Delhi / bad / in Beijing.
4 Rome / old / Damascus.
5 Ottawa / snowy / Moscow.
6 Mexico City has / big population / Tokyo.

b Work with a partner. Do you think the sentences in exercise **1a** are true (T) or false (F)?

c **10.16**))) Listen and check your answers.

2a Complete the sentences about your country with the superlative form of the adjective in (brackets).

1 The _____ (big) city is …
2 The _____ (old) university is in …
3 The _____ (long) river is the …
4 The _____ (hot) time of year is …
5 The _____ (good) place to live is …
6 One of the _____ (beautiful) areas is …

b Compare your answers with a partner.

3a Match the words in the box to illustrations 1–9.

| snow   windy   foggy   lightning   freezing   rain   cloudy |
| sunny   icy |

1 _____   2 _____   3 _____

4 _____   5 _____   6 _____

7 _____   8 _____   9 _____

b Work with a partner. Answer the questions.
1 What types of weather are there where you live?
2 Which months do you have them?

4a Match sentences 1–5 to the extra information a–e.

1 There are lots of **mountains** in the north of the country.
2 I'd love to visit a **rainforest**.
3 I saw a beautiful **waterfall** when I was in Venezuela.
4 Last year, we spent a week on an **island** near the **coast**.
5 In summer, I often spend the day at the **beach**.

a They're very hot and wet, but the plants and animals are amazing!
b I love swimming and surfing.
c You can ski there in winter.
d We went there by boat.
e The noise of the water was really loud!

b Work with a partner. Answer the questions.
1 Which places in **bold** in exercise **4a** do you have where you live?
2 Which are your favourite places to go to? Why?

5a Complete the table to show which adjectives can go with each noun.

	coffee	price	salary	accent	temperature	traffic
heavy	✗	✗	✗	✓	✗	✓
high						
light						
low						
strong						

b Write four questions to ask a partner using the words in the table.
Is there heavy traffic in your town?

c Work with a partner. Take turns to ask and answer your questions in exercise **5b**.

6a Complete the sentences about a city break.
1 Staying in the city centre is a better _____ than staying outside town.
2 In the city, comfortable shoes are _____ important than the clothes you take.
3 The _____ important thing to take is your phone.
4 I think you _____ always try the local food.
5 I'd _____ to use public transport, taxis are expensive.

b Compare your answers with a partner. Do you agree with the sentences in exercise **6a**? Why/Why not?

11 Working together

11.1 Community spirit

GOALS ■ Use verb + noun phrases (1) ■ Use *going to* for plans and intentions

Reading & Vocabulary verb + noun phrases (1)

1 Work in small groups. Answer the questions and give examples.
How often do you …
1 help people you know/don't know?   2 speak to your neighbours?

2a Work with a partner. Look at the title of the advert and the photos, and answer the questions.
1 What do you know about Nelson Mandela?
2 What do you think happens around the world on Mandela Day?

b Read the advert and check your ideas in exercise **2a**.

c Work with a partner. Do you think Mandela Day is a good idea? Why/Why not?

3a Work with a partner. Complete phrases 1–10 with verbs from the advert.
1 *teach*_____ someone a language
2 _____ a tree
3 _____ a sports event
4 _____ your workplace by keeping the kitchen clean
5 _____ elderly people with difficult jobs
6 _____ a neighbour's pet
7 _____ broken furniture
8 _____ an elderly neighbour
9 _____ money to charity
10 _____ sandwiches for homeless people

b Work with a partner. Which verbs in exercise **3a** do phrases 1–10 go with?
1 a party *organize*   6 a classmate with their homework
2 a present to someone   7 some flowers
3 your friend's bike   8 a friend's children for the evening
4 someone in hospital   9 someone to drive
5 a cake for a colleague's birthday   10 your local area by picking up rubbish

c **11.1**)) Listen, check and repeat.

4 Work in small groups. Which things in exercise **3a** and **3b** …
1 do you do already? Who do you do them for and when?
2 would you like/not like to do? Why/Why not?

I sometimes look after my sister's children.
I wouldn't like to teach someone to drive because I'm a terrible driver!

Sent: FRIDAY 11.30

Do Something for Mandela Day

Nelson Mandela worked all his life to change and improve South Africa. Now it's YOUR turn in YOUR community! Every year on 18th July, people around the world celebrate Mandela's life by doing something to help their local area. Here are some ideas:

- Look after a neighbour's pet.
- Teach someone a language.
- Paint the classrooms and repair some broken furniture at your local school.
- Visit an elderly neighbour and help them with difficult jobs.
- Make sandwiches for homeless people.
- Plant a tree.
- Improve your workplace by keeping the kitchen clean.
- Organize a sports event and sell tickets. Give the money to charity.

What are you going to do for Mandela Day? We'd love to hear your plans, so please email us or visit our website: www.mandeladay.com

Grammar & Listening   *going to*

5a   **11.2**))) Listen to three people's plans for Mandela Day and tick (✓) the activities they talk about.

1   walk to work   3   make some cakes   5   organize a game of football
2   organize a marathon   4   repair a bike   6   help a neighbour

b   Work with a partner. Which plan do you think is best? Give reasons.

6a   Match beginnings 1–6 to endings a–f to make six sentences from the listening in exercise **5a**.

1   We aren't going to   a   cycle to work?
2   Are you going to   b   his CV.
3   I'm going to organize   c   all the money to charity.
4   We're going to give   d   a game of football.
5   What am I going to   e   use any electricity.
6   We're going to improve   f   do on Mandela Day?

b   **11.2**))) Listen again and check your answers.

c   Use the sentences in exercise **6a** to complete the rules in the Grammar focus box.

GRAMMAR FOCUS *going to*

We use *going to* for future plans and intentions.

Positive (+)
Subject + *am/is*/**1**_____ + *going to* + infinitive without *to*
I'm going to walk to work.   *We're **going to** sell tickets.*

Negative (–)
Subject + **2**_____ /*is/are* + *not going to* + infinitive without *to*
*She **isn't going to** drive.*   *We **aren't going to** use any electricty.*

Questions (?)
(Question word) + *am*/**3**_____ /*are* + subject + **4**_____ + infinitive without *to* ?
*Are you **going to** cycle to work?*   *What **are** you **going to** do?*

→ Grammar Reference   page 156

7a   Work with a partner. Read the interview between a radio presenter (P) and an organizer (O) of Mandela Day. Complete the conversation using *going to* and the verbs in (brackets).

P   So, how are the plans for this year's Mandela Day?
O   Great, thanks! We're getting emails from people all around the world telling us how they **1**_____ (celebrate) the day.
P   That's good to hear. So what **2**_____ everyone _____ (do)?
O   Oh, all sorts of things. A lot of people **3**_____ (make) soup and sandwiches and give them to homeless people. I had an email from a man yesterday – he **4**_____ (not eat) for 24 hours and he **5**_____ (collect) money for his local hospital. And of course we **6**_____ (post) everything on our website for people to see.
P   **7**_____ you _____ (have) time to do something yourself?
O   No, I'm afraid I **8**_____ (not have) much time! But we **9**_____ (have) a big party here at the office and everyone needs to buy a ticket to come. And all the money goes to charity, of course.

b   **11.3**))) Listen and check your answers.

PRONUNCIATION *going to*

11.4))) In sentences with *going to* we do not usually stress *to*.
We're going to /tə/ look after a friend's daughter.
Are you going to /tə/ visit someone in hospital?

In negative sentences, we stress *not/ aren't/isn't.*

●
I'm not going to /tə/ organize an event.

8   **11.5**))) Listen and repeat the sentences.
1   We're going to organize a party.
2   I'm not going to visit my family this weekend.
3   What are you going to do for Mandela Day?

9a   **TASK** It is Mandela Day and you want to do something for your community. Think of three things you are going to do.

b   Work in small groups. Take turns to tell each other what you are going to do.

c   Choose the three best ideas from your group and present them to the class.

▶ VOX POPS VIDEO 11.1

11.2 Challenges

GOALS ■ Talk about technology ■ Say why you do things ■ Use the infinitive of purpose

Vocabulary & Speaking technology

1 Work in small groups. What is geocaching? Use the illustrations to help you guess.

2a Work with a partner. Read instructions 1–5 for geocaching and match them to illustrations a–e.

b Work in small groups and answer the questions.
   1 Were your ideas about geocaching in exercise **1** correct?
   2 Would you like to try geocaching? Why/Why not?

3a Use the highlighted words in the advert in exercise **2a** in singular or plural noun form to complete sentences 1–5.
   1 I have a _____, so I can use the internet when I'm out.
   2 I often buy _____ for my phone.
   3 I take my _____ everywhere, so I can work or study when I'm not at home.
   4 I check the news every day on my favourite newspaper _____ .
   5 I have _____ on my phone because I drive to lots of different places for work.

b **11.6**))) Listen and check your answers.

c Work with a partner. Tell each other which sentences in exercise **3a** are true for you. Ask for more information.
   A *I often buy apps for my phone.*
   B *Really? What kind of apps do you buy?*

4a **11.7**))) Listen to someone reading website and email addresses a–d. Match symbols 1–5 to the words in the box.
   a www.allinoneshopping.hu/personal
   b www.thefamouswebsite.org/join-in
   c k.m.customer-contact@cateringbizz.com
   d ania_cart9219@yahoo.co.uk

at	dash	dot	forward slash	underscore

   1 @   2 /   3 .   4 _   5 -

b Compare your answers with a partner.

c Work with a partner. Practise reading and listening to some more website and email addresses. Student A, turn to page 131. Student B, turn to page 135.

GEOCACHING:
A REAL-WORLD TREASURE HUNT FOR THE 21ST CENTURY!

a   b

c

d   e

'45*19'02n 093*39'07W

It's not difficult. You just need a smartphone or a tablet. Then you download an app and you're ready to go! Here's how it works.

1 One player fills a box with presents and hides it – in the city, in the countryside, anywhere!

2 He/She puts the coordinates of the box (or 'cache') on a geocaching website.

3 Other players use the coordinates and their GPS to try to find the cache. Many people do this as a team.

4 They find the cache, take a present from the box and put a new one in the box instead.

5 Then they post their photos and stories on the website.

Visit a geocaching website, like www.geocaching.com or www.opencaching.com and join in the fun!

Grammar & Speaking infinitive of purpose

5a Work with a partner. Why do you think people go geocaching?

b **11.8**))) Listen to four people talking about why they go geocaching. Match speakers 1–4 to reasons a–d.
   a They want to go to new places.
   b They want to do some exercise.
   c It's good fun.
   d They want to make new friends.

c Are the answers similar to your ideas in exercise **5a**?

6a **11.9**))) Listen to the people in exercise **5b** again and complete the sentences.
   1 I go geocaching _____ _____ fit.
   2 I do it _____ _____ new people.
   3 I go geocaching _____ _____ different places.

b **11.9**))) Listen, check and repeat.

7 Look at sentences 1–3 in exercise **6a** and complete the information in the Grammar focus box.

> **GRAMMAR FOCUS** infinitive of purpose
>
> • We use **1**_____ + infinitive to say why we do something.
>   *I do it to meet new people.*
>
> • We use the short form to answer a 'why' question.
>   A *Why do you go to the gym?*
>   B **2**_____ *keep fit.*
>
> • We can use the infinitive of purpose with all tenses.
>   *I'm going to call Suzi to talk about the party.*
>   *I walked home to save money.*
>
> → Grammar Reference page 157

8a Look at the photo and read about an unusual geocache. Do you think many people visit it? Why/Why not?

EASTER ISLAND CACHE

This geocache is in Rapa Nui (or Easter Island in English). It's a beautiful place, but it's not easy to get there. You can take a 5.5-hour flight from Chile. Or you could go by boat from New Zealand – it only takes 35 days!

Easter Island

b A geocacher is going to take the things in the box to Easter Island. Use phrases 1–6 and the infinitive of purpose to give a reason for taking each thing.

| camera | GPS | pen | plastic bags | presents | ~~torch~~ |

1 see in the dark
   I'm going to take a torch to see in the dark.
2 write some postcards to my family and friends
3 leave in the cache for other people
4 take some pictures of the statues
5 take my rubbish back to my hotel
6 help me find the cache

9 Rewrite sentences 1–7 using the infinitive of purpose, but don't change the meaning.
   1 People go to the gym because they want to keep fit.
      People go to the gym to keep fit.
   2 People shop online because they want to find the cheapest price.
   3 People take taxis because it saves time.
   4 In the future, more people are going to cycle to work because they want to do more exercise.
   5 People grew vegetables at home in the past because they needed to feed their families.
   6 People are going to learn more foreign languages in the future because it helps them find a job more easily.
   7 In the past, people moved to the city because they wanted to find a job.

10a Use the verbs in the box or your own ideas to write six sentences about you. Write two in the past tense, two in the present tense and two with *going to*.

| buy | visit | go | bring | move | start | call | talk to | join |

I bought a new bag yesterday.

b Think of a reason for each action, but don't write it down.
   I bought a new bag yesterday to carry my laptop to work.

c Work in small groups. Take turns to ask questions about each other's sentences in exercise **10a**. Start your answers with *to …*
   A *Why did you buy a bag yesterday?*
   B *To carry my laptop to work.*

▶ VOX POPS VIDEO 11.2

11.3 Vocabulary and skills development

GOALS ■ Deal with unknown words ■ Make adjectives stronger

Reading & Speaking unknown words

1 Work with a partner. Answer the questions.
1 What do you do when you read a word you don't know in your first language?
2 What do you do when you read a word you don't know in English?

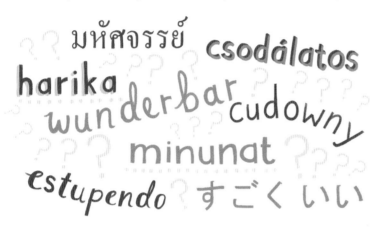

2a What do you think the highlighted word in this sentence means? What helped you guess? Compare your answers with a partner.

It's common to have rice for breakfast in Japan.

b Turn to page 131 and check your answer.

c Read the information in the Unlock the code box about unknown words. Did you use any of the ideas to help you do exercise 2a?

> 🔒 **UNLOCK THE CODE**
> unknown words
>
> When you read in English, you sometimes see words you don't know. Use these ideas to help you understand the words:
>
> 1 Identify the part of speech:
>   Is it a noun (a person or a thing)? e.g. *a team*
>   It is a verb (an action word)? e.g. *to work*
>   Is it an adjective (describes a noun)? e.g. *a good team*
>   Is it an adverb (describes a verb)? e.g. *work slowly*
>
> 2 Use the context – the words and sentences before and after the word:
>   *I'm so happy to hear your marvellous news.*
>   People say they're happy about good things, so *marvellous* is a positive word. It means *very good*.

3a Work with a partner. The words in **bold** are not real. Identify the part of speech for each word. What helped you decide?
1 I live in a **flissy** part of the city.
2 The college needs a new **flisser**.
3 Can you **fliss** him tomorrow?
4 We **flissed** the car yesterday.
5 My brother drives **flissly**.
6 I don't like **unflissy** people.

b Replace the words in **bold** in exercise **3a** with real words. Compare your answers with a partner.

I live in a busy part of the city.

4a Work with a partner. The words in **bold** are real. What are the parts of speech for each word and what do they mean? Use the context to help you.
1 Our new teacher is really **strict** – she isn't happy when students don't do their homework.
2 I think rich people and companies should pay more **tax** to the government.
3 My neighbour's dog **barks** very loudly.
4 My sister is always really **scared** when she sees a spider.
5 My phone at work rings **constantly** – it never stops!
6 You need to plant these flowers in good **soil**.
7 It's better to visit your dentist every six months than to go **annually**.
8 They live in a **massive** house with ten bedrooms.

b Compare your ideas in small groups. What helped you guess?

5a Work with a partner. Look at the photo and read the title of the magazine article. What is good about working alone or in a team?

Behind every winner, there is a team

In the past, it was common for a really brilliant scientist like Isaac Newton to work alone, but these days scientists usually work in teams. That's why some science magazines say the Nobel Prize for Physics should change. The writers believe it's wrong to award the prize to one person because there's usually a team that is working with the individual. But because only a maximum of three people can win the Nobel Prize at one time, some really crucial members of the team are often not included and don't win anything.

It's not only in science that just one person wins an award for the work of a team. In sport, for example, there is usually a team of people helping the player of individual sports. For example, the really great tennis players and Formula One drivers have a team of people working with them: from the coach or manager who helps them with their game or race to the dietician who tells them what to eat and drink.

So perhaps it's time to stop focusing only on the individual. We should remember that there is often a huge team of many more people working hard to make everything possible.

b Read the article and answer the questions with a partner.
1 What does the science magazine think is the problem with the Nobel Prize for Physics?
2 Why does the article mention sport?
3 What does the article think we should do about the problem?

6 Work with a partner. Guess the meaning of the highlighted words in the article. What helped you decide?

7 Work in small groups. Answer the questions.
1 Do you think people should focus more on the teams behind individuals? Why/Why not?
2 What other examples of individuals with a team can you think of?

Vocabulary & Speaking making adjectives stronger

8a Work with a partner. Complete the definition of the word from the text.

> huge (adjective) _____

a very small   b not very important   c very big

b Find these three strong adjectives in the article. What word comes before them in the article?

brilliant   crucial   great

c Read the information in the Vocabulary focus box and check your answers.

VOCABULARY FOCUS making adjectives stronger

- You can make many ordinary adjectives stronger by using *very* or *really*, or a strong adjective instead, e.g. *huge*. Brazil is a **very/really** big country. Brazil is a **huge** country.
- You can make strong adjectives stronger by using *really*, but not *very*. Their house is **really huge**. Not ~~Their house is very huge~~. It helps your vocabulary to remember ordinary and strong adjectives together, e.g. *big/huge*.

9a Work with a partner. Complete conversations 1–5 with strong adjectives from the box.

awful   excellent   delighted   tiny   lovely

1 **A** Were you very glad to get the job?
   B Of course! I was really _____!
2 **A** Was the weather very nice on your holiday?
   B Yes, it was really _____! We were very lucky.
3 **A** Is she very good at tennis?
   B Yes, she's really _____! She always wins.
4 **A** What's wrong? You don't look very happy.
   B It's really _____! I failed my driving test.
5 **A** Let's use my car. Your car is too small for five people.
   B You're right. My car is really _____!

b **11.10**))) Listen and check your answers. Notice the stress on *really*.

c Work with a partner. Take turns to practise the conversations in exercise **9a**.

10a Work with a partner. Write three short conversations similar to exercise **9a** using strong adjectives.

b Work with another pair. Read and practise their conversations. Are *very* and *really* in the correct places?

11.4 Speaking and writing

Reading & Writing   a notice

1   Work with a partner. Answer the questions.

1   How do you describe yourself?
    a really organized   **b** organized   **c** not very organized

2   Which of these do you sometimes organize?

> holidays   meetings   parties   study groups

2   Read notices 1 and 2 and discuss the questions with a partner.

1   Who do you think wrote them?

2   What type of person is going to answer them?

3a   Work with a partner. Which notice in exercise **2** is ...

1   more friendly and informal? Why?

2   more formal? Why?

b   Check your ideas in the Language for writing box.

LANGUAGE FOR WRITING   addressing your reader

- When you write something, it is important to know your reader and to write in a suitable way. Ask these questions: Who is the reader? What information does the reader need?

- Use formal language in notices with people you don't know very well, and informal language with people you know.

- To sound informal ...
  1   use ellipsis, e.g. ~~Are you~~ *Tired of studying alone?*
  2   use exclamation marks, e.g. *Working together is more fun!*

- To sound more formal ...
  1   write full sentences.
  2   don't use contractions, e.g. *we are* and not *we're*.
  3   use more formal expressions, e.g. *Would you like ...?*
      NOT ~~Do you want ...?~~

4a   Read lines 1–8 from two notices. Decide which are formal (F) and which are informal (I).

1   Come to the university gym at 7.00 p.m. on Sept 15th. *I*

2   Join the Maastricht University Basketball Club.

3   Do you want to help your community and do you have some free time?

4   If you are interested, call Mae Fox on 01110 8485576.

5   Want to get fit and make new friends?

6   Are you interested in working with young people?

7   We are looking for friendly people to help organize a youth club on Thursday evenings.

8   Wanted – basketball players

b   Put the lines in the two notices in a suitable order.

1

Are you a resident of East Harfield?

Are you worried about the local area? Would you like to help us keep it clean and tidy? The East Harfield Neighbourhood Committee spends every weekend doing jobs to improve our community and we are looking for new members. If you are interested, please email us at eastharfield@yahoo.com and tell us about yourself and how you would like to help.

2

Wanted – Year 2 English students!

Tired of studying alone? Want to study with other people and make new friends?

Come to our study group in Room 246 every Friday at 6.30 p.m.

Improve your English and have fun!

5a   Work with a partner. Plan a notice. Choose one of the ideas below or use your own ideas. Answer questions 1–4 to help you plan your notice together.

- sell something
- organize a charity event
- start a study group/book club/dance class, etc.
- rent a room in your house/flat
- start a football team/running group, etc. at work

1   Who is the reader, e.g. students, parents, colleagues, local people, etc.?

2   How well do you know them? How formal/informal should you be?

3   How can you make them 'notice' your notice?

4   What information do they need to know? Think of at least five things to ask/tell them, e.g. times, places, what you want, what to bring, etc.

b   Write your notice.

6   Work in small groups and read each other's notices. Which notices are the most interesting?

Listening & Speaking   offering to do something

7a Work with a partner. Match photos (a) and (b) to notices 1 and 2 in exercise **2**.

b **11.11**))) Listen to two conversations from the photos. Are the statements true (T) or false (F)?

Conversation 1
1   Dr Pedersen is at the meeting.
2   They are going to talk about the questions tomorrow.

Conversation 2
3   The local park is very small.
4   They want to paint the school.

c Compare your answers with a partner.

8a Work with a partner. Complete the sentences from the conversations with a word from the box.

Why   Would   I'll   Shall   Let

1   _____ I write that down?
2   _____ don't I give him the list then?
3   _____ take notes, so we don't forget.
4   _____ me help you with that.
5   _____ you like me to ask them?

b **11.12**))) Listen, check and repeat.

9a Match a situation 1–5 to an offer a–e.
1   It's really hot in here!
2   Excuse me, this fork is dirty.
3   These bags are heavy.
4   Are you still coming for dinner tonight?
5   I'm going to walk into the city centre.

a   Why don't I give you a lift?
b   Would you like me to open a window?
c   I'm sorry. I'll bring you another one.
d   Let me carry them for you.
e   Of course! Shall I bring a dessert?

b Work with a partner. Take turns to practise the conversations in exercise **9a**.

10a Read the information in the Language for speaking box about making offers.

LANGUAGE FOR SPEAKING making offers

When we offer to do something, we use:

Shall I (do) …?
Why don't I (do)?
Would you like me to (do) …?
I'll (do) ….
Let me (do) ….

b Work with a different partner. Choose a situation: work, study or social. Take turns to explain your problems and offer help, using the Language for speaking box to help you. Student A, turn to page 131. Student B, turn to page 135.

11.5 Video

Silicon Fen

1 Match the words to the definitions.

> a device   a graduate   an innovation   a processor
> resources   the Fens   to provide   to connect

1 an area of flat wet land in east England
2 to join two things together
3 a part of a computer that controls all the other parts
4 something that organizations have and can use
5 to give something to someone who needs it
6 a new idea or way of doing something
7 a small object or electronic machine, e.g. tablet
8 someone who has finished a university degree

2 Work with a partner. Look at the photos and the title of the video. What do you think the video is going to be about?

3 ▶ Watch the video and complete the sentences.

1 Silicon Fen is 'Europe's Silicon Valley' because …
2 ARM is different from when it began in 1990 because …
3 There are many technology companies here because …
4 The University helps Cambridge Science Park to develop because …
5 Cambridge is successful because …

4 ▶ Watch the video again and decide if the sentences are true (T) or false (F). Correct the false sentences.

1 The Fens area of England looks like a modern place.
2 There are 150 technology companies in Silicon Fen.
3 ARM employs over 3,000 people in the UK.
4 Apple and Samsung use ARM processors in their smartphones.
5 16% of the world's population use a device with an ARM chip in it.
6 Isaac Newton and Stephen Hawking worked at Cambridge University.
7 Cambridge Science Park isn't a good place for small businesses.

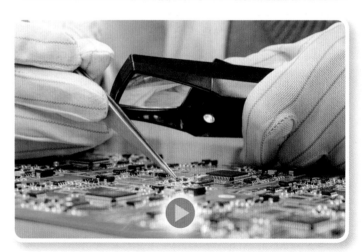

5a **TASK** Work with a partner. You are going to interview the founder of the company ARM. Write 6–8 questions that you would like to ask using the prompts.

• When did you start the company?
• Why … ?   • Where … ?   • What … ?
• How many … ?   • How big … ?   • Who … ?

b Work with another partner. Take turns to be the interviewer and the founder of ARM.

Review

1a **11.13**)) Listen to Mandy and Wanda talking about their New Year's resolutions. What promises did Wanda make to herself?

b Complete sentences 1–5 from the listening in exercise **1a** with the correct form of *going to* and the verbs in (brackets).

1 I _____ (spend) less time at work.
2 _____ (you/spend) more time with your friends and family?
3 _____ (he/look) for a new apartment?
4 We _____ (not/join) a gym.
5 We _____ (save) some money.

c **11.13**)) Listen again and check your answers.

d Write three resolutions you would like to do. Compare your answers with a partner.
I'm going to eat healthier food.

2a Complete sentences 1–8 with an infinitive of purpose phrase using the verbs in the box.

look after   organize   make   ~~paint~~   plant   repair
teach   visit

1 He got up early _____*to paint*_____ the living room.
2 She's going to move to Greece _____ English.
3 I go to Bob's house every weekend _____ his dog.
4 I went to my parents' house _____ my Mum's car.
5 I'm going to call all our friends _____ a birthday party for my best friend.
6 We're going to buy some eggs and sugar _____ a cake.
7 I'm going to take the afternoon off work tomorrow _____ my aunt in hospital.
8 I went to the garden _____ some flowers.

b **11.14**)) Listen and check.

c Work with a partner. Use the infinitive of purpose sentences in exercise **2a** or your own ideas to make true sentences for you and people you know.
I'm going to get up early tomorrow to go to the gym.
My friend moved to Germany last year to teach Spanish.

3a Cross out any words in italics that are not possible in answers a–e.

a I agree. They're *very / really* tiny.
b Yes, it's *very / really* brilliant.
c Yes, I did. It's *very / really* good.
d It's *very / really* cheap.
e Thanks. I think it's *very / really* lovely.

b Match sentences 1–5 to answers a–e in exercise **3a**.

1 This GPS is cheap.
2 That's a nice smartphone.
3 Those tablets are small.
4 Did you see the new music app?
5 They have a good website.

c Work in small groups. Use normal/strong adjectives and *very/really* to say things about the ideas in the box.

your family   your house   your English school/college
your city   your country

4a Put the words in the correct order to make offers.

a some / Why / sandwiches / I / make / don't ?
b repair / you / me / Would / to / like / it ?
c new / I / words / Shall / teach / some / you ?
d the / after / children / look / I'll .
e for / the / me / meeting / you / documents / organize / Let / for / the .

b **11.15**)) Listen to five sentences. Match each sentence to an offer in exercise **4a**.

c Write three problems you'd like help with.
I want to make more money.

d Work with a partner. Take turns to read your problems. Make offers to help your partner.
A *I want to make more money.*
B *Why don't you start your own business?*

Culture and the arts

12.1 Artistic ability

Grammar & Reading present perfect simple

1 Work with a partner. Answer the questions.
1 Are you good at singing, drawing or dancing? Do you play a musical instrument?
2 What kind of art would you like to be good/better at?

2a Look at the photos. What kinds of artist are they?

b Read the articles about two artists, Stephen Wiltshire and Tai Lihua. Answer questions 1–5 for each artist.
1 What couldn't Stephen/Tai do?
2 What is Stephen's/Tai's kind of art?
3 When did Stephen/Tai start doing this?
4 What did Stephen's/Tai's teachers do?
5 How do we know they are successful?

c Compare your answers with a partner.

3a Work with a partner. Look at sentences 1–4 from the articles and complete the rules in the Grammar focus box.
1 Thousands of people have watched her.
2 He has drawn many fantastic pieces of art.
3 He hasn't opened a gallery in New York.
4 She's danced in more than 75 countries.

GRAMMAR FOCUS present perfect simple

- We use the present perfect simple to talk about past experiences and events when:
  1 we don't know <u>when</u> the event happened.
  2 we are interested in <u>what</u> happened more than <u>when</u> it happened.
- We make the present perfect simple with:
  (+) I/You/We/They + ¹_____ / 've + past participle
  He/She/It + ²_____ / 's + past participle
  (–) I/You/We/They + haven't + past participle
  He/She/It + ³_____ + past participle

→ Grammar Reference page 158

b <u>Underline</u> other examples of the present perfect simple in the articles. Compare your answers with a partner.

Stephen Wiltshire is autistic and couldn't speak until he was five. His first words were 'paper' and 'pencil' – the same first words as Picasso's! At school, he started drawing pictures of London and his teachers gave him the name 'the human camera'. He has drawn many fantastic pieces of art and he's sold them all over the world. One of his drawings is a 5.7-metre-long picture of New York. He drew it after he spent just 20 minutes in a helicopter in the sky above the city. He has his own art gallery in London. He hasn't opened a gallery in New York, but he wants to – he's just looking for the right place to do it.

■ **autistic** having a mental condition that makes it difficult for somebody to communicate or form relationships with other people

Tai Lihua couldn't hear from the age of two after an illness. She is deaf, but this hasn't stopped her dream of dancing. When she was a child, the teacher at her school for deaf children asked the class to 'feel' the sound of a drum through their feet. From that moment, she wanted to be a dancer. Tai joined a dance company when she was 15 and she's become one of the most famous dancers in China. She's danced in more than 75 countries and thousands of people have watched her, including at the Beijing Paralympics.

■ **deaf** not able to hear

4a Work with a partner. Complete the article about another artist with the present perfect form of the verbs in (brackets).

Nobuyuki Tsujii was born blind, but he started playing on a toy piano at the age of just two. He began learning the piano two years later, and he gave his first big concert in Tokyo when he was 12 years old. He's in his twenties now, but he ¹_____ (give) concerts all over the world, and he ²_____ (win) many prizes and international competitions. He ³_____ (write) music for film and TV, too.

He ⁴_____ (not see) the written music, but he ⁵_____ (learn) to play some of the most difficult pieces of music in the world only through sound. His classical music fans ⁶_____ (say) this is amazing.

■ **blind** not able to see

b **12.1** Listen and check your answers.

PRONUNCIATION sentence stress

5a **12.2** In the present perfect, the stress is on the past participle in positive sentences, and on *haven't/hasn't* in negative sentences.

1 He's given concerts …

2 … he hasn't seen the written music …

b Work with a partner. Say the sentences about Stephen and Tai with the correct stress.
1 He's sold them all over the world.
2 He hasn't opened a gallery in New York.
3 This hasn't stopped her dream of dancing.
4 Thousands of people have watched her.

c **12.3** Listen, check and repeat.

6 Work in small groups. Which artist is the most amazing in your opinion and why?

I think … is the most amazing because …

Vocabulary & Speaking verb + noun phrases (2)

7 **12.4** Listen to three people, Phil, Jimmy and Albina talking about their experiences of art, and answer the questions. There may be more than one possible answer. Who talks about …
1 their family?
2 a new experience?
3 something they love?
4 something you can only do in big cities?
5 something they didn't finish?

8a Work with a partner. Write the words in the box next to the correct verb to make verb + noun phrases.

art galleries   in a band   ~~the cinema/theatre~~   dance drawing   ~~a film/movie~~   ~~the guitar~~   ~~music~~   a musical a music festival   the opera   painting   a play a rock/classical music concert   a salsa class   singing

go to   1   *the cinema/theatre*
       2 _____
       3 _____
       4 _____
       5 _____
       6 _____
see   7   *a film/movie*
       8 _____
       9 _____
play   10   *the guitar*
      11 _____
have   12   *music* / 13 _____ / 14 _____ /
      15 _____ / 16 _____ lessons

b **12.5** Listen, check and repeat.

9a **TASK** Work with a partner. Take turns to tell each other about your experiences. Use phrases from exercise **8a** and the ideas in the boxes to help you.

1 Music – types of music/instruments/lessons/ concerts/festivals/bands

2 Art and writing – drawing and painting lessons/art galleries/written something

3 Theatre, dance and cinema – plays/musicals/dance lessons/cinema/favourite actor

I've always wanted to play a musical instrument.
I haven't played in a band, but I would like to.

b Which of your experiences are similar and which are different?
We've both been to big concerts.

12.2 At the movies

GOALS ■ Talk about films ■ Use the present perfect and past simple

Vocabulary & Speaking films

1 Work with a partner. Read the quote about films and answer the questions.

> *'People who like movies have a favourite. People who love movies couldn't possibly choose.'*
> Nicole Yatsonsky, author

1 Do you agree with Nicole Yatsonsky? Why/Why not?
2 How often do you watch films at home?
3 How often do you go to the cinema?

2a **12.6**))) Listen to eight descriptions and number the types of film in the box.

> action films   animations   comedies   dramas   horror films
> musicals   romantic films   science fiction films

b **12.7**))) Listen, check and repeat.

c Work in small groups. Think of 2–3 more films for each type.

3a Work in small groups. Take turns to say which types of film you like and don't like.

I don't like action films because they're really boring. I prefer comedies.

b Tell the class about the films you like/don't like. Use the ideas in the box.
• Everybody likes/loves/hates …
• Nobody likes …
• Some of us like …

4 **12.8**))) Listen to two people talking about films. Which types of films in exercise **2a** are they talking about?

5a Work with a partner. Complete sentences 1–5 from the listening in exercise **4** using the words in the box.

> stars   favourite   about   It's   set

1 My _____ film is *Titanic*.
2 It _____ Kate Winslet and Leonardo DiCaprio.
3 It's _____ a huge ship and all the people on it.
4 _____ a science fiction film.
5 It's _____ in the future.

b **12.8**))) Listen again and check your answers.

c Change the sentences in exercise **5a** to make them true for your favourite film. Tell your partner.

Grammar & Listening present perfect and past simple

6a Read part of a web page and answer the questions.
1 What kind of film is *The Artist*?
2 Why did some people leave the cinema?

Film News & Reviews

It was black and white and silent, and it was the surprise success of 2012. The French film *The Artist* won the award for 'Best Picture' at the Oscars, but it wasn't popular with everyone. In some cinemas, people walked out early and asked for their money back. Why? Because they didn't know the film was silent when they bought the tickets!

b Work with a partner. Read the second part of the web page and answer the questions in it.

How often do people leave the cinema early and why do they do it? Have you ever left the cinema before the end of a film? Has it ever annoyed you when other people left the cinema early? Tell us your thoughts …

7 Look at the questions in exercise **6b** again and complete the rules in the Grammar focus box.

> **GRAMMAR FOCUS**
> present perfect questions and short answers
>
> • To make questions in the present perfect, we use:
>   1 _____ + I/you/we/they + past participle + ?
>   2 _____ + he/she/it + past participle + ?
>
> • With *yes/no* questions, we usually use short answers:
>   (+) Yes, I/you/we/they *have*.   (−) No, I/you/we/they *haven't*.
>   Yes, he/she/it *has*.   No, he/she/it *hasn't*.
>
> → Grammar Reference page 159

| **O—** Oxford 3000™

8a **12.9**))) Listen to four people answering the questions from the web page. Complete the first column of the table with a tick (✓) or a cross (✗).

	Have they ever left the cinema early?	Why/Why not?
Speaker 1		
Speaker 2		
Speaker 3		
Speaker 4		

b **12.9**))) Listen again and make notes in the second column of the table. Compare your answers with a partner.

9a **12.10**))) Listen and complete the sentences from the listening in exercise **8**. Compare your answers with a partner.

1 _____ never _____ the cinema early, but I've often wanted to.

2 A few months ago, I _____ to see a terrible film.

3 A _____ you ever _____ the cinema early?
   B Yes, I _____ . I _____ out once – it was last summer and it was a beautiful day.

b Work with a partner. Look at the sentences in exercise **9a** and complete the rules in the Grammar focus box. Write *past simple* or *present perfect*.

GRAMMAR FOCUS present perfect and past simple

* Use the ¹_____ to say something happened before now, but we don't know or don't say when. We often use it with *ever/never*.
* Use the ²_____ to say something happened before now and we know the time.
* We often start with the ³_____ and then change to the ⁴_____ to give more details.

→ Grammar Reference page 159

10a Work with a partner. Read part of an interview between a journalist (J), a film director, Pavel (P), and an actor, Wanda (W). Choose the correct form of the verbs.

J So Pavel, you're here for the Rio de Janeiro film festival. ¹ *Did you visit / Have you visited* Brazil before?

P Yes, ² *I did / I have* – twice. Actually, ³ *I came / I've come* here when I was a child and I ⁴ *was / have been* here three years ago for work, too.

J Interesting. And what about you, Wanda? ⁵ *Did you ever go / Have you ever been* to Rio?

W No, I ⁶ *didn't go / 've never been* here before, but it's a beautiful city!

J I'm very pleased to hear that! So, I ⁷ *saw / 've seen* your latest film 'Inbox me' last night and I ⁸ *thought / 've thought* it was really wonderful.

P Well, thank you very much!

J And everyone else in the cinema ⁹ *enjoyed / has enjoyed* it, too. When it ¹⁰ *finished / has finished*, people ¹¹ *stood / have stood* up and ¹² *clapped / have clapped* – I couldn't believe it!

P Really? I'm delighted to hear that. A lot of people ¹³ *said / have said* some lovely things about it.

W Last week someone ¹⁴ *told / has told* me it was their favourite film of the year!

J Great! So, tell me …

b **12.11**))) Listen and check your answers.

11a **TASK** Work in small groups. Take turns to ask about your experiences. Use the ideas in the box to help you, and your own ideas.

A *Have you ever been to a big concert?*
B *Yes, I have. I went to a Coldplay concert in Warsaw last year.*

> walked out of a film
> met a famous writer/singer/actor   acted in a play
> cry during a film   go to the opera
> stay awake all night watching films
> be in a film   ~~go to a big concert~~
> watch the same film three or four times

b Tell the class about your group. Have you had similar experiences?

Mario has never been to a big concert, but Elena and I have.

12.3 Vocabulary and skills development

Speaking & Vocabulary | past participles

1 Read the pairs of sentences. Which ones are true for you? Change any you can to make them true for you. Compare your sentences with your partner.

1 I've **been** to a lot of festivals.
   I **went** to a fantastic musical last year.
2 I've never **run** a marathon.
   I **ran** for the bus yesterday morning.
3 I've never **met** a famous person.
   I **met** my partner at university.
4 I've never **written** a comment on a website.
   I **wrote** a lot of emails yesterday.

2a Read the information in the Vocabulary focus box about past participles.

VOCABULARY FOCUS past participles

- The past simple and past participle forms of regular verbs are the same. They always end in -ed, e.g. visit**ed**, work**ed**.
- The past participle of irregular verbs can be different from or the same as the past simple form. Most verbs follow one of these rules:
  1 no change, e.g. *put*, *put*
  2 a vowel changes, e.g. *rang*, r**u**ng
  3 we add -n, e.g. *chose*, *chose***n**
  4 a vowel changes and we add -n, e.g. *wrote*, *wri***tte***n*
  5 the past participle is a different word, e.g. *was/were*, **been**

b Work with a partner. Put the words in the box into the correct column of the table.

began/begun	woke/woken	heard/heard	broke/broken
grew/grown	gave/given	went/gone	drove/driven
drank/drunk	ate/eaten	won/won	bought/bought
saw/seen	did/done	ran/run	met/met
spoke/spoken			

Rule	Past simple	Past participle
1 no change		
2 vowel change		
3 add -*n*		
4 vowel change + -*n*		
5 different word		

Listening & Speaking past simple and present perfect verb forms

3a **12.12**))) Listen and complete the verb phrases.

1 I _____ the door.
2 I _____ the door.
3 She _____ a marathon.
4 She _____ a marathon.
5 We _____ him.
6 We _____ him.
7 I _____ *Star Wars* twice this month.
8 I _____ *Star Wars* twice last month.

b Compare your answers with a partner.

4 **12.13**))) Read and listen to the information in the Unlock the code box about past simple and present perfect verb forms.

> 🔒 **UNLOCK THE CODE**
> past simple and present perfect verb forms
>
> There are three ways to tell the difference between past simple and present perfect verb forms. Listen for:
>
> 1 the difference in pronunciation between the past simple and the past participle form of the verb.
>   *ran   run*
>
> 2 the present perfect auxiliary *have* ('*ve*) or *has* ('*s*).
>   We **met** him.   We**'ve met** him.
>
> 3 time words and phrases.
>   *I've watched Star Wars twice* **this month**.
>   *I watched Star Wars twice* **last month**.

5a Work with a partner. What do you know about Bollywood?

b Read the first part of an interview between a presenter (P) and an actor, Mark Russell (M), about Bollywood. Complete the interview with the past simple or present perfect form of the verbs in (brackets).

P Good evening. Our guest tonight is Mark Russell, who is going to talk about the Indian film industry, Bollywood, and one of its biggest stars. Mark, welcome.

M Thanks, Steffi.

P Tell us a little bit about Bollywood. Many of us ¹_____ (hear) of it, but perhaps we don't all know much about it. Is it bigger than Hollywood these days?

M Yes, it is. In the last ten years, Bollywood ²_____ (make) more films and it ³_____ (sell) more tickets, too. For example, in 2009, Bollywood ⁴_____ (produce) over 1,200 films and Hollywood ⁵_____ (make) only about 500. Also, Bollywood films ⁶_____ (become) popular all over the world and they ⁷_____ (make) them in lots of countries.

c **12.14**))) Listen and check your answers.

6 **12.15**))) Look at the photo of Hema Sardesai, a Bollywood singer. Listen to the second part of the interview about Hema and choose the correct verb form.

1 I never heard / I've never heard
2 She recorded / She's recorded
3 She also had / She's also had
4 She's was / She's been
5 She visited / She's visited
6 India celebrated / India has celebrated
7 She sang / She has sung
8 People watched / People have watched

7 **12.15**))) Listen again and answer the questions with a partner.

1 What kind of singer is Hema?
2 Why is Hema so famous?
3 Is it OK for actors in films not to sing? Should people like Hema be more famous? Why/Why not?

8a **TASK** Write three true and two false sentences about yourself using the past simple or present perfect.

b Work with a partner. Take turns to read a sentence and say what verb form you heard. Guess which sentences are false.

12.4 Speaking and writing

GOALS ■ Speak on the phone ■ Write a review ■ Use pronouns in writing

Listening & Speaking on the phone

1 Work with a partner. Answer the questions.

What do you say when you answer the phone …
1 in your language?
2 in English?

2 **12.16**))) Listen to two conversations and answer the questions. Compare your answers with a partner.
1 Why does Marcus call Caitlin?
2 What is Caitlin going to do after speaking to Marcus?
3 What question does she ask the person at the comedy club?
4 Why can't she find out the information she wants?

3a Work with a partner. Complete sentences 1–8 with the words in the box.

Can here have back (x2) Could speak Hang it's afraid

1 Hi Francis, _____ Marcus. Is Caitlin there?
2 Hello. Could I _____ to the ticket office manager, please?
3 She's not _____ at the moment.
4 I'm _____ he's not available at the moment.
5 _____ you tell her to call me _____, please?
6 _____ you ask him to call me _____, please?
7 Could I _____ your number, please?
8 _____ on a minute. I'll just get her.

b **12.17**))) Listen, check and repeat.

c Work with a partner. Which sentences in exercise **3a** are formal and which are informal?

4 Work with a partner. Take turns to have two phone conversations. Use the prompts and the Language for speaking box to help you.

Conversation 1
Ask to speak to your friend, Misha.

Conversation 2
Ask to speak to the manager of a company.

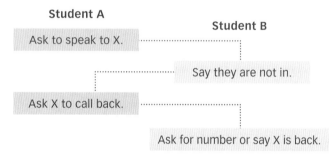

Student A
Ask to speak to X.

Student B
Say they are not in.

Ask X to call back.

Ask for number or say X is back.

LANGUAGE FOR SPEAKING on the phone

Informal
Hi (X), it's (Y). Is (Z) there?
I'm afraid she's not here at the moment.
Can you tell her to call me back, please?
Hang on a minute. I'll just get her.

Formal
Hello. Could I speak to the manager, please?
I'm afraid he's not available at the moment.
Could you ask him to call me back, please?
Could I have your number, please?

5 Work with a partner. Practise some more phone conversations. Student A, turn to page 131. Student B, turn to page 135.

Reading & Writing a review

6 Work in small groups. Number the types of entertainment from 1 (you like the most) to 8 (you like the least). Compare your answers and explain your reasons.

____ classical music concerts   ____ art galleries
____ pop/rock concerts   ____ circuses
____ plays (at the theatre)   ____ comedy clubs
____ films (at the cinema)   ____ museums

I put films first because I love them and I usually go to the cinema about once a week.

7 Read the first part of each review and match them to a photo. Compare your answers with a partner.

○○○

| HOME | ABOUT ME | MUSIC | FASHION |

¹ <u>I didn't expect it to be good.</u> I hated it when I was a child but I enjoyed the show last week ² <u>because there weren't any animals, just acrobats doing amazing things.</u> I really liked their clothes, too. Some of them were very colourful. My daughter Miriam and I sat very close to the stage. She has talked about it a lot at school and now all her friends want to go, too! ³ <u>I thought it was fantastic</u> and ⁴ <u>I recommend it to everyone.</u>

○○○

| HOME | ABOUT ME | MUSIC | FASHION |

⁵ <u>I was really excited about going</u> because they're my favourite band. But I've seen them before and they were much better then. I didn't enjoy it last night ⁶ <u>because the singer was too quiet</u> and the guitar player was terrible! They're playing again tonight but ⁷ <u>I don't recommend going.</u> ⁸ <u>I thought they were awful.</u> But at least it was quite cheap!

8 Work with a partner. Read the reviews. Which is positive? Which is negative? How do you know?

9 Match the <u>underlined</u> phrases 1–8 in the reviews to categories a–d. There are two answers for each one.

a what the writer thought before the show   <u>1, 5</u>
b what the writer thought about the show   ____
c why the writer liked/didn't like the show   ____
d the writer's advice to other people   ____

10a Think of an event you have been to. Use an idea from exercise **6** or your own ideas. Write notes in each of the categories.

1 what you thought before
2 what you thought after it
3 why you liked/didn't like it
4 your advice to other people

b Work with a partner. Tell them about the event. Use the phrases in the Language for writing box to help you.

LANGUAGE FOR WRITING a review

I was(n't) excited about (it/the show/the concert).
I expected/didn't expect (it/the circus) to be …
I liked/loved/enjoyed the (play) because …
I didn't like/enjoy the (concert) because …
I thought it was/they were (great/awful/a bit long/too loud).
I (don't) recommend (it/seeing this film/going to this show).

11a **TASK** Write your review. Use the ideas you talked about in exercise **10a**.

b Work with a partner and read their review. Would you like to go to the show they reviewed? Why/Why not?

12.5 Video

Park Theatre

1 Work with a partner. When was the last time you saw a play? Where was it? What was it? Did you enjoy it? Why/Why not?

2 Look at the photos. Which of these things do you see in the them?

> Ancient Greece audience balcony floor pantomime
> seats Shakespearean theatre theatre ticket stage

3 ▶ Watch the video and answer the questions.
   1 How has theatre changed since Shakespeare's day? Is this a positive or negative change? Why/Why not?
   2 How is Park Theatre changing modern theatre? Is this a positive or negative change? Why/Why not?

4 ▶ Watch the video again and choose the correct option.
   1 In Shakespeare's time most people *could / couldn't* afford the theatre.
   2 In Shakespeare's time, rich people watched plays *at the same time as / at a different time to* poor people.
   3 Park Theatre is a very *old / modern* theatre in *a modern / an old* office block.
   4 The Park Theatre puts on plays in *two / three* different rooms.
   5 Every ticket costs less than *twelve / twenty* pounds so it's affordable.
   6 Park Theatre shows old classics and modern *music / musicals*.
   7 Crystal Springs is a modern play about *teenagers / teachers*, parents and social media.
   8 In its short history Park Theatre has been *unsuccessful / very successful*.

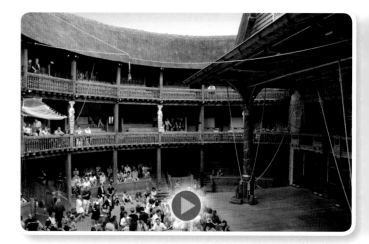

5a **TASK** Imagine you have a voucher to go to a show. What type of show would you like to go to? Write down what you would like to see and why. Use these ideas to help you.
   • performers
   • play, film, music concert, etc.
   • what reviews it has had
   • where it is

b Work in small groups. Tell each other what show you would like to see and why. Decide as a group which one to choose.

c Tell the class what show your group has chosen. Try to choose one show for the whole class.

Review

1a Complete gaps 1–6 with *go*, *play*, *see* or *have* and match the phrases to photos a–f.

1 _____ to a music festival
2 _____ an instrument
3 _____ dance lessons
4 _____ a film/movie
5 _____ to art galleries
6 _____ a play or a musical

b Work with a partner. Which things from exercise **1a** have you done and which things have you never done?

I have been to lots of music festivals. I went to the Festival in the Desert in Mali three years ago and it was fantastic.

I've never had a dance lesson. I don't like dancing!

2a Put the words in the correct order to make sentences we use on the phone.

1 a / Hang / minute / on .
2 Ms. Martinez / speak / please / Could / to / I ?
3 tell / back / you / her / me / Can / to / please / call ?
4 office / I'm / the / moment / the / afraid / of / out / at / she's .

b 12.18))) Listen to a phone conversation. Which sentences in exercise **2a** did you hear?

c Work with a partner. Write a phone conversation and practise it.

d Work with another pair. Read and practise their conversation. Is the conversation formal or informal?

3 Complete the text with the past simple or present perfect form of the verbs in (brackets).

These days, Verona coliseum is famous for its opera festival, but it ¹_____ (be) a place to see other types of entertainment over the years. The Romans ²_____ (build) the coliseum almost two thousand years ago for sports and games called 'ludi'. The most famous of these games ³_____ (be) fights between gladiators. These events ⁴_____ (be) very popular and people ⁵_____ (come) from far away to see them. In 1117, there ⁶_____ (be) a big earthquake in Verona and people ⁷_____ (not use) the coliseum for a long time. However, centuries later, the Venetians ⁸_____ (decide) to repair the building and use it for concerts. From that time, hundreds of thousands of people ⁹_____ (come) to Verona to listen to music and many famous opera singers and ballet dancers ¹⁰_____ (perform) there.

b 12.19))) Listen and check your answers.

4a What types of film do items 1–8 make you think of?

1 laughing *comedies*
2 people in love
3 a cartoon for children
4 fast cars
5 singing and dancing
6 Dracula and Frankenstein
7 travelling into the future
8 going to live in a new country

b Think of a famous film you know. Write three sentences about it, but don't use the name of the film. Use questions 1–4 in the box to help you, and your own ideas.

1 What type of film is it?
2 What is it about?
3 Who does it star?
4 Where does it happen?

It's set in Barcelona and it stars Scarlett Johansson.

c Work with a partner. Take turns to read your sentences and guess the films.

Communication

1.1 All students
Exercise 2

Read the factfiles and check your answers.

LONDON, ENGLAND	FACTFILE
Nationality	British
Other nationalities	Asian (e.g. Indian, Pakistani, Chinese), European (e.g. Irish, Polish), African (e.g. Nigerian, Somali), West Indian (e.g. Jamaican), etc.
Main language	English
Other languages	Polish, Urdu, etc.

SAN FRANCISCO, USA	FACTFILE
Nationality	American
Other nationalities	Central or South American (e.g. Mexican, Chilean), Chinese, Filipino, etc.
Main language	English
Other languages	Spanish, Chinese, Filipino, etc.

MELBOURNE, AUSTRALIA	FACTFILE
Nationality	Australian
Other nationalities	British, Italian, Greek, Vietnamese, etc.
Main language	English
Other languages	Italian, Greek, Vietnamese, etc.

DUBAI, UAE	FACTFILE
Nationality	Emirati
Other nationalities	Indian, Pakistani, Bangladeshi, Filipino, etc.
Main language	Arabic
Other languages	English, Urdu, Hindi, Filipino, etc.

1.3 Student A
Exercise 9

1 Complete gaps 1–5 in table A.

Table A

Singular	Plural
1 _____	stories
a glass	2 _____
3 _____	lives
a dress	4 _____
5 _____	children

2 Ask your partner questions to check your answers for table A.

What's the singular of stories?
What's the plural of …?
How do you spell that?

3 Listen to your partner's questions for table B and answer them. Then complete gaps 6–10.

Table B

Singular	Plural
a knife	6 _____
7 _____	people
a city	8 _____
9 _____	matches
a woman	10 _____

1.4 Student A
Exercise 6

1 Complete the table with information about you.

2 Ask questions to complete your partner's information.

	You	Your partner
Name		
Job		
Nationality		
Email address		

2.2 All students
Exercise 1

1 False. The basic training takes about two years. Then, before each trip into space, they need to do another two–three years of training.

2 True. Valeri Polyakov stayed in space for 437.7 days in 1994–5. Sergei Avdeyev stayed in space for 379.6 days in 1998–9.

3 True. Astronauts can wear glasses.

2.4 Student A
Exercise 4

1 You are in Lagos with Student B. Read factfile A. Suggest meeting Student B and make arrangements.

2 You are in Buenos Aires with Student B. Read factfile B. Listen to Student B and reply.

LAGOS, NIGERIA Places to go and things to do	FACTFILE A
National Museum of Nigeria	9 a.m. – 4 p.m.
Lekki Conservation centre (see monkeys, crocodiles, birds)	9 a.m. – 6 p.m.
Yellow Chilli (Nigerian restaurant)	12 p.m. – 10.30 p.m.
New Afrika Shrine (live music, African dance and theatre)	6 p.m. – 6 a.m.
Eleko Beach (bar, live music, picnics, tents to sleep in)	24 hours a day

BUENOS AIRES, ARGENTINA Places to go and things to do	FACTFILE B
MNBA (art gallery and museum)	9.30 a.m. – 8.30 p.m.
Fundación Tango Argentino (dance classes)	8 p.m. – 10 p.m.
La Cabrera (restaurant famous for beef)	12.30 p.m. – 4.30 p.m. 8.30 p.m. – 1.00 a.m.
Football matches	7.15 p.m. – 9.15 p.m.
Jet Lounge (house music, fashion parties, sushi, cocktails)	12.30 a.m. – 8 a.m.

4.1 Student A
Exercise 11

1 You want to go on a weekend break. Read the information about Bruges and the things you want to do.

Bruges
- Airport (Brussels) – 90 km from Bruges
- Railway station in the centre
- Campsite near the city centre
- Lots of museums including Choco-Story (a chocolate museum), Diamant Museum (a diamond museum) and Expo Picasso (an art museum)
- More than five different (street) markets every week
- Four youth hostels and 300 hotels
- An Olympic swimming pool

You want to ...
- fly there
- stay in a cheap hotel
- visit museums
- go to the cinema
- go swimming

2 Ask your partner about Krakow and answer their questions about Bruges.

A *Is there a cinema in Krakow?*
B *Yes, there are more than three.*

3 Decide together which town is better for your weekend break.

4.2 Student A
Exercise 6

Ask questions and describe your studio flat to your partner to find seven differences.

A *Is there a cooker next to the fridge?*
B *Yes, there is./No, there isn't.*

4.4 Student A
Exercise 7

On your map there are four places with no name. Ask your partner for directions from the traditional market in Denpasar to the four places below. Write them in the correct place on the map.

- bus station
- market
- Jagatnatha temple
- hotel

A *Excuse me, how do I get to the bus station?*
B *Well, go straight on and …*

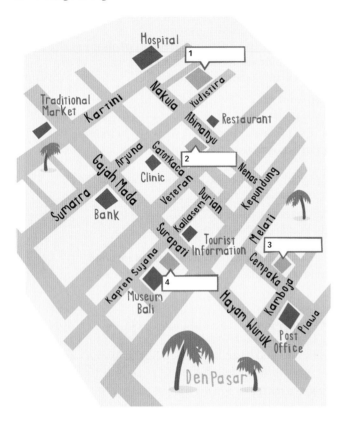

4.4 All students
Exercise 11

Choose a situation 1, 2 or 3 and write an email giving information and instructions. Include the following:

- why you need to meet
- the place and time
- any other details, e.g. how to get there.

Remember to use imperatives when you give instructions.

1 You need to organize the office meeting for lunchtime on Thursday. Everyone needs to bring their laptop or tablet. No food or drink.

2 You want to organize a dinner for your English class at your flat. Everyone needs to bring something to eat and drink.

3 You want to organize a group of students to study English with. People need to bring their coursebooks, and tablets or notebooks. You must speak English only.

5.2 Student A
Exercise 12

1 Work with another Student A. Look at prompts 1–6 and decide which questions are present simple and which are present continuous.

> *Is the shop assistant standing?* ✓
> **NOT** ~~*Does the shop assistant stand?*~~ ✗

1 the shop assistant/stand?
2 what time/the shop/open?
3 the shop/take/credit cards?
4 what/the young man/hold?
5 what/the old man/wear?
6 what/shop assistant/wear?

2 Work with Student B. Take turns to ask and answer your questions and find the six differences.

A *Is the shop assistant standing?*
B *Yes, she is./No, she isn't.*

6.2 Student A
Exercise 6

1 Read and complete the sentences with the past simple of the verbs in (brackets).

a He ¹_____ (return) the money to his boss who ²_____ (call) the owner of the bag.
b Adam Woldemarim ³_____ (work) as a taxi driver in Las Vegas.
c When he ⁴_____ (look) between the seats he ⁵_____ (notice) a bag.
d He ⁶_____ (thank) Adam and gave him $2,000.

2 Read your sentences to your partner and listen to theirs. Put your sentences and your partner's sentences together to make a complete story.

6.4 Student A
Exercise 6

1 Tell your partner the pieces of news a–e.

  a We moved house three times last year.

  b Someone shouted at me in the street yesterday.

  c I've got a new job!

  d I walked ten miles on Sunday.

  e I've got too much work at the moment.

2 Respond to your partner's news.

7.4 All students
Exercise 13a

Students	At the beginning of the year, the university made a rule that all students need to go to the gym for two hours of exercise a week.
Employees	The company gave employees a choice: work 40 hours a week at their desks or work 39 hours a week and spend one hour in the company gym.
Everyone	A new law says that everyone under 16 can go to big sports events for free. This is because the government wants children to see and do more sport.

8.4 Student A
Exercise 4

1 You work at the ticket office in New Delhi station in north India. Look at the information about the next train to Varanasi and answer Student B's questions.

	Times	Journey time	Ticket price (rupees)	Platform
New Delhi to Varanasi	depart: 16.20 arrive: 05.28	13 hours 08 mins	470 (sleeper)	7

2 You are a passenger at Mysore station in south India. You want to get a single first class ticket for the next train to Bangalore. Ask ...

- when it departs/arrives
- the journey time
- the price
- the platform number

9.1 Student A
Exercise 11

1 Look at the illustration. Take turns to ask and answer questions to find the differences between your illustration and your partner's. Use *some* and *any* in your questions and answers.

  A *Do you have any salad?*

  B *Yes, I do, but I don't have any jam. Do you have any?*

  A *Yes, I do, so that's one difference.*

2 How many differences did you find?

9.2 Student A
Exercise 10b

Work with Student B. Ask questions to complete your recipe.

Do you cut the butter into small pieces?

MUSHROOM SOUP

INGREDIENTS
- 4 potatoes • 2 carrots • 400 grams of mushrooms
- 250 millilitres of milk • 750 millilitres of water
- 50 grams of butter

METHOD

1 Cut the _____ into small pieces with a knife.

2 Chop the mushrooms and the carrots.

3 Heat the butter in a saucepan and add the mushrooms. Stir with a spoon.

4 _____ the water in the kettle and add to the saucepan.

5 Add the _____ and _____ to the saucepan. Boil for ten minutes.

6 Add the milk and boil for five more minutes.

7 Put everything in the food-processor for one minute to make the soup.

9.3 Student A
Exercise 10

1 Work with another Student A. Put the words in order to make questions about the Philippines.

1 the / is / population / What ?
2 live / What percentage / the biggest city / in ?
3 the maximum and minimum / What / temperature every year / is ?
4 is / Day / When / Independence ?

2 Look at the table and answer Student B's questions about Malaysia.

	Malaysia	The Philippines
Population	30,000,000	_____
Percentage living in biggest city (Kuala Lumpur)	3%	_____
Temperature	Max = 38°C Min = 15°C	Max = _____ Min = _____
Important day	31/08 (Hari Merdeka – National Day)	_____

3 Ask Student B the questions from exercise 1 to complete the column for the Philippines.

9.4 All students
Exercise 10

Take turns to be the waiter and the customer. Order the food you want from the menu.

A *Hi, would you like to order?*
B *Yes, please.*
A *OK, would you like a starter?*

STARTERS
Chicken and vegetable soup
Cambodian beef salad
Fishcakes with a side salad
Mixed green salad

MAINS
Chinese beef and mushrooms in a black bean sauce with noodles
Grilled lamb with rice and salad
Baked fish with roast or boiled potatoes and steamed vegetables
Gio's special pasta with green beans, tomatoes, olives and parmesan cheese

DESSERTS
Apple pie with cream
Chocolate cake with cream
Ice cream: chocolate, strawberry, mango
French cheese

DRINKS
Tea
Coffee
Mineral water
Coke
Orange juice

10.2 All students
Exercise 4d

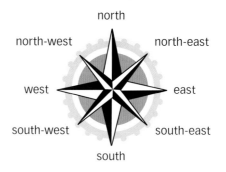

10.2 Student A
Exercise 5

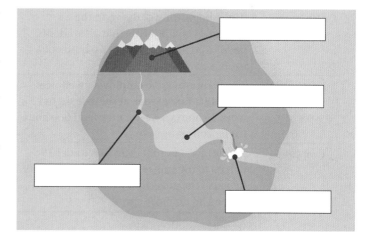

1 Label the map.

2 Describe your map to your partner.
In the north-west of my island there are …

3 Listen to your partner and draw what they describe on your map. Compare your maps. Are they the same?

10.4 Student A
Exercise 2

1 Read definitions a–e and label the illustrations on page 102 with the words in **bold**.

a You use **a first-aid kit** when you hurt yourself.
b **A GPS** helps you find your way to the right place.
c You use **a torch** to help you see in the dark.
d You use **a map** to see where you are and find your way to the right place.
e You sleep in **a tent** when you go camping.

2 Read your definitions to your partner.

3 Listen to your partner's definitions and label the other illustrations. If you don't know how to spell a word, ask …
How do you spell that?

10.4 All students Exercise 11

Australia
North usually very hot
Great Barrier Reef – 2,000 km long
Snow on higher mountains – can ski
Swim and dive on the reef – colourful fish
An island – sixth largest country in world
Uluru (Ayers Rock) 348 m – red – in the middle of
the country
Animals you can't see anywhere else – koalas, kangaroos
South can be cool

11.2 Student A Exercise 4c

1 Read the websites and email addresses to your partner.

www.myspace.com/zootwoman
Jack_memperton456@hotmail.com
www.chrisbrock.co.uk/personal/
star-student74@thetopschool.org

2 Listen to your partner's websites and email addresses and write them down.

11.3 All students Exercise 3b

The meaning of *common* here is *usual* or *frequent*.

11.4 Student A Exercise 10b

Work
You are going to have a meeting with your colleague, Student B.
1 You don't know where the meeting room is.
2 It's important someone makes notes.
3 You want to organize another meeting, but you are very busy.

Study
Student B is doing the same course as you.
1 You don't understand question number 4.
2 You missed the class this morning.
3 You don't have any paper to write notes.

Social
You are going on holiday with Student B.
1 You can't remember what time the taxi is going to arrive.
2 You can't find the plane ticket.
3 You need something to read for the journey.

12.4 Student A Exercise 5

Do Conversation 1 and choose one situation from Conversation 2.

Conversation 1
Social

You want to speak to your friend Fazad about going out tonight. Call the flat he shares with his flatmate and ask to speak to him.

Conversation 2
Study

You are a secretary at a university and you answer the phone for the teachers and professors. Professor Clark can't speak to anyone now because she is busy. Answer the phone.

Work

Your company does a lot of business with another company in a different city. You need to speak to Mr Tagako at the other company. Call and ask to speak to him.

1.3 Student B Exercise 9

1 Complete gaps 1–5 in table B.

Table B

singular	Plural
1 _____	knives
a person	2 _____
3 _____	cities
a match	4 _____
5 _____	women

2 Listen to your partner's questions for table A and answer them. Then complete gaps 6–10.

Table A

Singular	Plural
a story	6 _____
7 _____	glasses
a life	8 _____
9 _____	dresses
a child	10 _____

3 Ask your partner questions to check your answers for table B.

What's the singular of knives?
What's the plural of … ?
How do you spell that?

1.4 Student B
Exercise 6

1   Complete the table with information about you.

2   Ask questions to complete your partner's information.

	You	Your partner
Name		
Job		
Nationality		
Email address		

2.4 Student B
Exercise 5

1   You are in Lagos with Student A. Read factfile A. Listen to Student A and reply.

2   You are in Buenos Aires with Student A. Read factfile B. Suggest meeting Student A and make arrangements.

LAGOS, NIGERIA Places to go and things to do	FACTFILE A
National Museum of Nigeria	9 a.m. – 4 p.m.
Lekki Conservation centre (see monkeys, crocodiles, birds)	9 a.m. – 6 p.m.
Yellow Chilli (Nigerian restaurant)	12 p.m. – 10.30 p.m.
New Afrika Shrine (live music, African dance and theatre)	6 p.m. – 6 a.m.
Eleko Beach (bar, live music, picnics, tents to sleep in)	24 hours a day

BUENOS AIRES, ARGENTINA Places to go and things to do	FACTFILE B
MNBA (art gallery and museum)	9.30 a.m. – 8.30 p.m.
Fundación Tango Argentino (dance classes)	8 p.m. – 10 p.m.
La Cabrera (restaurant famous for beef)	12.30 p.m. – 4.30 p.m. 8.30 p.m. – 1.00 a.m.
Football matches	7.15 p.m. – 9.15 p.m.
Jet Lounge (house music, fashion parties, sushi, cocktails)	12.30 a.m. – 8 a.m.

4.1 Student B
Exercise 11

1   You want to go on a weekend break. Read the information about Krakow and the things you want to do.

Krakow

- Airport 11 km from the centre of Krakow
- More than twenty youth hostels and 250 hotels
- Railway station in the centre
- Campsites near the city centre
- Lots of museums including Krakow National Museum and City of Krakow Historical Museum
- More than three cinemas
- Hala Targowa flea market
- Two open-air and one indoor swimming pool

You want to …

- go by train
- stay on a campsite
- go swimming
- go to markets
- visit an art museum

2   Ask your partner about Bruges and answer their questions about Krakow.

   B   *Is there a campsite in Bruges?*
   A   *Yes, there is. It's near the city centre.*

3   Decide together which town is better for your weekend break.

4.2 Student B
Exercise 6

Ask questions and describe your studio flat to your partner to find seven differences.

A   *Is there a cooker next to the fridge?*
B   *Yes, there is./No, there isn't.*

4.4 Student B
Exercise 7

On your map there are four places with no name. Ask your partner for directions from the traditional market in Denpasar to the four places below. Write them in the correct place on the map.

- post office
- bank
- tourist information
- hospital

A *Excuse me, how do I get to the post office?*
B *Well, go straight on and …*

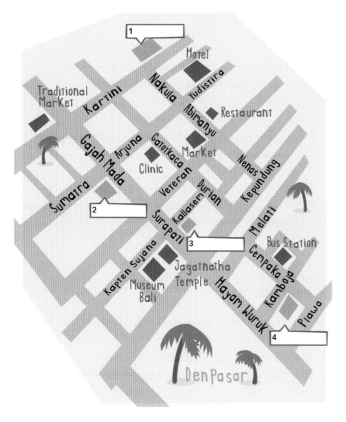

5.2 Student B
Exercise 12

1 Work with another Student B. Look at prompts 1–6 and decide which questions are present simple and which are present continuous.

What time does the shop close? ✓
NOT ~~What time is the shop closing?~~ ✗

1 what time/the shop/close?
2 what/the old man/do?
3 what languages/the shop assistants/speak?
4 what/the young man/hold?
5 what/the young woman/wear?
6 what/the young man/wear?

2 Work with Student A. Take turns to ask and answer your questions and find the six differences.

A *What time does the shop close?*
B *It closes at five o'clock.*

9.3 All students
Exercise 9

1 The lowest natural temperature recorded on Earth is -89.2 °C in Antarctica, on July 21st 1983.
2 Man first landed on the moon on 20th July 1969.
3 Belgium produces 172,000 tons of chocolate a year.
4 An average person laughs 15 times a day.
5 Children laugh 400 times a day.
6 41% of people use Facebook at work according to Forbes.
7 People spend 3.66 years of their life eating.

6.2 Student B
Exercise 6

1 Read and complete the sentences with the past simple of the verbs in (brackets).

a He ¹_____ (open) it and there was a large amount of money – over $200,000!
b Adam ²_____ (decide) to send some of the money to his family in Ethiopia.
c The owner was very happy when he ³_____ (collect) his lost money.
d One night he ⁴_____ (finish) work at 2.00 a.m. and ⁵_____ (start) to clean his cab.

2 Listen to your partner's sentences and read yours to them. Put your sentences and your partner's sentences together to make a complete story.

6.4 Student B
Exercise 6

1 Tell your partner the pieces of news a–e.

a I booked a holiday to Australia.

b I couldn't sleep last night.

c I was on TV when I was a child.

d I've got a cold.

e I watched a great film on TV last night.

2 Respond to your partner's news.

8.4 Student B
Exercise 4

1 You are a passenger at New Delhi station in north India. You want to get a single sleeper ticket for the next train to Varanasi. Ask …

- when it departs/arrives
- the journey time
- the price
- the platform number

2 You work at the ticket office in Mysore station in south India. Look at the information about the next train to Bangalore and answer student A's questions.

	Times	Journey time	Ticket price (rupees)	Platform
Mysore to Bangalore	depart: 14.15 arrive: 16.25	2 hours 10 mins	995 (1st class)	3

9.1 Student B
Exercise 11

1 Look at the illustration. Take turns to ask and answer questions to find the differences between your illustration and your partner's. Use *some* and *any* in your questions and answers.

A *Do you have any salad?*

B *Yes, I do, but I don't have any jam. Do you have any?*

A *Yes, I do, so that's one difference.*

2 How many differences did you find?

9.2 Student B
Exercise 10b

Work with Student A. Ask questions to complete your recipe. *Do you fry the mushrooms and the carrots?*

MUSHROOM SOUP

INGREDIENTS

- 4 potatoes   • 2 carrots   • 400 grams of mushrooms
- 250 millilitres of milk   • 750 millilitres of water
- 50 grams of butter

METHOD

1 Cut the potatoes into small pieces with a knife.

2 _____ the mushrooms and the carrots.

3 Heat the _____ in a saucepan and add the _____ . Stir with a spoon.

4 Boil the water in the kettle and add to the saucepan.

5 Add the potatoes and carrots to the saucepan. Boil for ten minutes.

6 Add the _____ and boil for five more minutes.

7 Put everything in the food-processor for one minute to make the soup.

9.3 Student B
Exercise 10

1 Work with another Student B. Put the words in the right order to make questions about Malaysia.

1 the / is / population / What ?

2 live / What percentage / the biggest city / in ?

3 the maximum and minimum / What / temperature every year / is ?

4 is / day / an / When / important ?

2 Ask Student A the questions from exercise 1 to complete the column for Malaysia.

	Malaysia	The Philippines
Population	_____	99,000,000
Percentage living in biggest city (Quezon)	_____	2.00%
Temperature	Max = _____ Min = _____	Max = 28°C Min = 16°C
Important day	_____	12/06 (Independence Day)

3 Look at the table and answer Student A's questions about the Philippines.

10.2 Student B Exercise 5

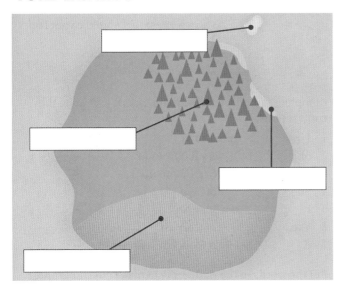

1 Label the map.

2 Listen to your partner and draw what they describe on your map.

3 Describe your map to your partner.
   In the north-east of my island there is ...

4 Compare your maps. Are they the same?

10.4 Student B Exercise 2

1 Read definitions a–e and label the illustrations on page 102 with the words in **bold**.

   a **A stove** is a small kind of cooker.

   b You use **a lighter** to start a fire.

   c Plates, bowls, spoons, knives and saucepans are all examples of **equipment for cooking and eating**.

   d You sleep in **a sleeping bag** to keep warm when you sleep outside.

   e You use **a compass** to find where north, south, east and west are.

2 Listen to your partner's definitions and label the other illustrations. If you don't know how to spell a word, ask ...
   How do you spell that?

3 Read your definitions to your partner.

11.2 Student B Exercise 4c

1 Listen to your partner's websites and email addresses and write them down.

2 Read the websites and email addresses to your partner.
   • s.lorenzo-jefferson@hgg.org
   • www.theblacksea.eu
   • every_apple333@gmail.com
   • www.nationaltheatre.gnbo.com.ng/

11.4 Student B Exercise 10b

Work
You are going to have a meeting with your colleague, Student A.
   1 You need more copies of a document.
   2 You don't have a pen.
   3 You don't know how to use the software.

Study
Student A is doing the same course as you.
   1 You need to contact the teacher, but you don't have her email address.
   2 You don't understand what the teacher says.
   3 You didn't have time to do the homework.

Social
You are going on holiday with Student A.
   1 You don't have any euros.
   2 You have too many bags.
   3 You can't find your guidebook.

12.4 Student B Exercise 5

Do Conversation 1 and choose one situation from Conversation 2.

Conversation 1
Social
You share a flat with your friend Fazad. He is out at the moment and you don't know when he's going to be back. Answer the phone.

Conversation 2
Study
You are a student and you have a problem with the course you are doing. Call the university and ask to speak to your teacher, Professor Clark.

Work
You are a receptionist at a big company and you answer the phone for your boss, Mr Tagako. He's busy and can't talk to anyone at the moment. Answer the phone.

Grammar reference

1.1 The verb *to be*

GR1.1a 》

Positive (+)	Negative (–)
I **am** from Thailand. I**'m** from Thailand.	I **am not** Swiss. I**'m not** Swiss.
You **are** Thai. You**'re** Thai.	You **are not** from Egypt. You **aren't** from Egypt.
He **is** from Brazil. He**'s** from Brazil.	He **is not** happy. He **isn't** happy.
She **is** Brazilian. She**'s** Brazilian.	She **is not** hungry. She **isn't** hungry.
It **is** late. It**'s** late.	It **is not** Friday today. It **isn't** Friday today.
We **are** married. We**'re** married.	We **are not** from Chile. We **aren't** from Chile.
They **are** teachers. They**'re** teachers.	They **are not** Italian. They **aren't** Italian.

We use the verb *to be* …
* when we describe someone or something, e.g. *He's big*.
* to talk about age, e.g. *I'm forty*.

In everyday conversation and informal writing we use contractions:
're not/aren't, 's not/isn't, 'm not.
' = a missing letter, e.g. He is → He's.
In formal writing we use full forms, e.g. *They are not*.

yes/no questions and short answers

GR1.1b 》

1 **A** ***Are*** they twins?   2 **A** ***Is*** it ten o'clock?
   B *Yes, they **are***.   **B** *No, it **isn't***.

Questions (?)		Short answers	
Am I		Yes, I **am**.	No, I**'m not**.
Are you	late?	Yes, you **are**	No, you **aren't**.
Is he/she/it	French?	Yes, he/she/it **is**.	No, he/she/it **isn't**.
Are we/they		Yes, we/they **are**.	No, we/they **aren't**.

In questions, we put *am, is, are* before *I, you, he, she, it, we, they*.

In positive short answers we use full forms.

A *Are you German?*
B *Yes, I am.* NOT ~~Yes, I'm.~~

In negative short answers we use full forms or contractions.

A *Are we early?*
B *No, we are not./No, we aren't.*

---

1 Complete sentences 1–7 with *am, is, are*, and write the contractions.

1 I __am__ from Korea   → *I'm*
2 She _____ very happy today.   → _____
3 They _____ from Vietnam.   → _____
4 She _____ not here.   → _____
5 I _____ not Spanish.   → _____
6 You _____ not worried.   → _____
7 It _____ not a French restaurant.   → _____

2 Put the words in the right order to make questions and short answers.

1 **A** Russian / Are / you ? *Are you Russian?*
   B not / No, / I'm *No, I'm not.*
2 **A** Ben / Is / name / your ? _____
   B it / Yes, / is _____
3 **A** I / late / Am / class / for / today ? _____
   B Yes, / are / you _____
4 **A** Are / British / they ? _____
   B No, / American / they're _____
5 **A** Austria / Are / you / from ? _____
   B we / No, / aren't _____
6 **A** she / Is / a / teacher ? _____
   B she / No, / isn't _____

3 Make questions and short answers.

1 _Is_ he a student?   ✓ *Yes, he is.*
2 _____ you from Malaysia?   ✗ *No,*
3 _____ I in the right room?   ✗ _____
4 _____ it your first day here?   ✓ _____
5 _____ we in the same class?   ✓ _____

4 Put the conversation in the right order.

A Hi, my name's Luigi.   _1_
A No, I'm Italian.   ____
B Hi, I'm Asli. Are you from Spain?   ____
A No, not Rome. I'm from Naples in the South. Where are you from?   ____
B Oh, are you from Rome?   ____
A Oh good!   ____
B Yes, they are, and the teacher is nice.   ____
A Yes, I am. It's my first day. Are the students friendly?   ____
B I'm from Istanbul in Turkey. Are you a student in this class?   ____
B OK! Let me introduce you to my friends.   _10_

1.2 Possessive determiners and possessive 's

Possessive determiners: *my, your*, etc.

GR1.2a))

I'm a twin.   **My** *twin sister lives in Zagreb.*
You're not in this class today.   **Your** *class is in room 401.*
He's from a big family.   **His** *brothers live in Singapore.*
She's a good friend.   **Her** *name is Hannah.*
It's a typical French village.   *It's famous for* **its** *food.*
We're fluent in Chinese.   **Our** *father is from Shanghai.*
They're my half sisters.   **Their** *names are Kana and Keiko.*

Personal pronoun	I	you	he	she	it	we	they
Possessive determiner	my	your	his	her	its	our	their

We use a possessive determiner to say that something or someone belongs to a person, a place or a thing. The possessive determiner always comes before a noun or a noun phrase.

We use …

- *his* to say that something or someone belongs to a man/boy
  John loves **his** *daughter.*
  NOT *John loves her daughter.*

- *her* to say that something or someone belongs to a woman/girl
  Amari and **her** *husband are here.*
  NOT *Amari and his husband are here.*

- *its* to say that something or someone belongs to a thing
  The city is famous for **its** *universities.*
  NOT *The city is famous for their universities.*

- Possessive determiners have one form for singular and plural, e.g. *our friend/our friends* NOT *ours friends*.

it's ≠ its
It's (= It is) *a big city.*
Its (possessive) *buildings are beautiful.*

Possessive 's

GR1.2b))

1 Sam is my father**'s** boss.
2 They are my children**'s** cars.
3 Bob and Paula are my paren**ts'** friends.
4 Petra and Bill**'s** new house is big.

We use the possessive 's to say that something or someone belongs to a person, a place or a thing. The possessive 's always comes after a noun.

- With regular plural nouns we use ' not 's, e.g. *They're my parents' friends.* NOT *They're my parent's friends.*

- If there is more than one subject, we put the 's on the last name, e.g. *Sara and Ricardo's daughter.* NOT *Sara's and Ricardo's daughter.*

John's in the office. (= is)
John's office is big. (= the office that belongs to John)

1 Complete the sentences with a possessive determiner.
   1 My brother has a daughter. _Her_ name is Brigitte.
   2 I have two nephews. _____ names are Tim and Ned.
   3 Dubai is famous for _____ tall buildings.
   4 My teacher is from New Zealand and _____ wife is from Tasmania.
   5 You're in room 14 and _____ teacher's name is Angela.
   6 We're Mexican, but _____ parents live in Brazil.
   7 I'm from Sweden and _____ name is Oskar.
   8 'Is this _____ book?' 'Oh, yes, it is! Thank you.'

2 Make possessive forms by adding 's or '.
   1 My country _'s_ people are happy.
   2 My two brothers _'___ cars are expensive.
   3 We're Peter and Vera___ neighbours.
   4 Are these Lucas___ glasses?
   5 This is their grandparents___ house.
   6 They are his grandson___ pencils.
   7 These are our bosses___ offices.

3 Circle the correct option.
   1 The *mechanic's car* / *mechanics car* is very nice.
   2 This is my *aunt and uncle's* / *aunt's and uncle's* house.
   3 *His* / *He's* my daughter's teacher.
   4 Maria and *her* / *their* parents live in Portugal.
   5 Tom is *Magda's nephew* / *nephew's Magda*.
   6 *Jane's children* / *Jane's children's* speak Mandarin.
   7 *My glasses* / *My glasses'* are in the classroom.
   8 It's famous for *it's* / *its* music.

4 Complete the text about Balinese names using the words in the box.

are child's father's husband's I'm is its mother's names Our their

Hi! I'm Wayan and ¹ _I'm_ Balinese. Bali ² _____ an island in Indonesia. It's famous for ³ _____ music and dancing. In a Balinese family, the first child's name is Wayan, Putu or Gede. It's the same for a boy or a girl. The second ⁴ _____ name is Made, Kadek or Nengah. The third is Nyoman or Komang and the fourth is Ketut. If there is a fifth child, he or she is often called Wayan Balik (= Wayan 'again'). Balinese do not usually use last names.

In my family there ⁵ _____ six children. We all have typical Balinese names. I have two sisters, ⁶ _____ names are Wayan and Komang, and three brothers, Ketut, Made and Putu. ⁷ _____ parents' ⁸ _____ are Ketut and Ketut. Women have the title 'Ni' before their name, so my ⁹ _____ name is Ni Ketut, and men use 'I', so my ¹⁰ _____ name is I Ketut. My sister, Komang, is married and her ¹¹ _____ name is also Komang.

2.1 Present simple and adverbs of frequency

Present simple positive

GR2.1a))

1 I **go** to the beach on Saturdays.
2 He **gets up** at six o'clock every day.
3 She **comes** from Turkey.
4 They **have** four children.

Present simple positive (+)

I	cook	
You	cook	
He/She/It	cook**s**	at weekends.
We	cook	
They	cook	

Spelling rules
- Verbs ending in -ch, -sh, -s, -ss, -z, -o, and -x

watch	→	watches	miss	→	misses
wash	→	washes	go	→	goes
relax	→	relaxes	do	→	does

- Verbs ending in consonant + -y
  study → studies
- The third person he/she/it form of have is has.

- We use the present simple to talk about habits or routines.
  He goes to work every day.
- We also use it to talk about a fact or something we think is true for a long time.
  Penguins eat fish. She lives in Bonn.

Adverbs of frequency
- We use adverbs of frequency with the present simple to say how often we do something.

GR2.1b))

100%					0%
always	usually	often	sometimes	hardly ever	never

1 I **always** go to bed before ten o'clock.
2 Do you **usually** have toast for breakfast?
3 We're **sometimes** tired in the afternoon.
4 They **hardly ever** go to the cinema.

- We usually put the adverb *after* the verb *to be* and *before* all other verbs.
  Silvia is often at home on Saturdays.
  Andy never goes to work on Sundays.
- *Sometimes* and *usually* can come at the beginning or end of sentences.
  Sometimes I listen to music at work.
  Winters are very cold here, usually.

---

1 Complete the sentences with the correct form of the verb in (brackets).

1 Four scientists _work_ at the research centre. (work)
2 They _____ their jobs. (love)
3 Our friend _____ lots of photos. (take)
4 We _____ a lot of free time. (have)
5 She _____ in the evening. (relax)
6 I _____ a book on the bus. (read)
7 He _____ films at weekends. (watch)
8 You _____ your clothes here. (wash)

2 Put the words in the right order to make sentences.

1 go / We / to /often / beach / the
  We often go to the beach.
2 He / big / always / dinner / makes / a
  _____
3 visit / islands / other / They / sometimes
  _____
4 You / work / the / in / lab / usually
  _____
5 sleep / have / never / enough / We
  _____
6 listen / never / at / music / to / work / I
  _____
7 It / ever / rains / the / on / island / hardly
  _____
8 my / in / city / never / It / cold / is
  _____
9 I / worried / ever / hardly / am
  _____
10 houses / in / cold / The / sometimes / are / winter
  _____

3 Complete the text with the correct form of the words in the box.

enjoy   finish   go   hardly   have   listen   never   ~~study~~
usually   work

Cara is a scientist and she **1** _studies_ the sun. She lives in Calama in Chile. During the week she gets up early and **2** _____ to the research centre. She **3** _____ has a small breakfast – a biscuit and a cup of coffee. She **4** _____ with five other researchers. They all **5** _____ their jobs. She **6** _____ work at five o'clock.

In the evening, she **7** _____ dinner with her husband and they often watch a DVD or **8** _____ to music. They **9** _____ watch TV because they think it's boring and they **10** _____ ever talk about work.

2.2 Present simple negative

GR2.2a)))

1 I **don't have** a lot of free time.
2 He **doesn't wear** special clothes for work.
3 We **don't get up** early at weekends.

Present simple negative (–)

I You	don't	
He She It	doesn't	like tea.
We They	don't	

- We form the present simple negative with do/does + not + infinitive without to.
- We often use contractions:
  don't (= do not) and doesn't (= does not).
- For the third person he/she/it form we don't add -(e)s to the verb.
  She doesn't sleep in a bed.
  NOT She doesn't sleeps in a bed.

Adverbs of frequency in negative sentences

GR2.2b)))

1 We don't **often** watch a film in the evening.
2 He doesn't **always** have breakfast.
3 They don't **usually** go out on Fridays.
4 She hardly ever **takes** photos.

- Adverbs of frequency go between don't/doesn't and the verb.
- We don't use a negative verb with hardly ever or never.
  You **hardly ever** write.
  NOT You don't hardly ever write.
  It **never** rains in the summer.
  NOT It doesn't never rain in the summer.

1 Circle the correct option.
1 The sun *doesn't* / *don't* rise in the south.
2 Sara *doesn't* / *don't* want breakfast.
3 The shop doesn't *close* / *closes* in the evening.
4 I *don't* / *doesn't* sleep a lot.
5 They don't *have* / *has* classes today.
6 We don't *always eat* / *eat always* fresh fruit.
7 You *don't never go* / *never go* to work at night.
8 He *doesn't often* / *don't often* get up late.

2 Change sentences 1–10 to make them negative.
1 I need perfect eyesight.
  You don't need perfect eyesight.
2 I work hard.
  He _____
3 You stop for a break at lunchtime.
  She _____
4 He watches films on Fridays.
  They _____
5 She agrees with me.
  You _____
6 They exercise a lot.
  I _____
7 It rains every day.
  It _____
8 He changes his clothes every day.
  We _____
9 I feel good in the morning.
  She _____
10 We sleep for eight hours a night.
  They _____

3 Complete the text about Sabina's day. Use the words in the box.

am   doesn't   doesn't   don't   ~~don't~~   eat   like   likes

I get up early every day. I **1** _don't_ have breakfast because I **2** _____ never hungry in the morning. I have a shower and then I run to catch the bus. It **3** _____ wait for me! At work I **4** _____ drink coffee – only water. I usually **5** _____ lunch with my friend. I have a sandwich, but my friend doesn't **6** _____ bread, so she has fruit and yoghurt. My mum **7** _____ to talk to me every day, so I usually phone her in the evening. She **8** _____ stop talking!

3.1 *Yes/No* questions

yes/no questions with *be*

GR3.1a 》)

1 **A** *Are* you an outdoor person?
  B *No, I'm not*.
2 **A** *Is* she retired?
  B *Yes, she is*.

In present simple questions with *to be* we use *am/is/are* + subject.

Questions (?)	Short answers
Am I friendly to other people?	Yes, you **are**./No, you**'re not**.
Are you a tidy person?	Yes, I **am**./No, I**'m not**.
Is he rich?	Yes, he **is**./No, he **isn't**.
Are we free tomorrow?	Yes, we **are**./No, we **aren't**.
Are they musicians?	Yes, they **are**./No, they **aren't**.

In positive short answers, we don't use contractions.
Yes, he is. NOT ~~*Yes, he's*~~.

yes/no questions with other verbs

GR3.1b 》)

1 **A** *Do* you enjoy meeting new people?
  B *Yes, I do*.
2 **A** *Does* he work freelance?
  B *No, he doesn't*.

We form present simple *yes/no* questions with *Do/Does* + subject + infinitive without *to*.

Questions (?)	Short answers
Do you like your job?	Yes, I **do**./No, I **don't**.
Does she get up early?	Yes, she **does**./No, she **doesn't**.
Does it rain a lot?	Yes it **does**./No, it **doesn't**.
Do we usually go home early?	Yes, we **do**./No, we **don't**.
Do they work long hours?	Yes, they **do**./No, they **don't**.

In short answers, we use *do/don't* or *does/doesn't*. We don't use the main verb.
Do you like taking photos? Yes I do./No, I don't.
NOT ~~*Yes, I like./No, I don't like*~~.
Does she make a lot of money? Yes, she does.
NOT ~~*Yes, she makes./No, she doesn't make*~~.

1 Match questions 1–8 to answers a–h.
  1 Are you a photographer?
  2 Do you work full-time?
  3 Does your sister like being busy?
  4 Do your parents like working with computers?
  5 Is he a fast worker?
  6 Does it rain a lot in summer?
  7 Am I often late?
  8 Does your son enjoy helping people?

  a No, they don't.
  b Yes, he does.
  c Yes, you are.
  d Yes, it does.
  e Yes, she does.
  f Yes, I am.
  g Yes, he is.
  h No, I don't.

2 Complete the questions and short answers.
  1 _Do_ I know your friend?　　　　Yes, _you do_ .
  2 _____ you work freelance?　　　　No, _____.
  3 _____ your niece badly-paid?　　　Yes, _____.
  4 _____ Ahmad often late?　　　　　Yes, _____.
  5 _____ the film start at 6 p.m.?　　No, _____.
  6 _____ we have enough time?　　　No, _____.
  7 _____ your sisters like their presents?　Yes, _____.
  8 _____ our jobs make us happy?　　No, _____.
  9 _____ they nurses?　　　　　　　Yes, _____.
  10 _____ she like this city?　　　　　No, _____.

3 Complete the conversation. Use contractions where possible.
  Dana　¹ _Are_ you a nurse?
  Beth　Yes, I ² _____.
  Dana　³ _____ you like your job?
  Beth　Yes, I love it. I enjoy helping people.
  Dana　⁴ _____ you work full time?
  Beth　Yes, I ⁵ _____. I work long hours.
  Dana　⁶ _____ you well-paid?
  Beth　No, I ⁷ _____ not!
  Dana　⁸ _____ you like the people you work with?
  Beth　Yes, I work with my sister.
  Dana　⁹ _____ she a nurse?
  Beth　No, she ¹⁰ _____ a doctor.

3.2 *Wh-* questions

- We form present simple *wh-* questions in a similar way to *yes/no* questions, but we start with a question word.

Present simple *Wh-* questions with *be*

GR3.2a)))

1 **A** *Who's your teacher?*
 B *Ben Lewis.*
2 **A** *Why are you unhappy?*
 B *Because I hate my job.*
3 **A** *Where are they?*
 B *At home.*

Question word	*to be*	subject	
Where	**are**	you	from?
Why	**is**	she	sad?

Present simple *Wh-* questions with all other verbs

GR3.2b)))

1 **A** *What do you do in the evenings?*
 B *I relax with friends.*
2 **A** *What time does the lesson start?*
 B *At nine o'clock.*
3 **A** *How often do you go shopping?*
 B *I go shopping once a week.*

Question word	*do/does*	subject	infinitive without *to*
Where	**do**	you	live?
What	**does**	his cousin	do?

- We use different question words to ask about different types of information.

 What – to ask for information about things or activities.
 Who – to ask about a person.
 When/What time – to ask about time.
 Where – to ask about places.
 Why – to ask for a reason.
 How often – to ask about frequency.

1 Complete the questions.

1 **A** _Why_ do you want to learn English?
 B I want to be a pilot, so I need it for my job.
2 **A** _____ often _____ you use English for your job?
 B Every day!
3 **A** _____ does she work?
 B She works in Kuwait.
4 **A** What _____ do you have breakfast?
 B Usually at about seven o'clock.
5 **A** _____ is your teacher?
 B My teacher's called Ben.
6 **A** _____ are hairdressers usually happy?
 B Because they make their customers feel good.
7 **A** Who _____ you work for?
 B I work a for a big company.
8 **A** How often _____ he work from home?
 B Once a week.

2 Put the words in the right order to make questions.

1 outside / How often / his brother / work / does ?
 How often does his brother work outside?
2 do / the students / use / the internet / When ?
3 does / Who / work for / your friend ?
4 are / Why / the children / bored ?
5 does / their team / play / Where ?
6 do / you / What / wear / to work / usually ?
7 for class / How often / you / late / are ?

3 Complete the gaps. Use a question word and *do* or *does*.

1 **A** _What does_ your father do?
 B He's a teacher.
2 **A** _____ you not like your job?
 B Because it's badly paid.
3 **A** _____ your nephew live with?
 B My brother.
4 **A** _____ our classes finish?
 B At 5.30.
5 **A** _____ you go on holiday?
 B Once a year.
6 **A** _____ her children do in the evenings?
 B They play computer games.
7 **A** _____ your parents come from?'
 B Korea.
8 **A** _____ they sing in the band with?
 B Two girls.
9 **A** _____ she want a new phone?
 B Her old one doesn't work.
10 **A** _____ he want to go shopping?
 B Tomorrow afternoon.

4.1 *There is/There are*

We use *there is* with singular nouns and *there are* with plural nouns.

GR4.1)))

Positive (+)	Negative (–)
There's an airport.	**There isn't** a hotel.
There are some restaurants.	**There aren't** any museums.
There are lots of trees.	**There aren't** a lot of trees.

Questions (?)	Short answers
Is there a train station?	Yes, **there is.**/No, **there isn't**.
Are there any shops?	Yes, **there are.**/No, **there aren't**.

We often use positive and negative contractions:
there is → there's but NOT ~~there're~~
there is not → there isn't
there are not → there aren't.

- We use *there is/there are* to say that something or someone exists somewhere.

  There's a chemist on Woodstock Road.
  There are twenty-four rooms in the hotel.

- We use *there is/there are* the first time we talk about something and *it is/they are* the next time.

  There's a nice hotel in the town. **It's** very comfortable.
  There are lots of shops here, but **they are** all closed today.

- We often use *there is/there are* to describe places.

  In my town **there are** a lot of restaurants.

- In a list of things we use *there is* if the first word is singular and *there are* if the first word is plural.

  In my city **there are** lots of restaurants, a campsite and an old church.
  In the hotel **there is** a swimming pool, a hairdresser's and ninety-five bedrooms.

- In positive sentences we usually use *some* or a number before plural nouns.

  There are **some** glasses on the table.
  There are **twenty** students in the room.

We usually use *any* before plural nouns in negative sentences and questions.
There aren't **any** chairs. (= There are no chairs.)
Are there **any** tables?
We also use *many* before plural nouns in negative sentences when we want to say there are fewer than we would like or expect.
There aren't **many** tables. (= There are some tables, but not enough or not as many as I expected.)

---

1 Complete the sentences with the positive, negative or question form of *there is/there are*.

1 ___Is there___ a hospital in your town?
2 _____ lots of hotels and a theatre.
3 _____ a library near his house?
4 _____ any trees in your garden?
5 _____ a kitchen and two bathrooms in my flat.
6 _____ any trains in my country.
7 _____ a chemist in the hospital.
8 _____ any cheap hotels in the city centre?
9 _____ a museum or a theatre here, so I think it's boring.
10 _____ a factory in my town. My father works there.

2 Use the symbols (✓) or (✗) to write positive or negative short answers.

1 Is there a toilet in the cinema? ✓ ___Yes, there is.___
2 Are there any shops open now? ✗ ___No,_____
3 Are there any nice beaches on the island? ✓ _____
4 Is there a theatre in your town? ✗ _____
5 Are there lots of restaurants near here? ✓ _____
6 Is there a museum in the city centre? ✓ _____
7 Are there any hotels? ✗ _____
8 Are there lots of people here in the summer? ✓ _____

3 Complete the text about Beijing's underground city, Dixia Cheng. Use *there is, there isn't, there are* or *there aren't*.

Underneath the city of Beijing in China ¹ ___there is___ a small city. It's about 50 years old. ² _____ any people living there now, but sometimes tourists can visit. ³ _____ lots of restaurants, schools, theatres, factories and many public places, but they are all empty. ⁴ _____ a big picture of Mao Zedong in nearly every large space. ⁵ _____ bedrooms for about 300,000 people, but they aren't comfortable. In one bedroom ⁶ _____ a desk and six beds. In another room ⁷ _____ a lot of baths. ⁸ _____ any windows. ⁹ _____ any trees or flowers. It's never very cold and never hot because it's underground. It's not popular with tourists because it's dark and dangerous. Not many people in Beijing know that ¹⁰ _____ a city under their feet.

4.2 Articles *a/an, the, –*

a/an and no article

GR4.2a)))
1 *There's **an** orange on the table.*
2 *I'm not **a** student.*
3 *She's **an** English teacher.*
4 *There's **a** nice restaurant in my street.*
5 *I have two children.*
6 *He doesn't work on Saturdays.*

- The first time we talk about one person/thing, we use *a* or *an*.
  *Jan lives in **an** old house in **a** village near Hull.*

  We use *a* before consonant sounds, e.g. *a shelf, a university*.
  We use *an* before vowel sounds, e.g. *an airport, an hour*.

- The first time we talk about people or things using a plural noun, we don't use an article.
  Jo knows people all over Europe.
  I like penguins.

- We also use *a/an* (singular) and no article (plural) to talk about jobs, or to talk about what things are.
  *She's **an** engineer.   Is that **a** new tablet?*
  Alex and Jan are journalists.   Those are beautiful earrings!

- We use *a* in some phrases, e.g. ***a** lot of, once **a** week*.
- We use no article…
  1 for names, cities, streets and most countries
    My name's David.   I'm from Bath.   I think this is Bond Street.
    We live in Venezuela. (but **the** *USA*, **the** *UK*)
  2 with days, times and meals
    I'm free on Friday at nine o'clock. I have lunch at one o'clock.

the

GR4.2b)))
1 *My friend's house is in **the** city centre.*
2 *Lima is **the** capital of Peru.*
3 *Sheena is from **the** USA.*
4 *We have dinner at seven o'clock in **the** evening.*

- We use *the* to say 'you know which one(s) I mean'. This can be …
  1 because we have already talked about it/them
    *Jan lives in an old house in a village near Hull. **The** house was built in 1485. **The** village is near a lake.*
  2 because we make it clear in the sentence, e.g. **the** *shops on my street*, **the** *woman who answered the phone*
  3 when there is only one, e.g. **the** *moon*, **the** *Burj Khalifa*, **the** *city centre*, **the** *capital of Australia*, **the** *Nile*

- We also use *the* for parts of the day: *in **the** morning, in **the** afternoon* (but *at night*).

1 Complete the sentences with *a, an, the* or – (no article).
  1 What's that? It's ___an___ umbrella.
  2 What's his job? He's _____ journalist.
  3 There isn't _____ office here.
  4 We live in _____ UK.
  5 They're in _____ city centre.
  6 Are you free in _____ evenings?
  7 I like _____ Brazil because I love _____ sun!
  8 I've got _____ three bedrooms.
  9 You're _____ fantastic student.
  10 There are _____ lot of shops.

2 Make sentences or questions. Add articles where necessary.
  1 There isn't / museum in / my town
    There isn't a museum in my town.
  2 There are / twenty noisy children in / garden
    _____.
  3 Is there / tourist information centre / here ?
    _____.
  4 Meet me in / city centre /at / eight o'clock
    _____.
  5 There are / lot of / shops open in / evening
    _____.
  6 There's / swimming pool in / my friend's house
    _____.
  7 Is there / toilet at / railway station ?
    _____.
  8 There isn't / bathroom in / my hotel room
    _____.

3 Complete the text with the correct articles. Sometimes no article is necessary.

My best friend lives in St Petersburg, Russia. She lives in
¹ _a_ beautiful house in ² _____ centre of the city near
³ _____ Neva River. There are ⁴ _____ six bedrooms, three
bathrooms and ⁵ _____ swimming pool. Her house is near
⁶ _____ shopping centre. I usually visit her once ⁷ _____
year in summer. There are lots of fantastic restaurants in
St Petersburg and we eat in ⁸ _____ different place every day.
We always visit ⁹ _____ theatre next to her house because
we both love watching ¹⁰ _____ plays. We never feel bored.

5.1 *Can, can't, could, couldn't*

can and *can't*

> **GR5.1a**))
>
> 1 *I **can** swim, but I **can't** ride a bicycle.*
> 2 *You **can** visit the museum, but you **can't** visit the mine.*

We use *can* and *can't* to talk about ability and possibility in the present.

Positive (+)
*He **can** play tennis very well.* (he knows how to do this.)
*People **can** buy clothes on the internet.* (it's possible to do this.)

Negative (–)
*We **can't** speak Russian.* (we don't know how to do this.)
*You **can't** drive in the city centre.* (it's not possible to do this.)

Questions
A *Can your children ride bicycles?*
B *Yes, they **can**. They cycle to school every day.*

A *Can I take a train to Muscat?*
B *No, you **can't**. There aren't any trains in Oman.*

could and *couldn't*

> **GR5.1b**))
>
> 1 *He **could** write when he was five, but he **couldn't** read.*
> 2 A ***Could** people travel by underground in the 1840s?*
>   B *No, they **couldn't**.*

We use *could* and *couldn't* to talk about ability and possibility in the past.

Positive (+)
*I **could** read when I was four years old.* (I knew how to do this)
*People **could** buy things from machines in 1890.* (it was possible to do this)

Negative (–)
*When I was four years old, I **couldn't** swim.* (I didn't know how to do this)
*In the 1880s, people **couldn't** fly to different countries.* (it was not possible to do this)

Questions
A *Could you write when you were eight years old?*
B *Yes, I **could**. I could also play the violin.*

A *Could you buy food online in 1993?*
B *No, you **couldn't**. But you could in 1997.*

> • After *can/could* we use the infinitive without *to*.
>   *You **can't buy** hot drinks online.*
>   NOT ~~You can't to buy hot drinks online.~~
> • We don't add *-s* in the third person singular.
>   *She **can play** the piano.*
>   NOT ~~She cans plays~~
> • We don't use *do/does* to make the question forms.
>   *Can you park in the city centre?*
>   NOT ~~Do you can park in the city centre?~~

1 Complete the questions about ability and possibility and write the short answers.

1 A <u>*Can*</u> you swim in very cold water?
   B No, <u>*I can't.*</u>
2 A _____ I drink the water in your country?
   B Yes, _____ .
3 A _____ you carry this heavy bag?
   B No, _____ .
4 A _____ you hear the traffic outside yesterday?
   B No, _____ .
5 A _____ you cook when you were at university?
   B Yes, _____ .
6 A _____ she draw well?
   B Yes, _____ .
7 A _____ they answer this difficult question?
   B No, _____ .
8 A _____ people fly to Antarctica in the 1920s?
   B No, _____ .

2 Complete the sentences with the correct form of *can/could* and the words in the box.

download   not buy   not live   not play   ~~send~~   swim   use

1 <u>*Could*</u> you <u>*send*</u> an email in 1990?
2 In the 1980s, people _____ clothes online.
3 These days, you _____ music onto your computer.
4 _____ you _____ in the sea here? Is it safe?
5 _____ you _____ euros in France in 1990?
6 We _____ on Mars at the moment.
7 In the 1980s, children _____ online games.

3 Complete the conversation with the words in the box.

can   can't   could x4   ~~couldn't~~   pay   talk   travel

Agata Tell me about your life in the 1970s. Was it very different?

Barb In some ways, yes. There was no internet, so you [1] <u>*couldn't*</u> get information easily, but there were good libraries and I [2] _____ borrow lots of books.

Agata [3] _____ you talk to your friends in other countries easily?

Barb I could [4] _____ to them on the phone, but it was very expensive, so we usually wrote letters.

Agata Could you [5] _____ to other countries on holiday?

Barb Yes, we [6] _____, but travelling was also very expensive, so our family didn't often go on holiday.

Agata Well, it's not always cheap today, but sometimes you [7] _____ find a cheap flight. What else was different?

Barb I [8] _____ play outside all day with my friends. You [9] _____ do that today because of the dangers.

Agata Could you [10] _____ for things by credit card?

Barb Yes, but not in all shops. I usually paid in cash.

5.2 Present continuous

GR5.2))
1 They're wearing hoodies.
2 She isn't waiting for Peter.
3 A Are you going to the wedding? B Yes, I am.
4 A What is he doing? B He's talking on the phone.

We form the present continuous with subject + to be + verb + -ing.

Positive (+)	Negative (–)	
I'm	I'm not	
You're	You aren't	
He/She/It's	He/She/It isn't	working today.
We/They're	We/They aren't	

yes/no questions (?)		Short answers	
Am I		Yes, I am.	No, I'm not.
Are you		Yes, you are.	No, you aren't.
Is he/she/it	reading?	Yes, he/she it is.	No, he/she/it isn't.
Are we/they		Yes, we/they are.	No, we/they aren't.

Wh- questions

To make a Wh- question we add a Wh- word before am/is/are.

Where **are** you go**ing**? Who **are** they talk**ing** to?

Spelling rules
- Most verbs add -ing, e.g. wear → wearing.
- For verbs ending in -e, we drop the -e and add -ing, e.g. live → living.
- For verbs ending with one vowel + one consonant, we double the final consonant and add -ing. We don't double -x or -y.
  get → getting   begin → beginning   pay → paying

Present continuous or present simple?

Present continuous	Present simple
I'm wearing a jacket today.	I often wear a jacket.
You aren't wearing shoes.	You never wear shoes at home.
He's working from home this week.	He doesn't usually work from home.

- We use the present continuous to talk about something happening at this moment or around now (today, this week).
- We use the present simple to talk about habits or routines, and things that happen all the time.

What do you do? or **What are you doing?**
A What do you do?	A What are you doing?
(= What's your job?)	(= now?)
B I'm a dentist.	B I'm having lunch.

1 Complete the questions in the present simple or continuous and use the symbols (✓) or (✗) to write positive or negative short answers.

1 _Are_ you wearing socks?   ✓ _Yes, I am._
2 _____ I sitting in your seat?   ✗ _____
3 _____ they waiting?   ✗ _____
4 _____ he usually drive carefully?   ✓ _____
5 _____ you read the news every day? ✗ _____
6 _____ she enjoying this lesson?   ✓ _____
7 _____ we staying at this hotel?   ✓ _____
8 _____ it raining?   ✗ _____
9 _____ penguins live in Antarctica? ✓ _____
10 _____ he always speak quickly?   ✓ _____

2 Circle the correct option.

1 Elvira's wearing / wears a black skirt and designer shoes today.
2 The children are walking / walk to school every morning.
3 I'm working / work in Mumbai this month.
4 They aren't taking / don't take any photos today.
5 We're never playing / never play computer games.
6 'Why are you running / do you run?' 'I'm late!'
7 'How often are you watching / do you watch TV?' 'Every evening.'
8 'Is he having / Does he have a shower?' 'No, he's in bed.'
9 'Who's dancing / dances in the garden?' 'That's Ella. She's a very good dancer.'
10 'What's your brother doing / does your brother do?' 'He's an engineer.'
11 Come now! The film 's starting / starts.
12 Please talk quietly. The babies are sleeping / sleep.

3 Complete the conversation using the present simple or continuous of the verbs in (brackets).

A Hi Mandy! How are you? What [1] _are you doing_ (you do) here?
B Hi Jakob! I'm fine. Good to see you. I [2] _____ (visit) my sister. She [3] _____ (live) here. I [4] _____ (stay) with her for three days.
A Oh nice! What [5] _____ (your sister do)?
B She's a dentist. She [6] _____ (work) in the city centre. What about you? What [7] _____ (you do) these days?
A I [8] _____ (learn) to fly. I want to be pilot.
B Wow. That's great! Where [9] _____ (you learn)?
A In Aptex Training Centre, near the airport. Hey, do you have time for a coffee?
B No, sorry, I [10] _____ (wait) for my sister. She's in the bank. Look, that's her there. She [11] _____ (wear) a red dress and [12] _____ (talk) to the cashier.
A OK, another time. Call me!

6.1 Past simple of to be: was and were

Was and wasn't (was not) are the past forms of is and isn't.
Were and weren't (were not) are the past forms of are and aren't.

Positive (+)		Negative (–)		
I He She It	**was**	I He She It	**wasn't**	at home.
We You They	**were**	We You They	**weren't**	

Yes/No questions and short answers

Yes/No questions (?)			Short answers				
Was	I he she it	at home?	Yes, I Yes, he Yes, she Yes, it	**was.**	No, I No, he No, she No, it	**wasn't.**
Were	we you they		Yes, we Yes, you Yes, they	**were.**	No, we No, you No. they	**weren't.**

• We often use was/were with past time expressions, e.g. last week, in 2003, 500 years ago, yesterday.

  I **was** at work two hours ago.
  It **wasn't** very hot yesterday.

We use was/were with born.
I was born in 1990.

Wh- questions

To make a Wh- question we use a Wh- question word before was/were.

The word order is the same as for yes/no questions.

What was your last job?
Why was she in Spain last week?
When were they born?

1 Complete the sentences and short answers with the past simple form of the verb to be.

1 We are in Venice now.
   We _were_ in Rome last month.
2 They are in the office today.
   _____ they in the office last night? No, they _____ .
3 I'm on the bus now.
   I _____ on the train two hours ago.
4 She's in class now.
   _____ she in class at 9 a.m. this morning?
   Yes, she _____ .
5 We are at the post office now.
   We _____ at the police station at 3.30 p.m. yesterday.
6 It is cold today.
   _____ it cold yesterday? No, it _____ .
7 They are at the cinema now.
   _____ they at the cinema last Friday? Yes, they _____ .
8 My glasses are in my bag.
   My glasses _____ on my head five minutes ago.

2 Complete the past simple questions 1–10 using the words in (brackets).

1 _Where were_ you and your wife last week? (Where)
2 _____ your first boss? (Who)
3 _____ your father born? (When)
4 _____ your favourite toy when you were five? (What)
5 _____ you quiet in the meeting yesterday? (Why)
6 _____ good last night? (the film)
7 _____ on holiday last week? (they)
8 _____ our colleagues two hours ago? (Where)
9 _____ your desk messy yesterday? (Why)
10 _____ the hotel cheap? (Why)

3 Match answers a–j to questions 1–10 in exercise **2**.

a No, it wasn't.
b Mr Chen.
c It wasn't close to the beach.
d I was tired.
e In 1966.
f In Paris.
g Yes, they were.
h I was very busy.
i In a meeting.
j My toy car.

4 Complete the text. Use was/were or wasn't/weren't.

This year I'm unemployed and unhappy. Last year was different. Last year the sky ^{1} _was_ blue all summer and I ^{2}_____ happy. I ^{3}_____ an engineer. My house ^{4}_____ full of flowers and music. My children ^{5}_____ at an expensive school. There ^{6}_____ lots of interesting books on my desk. In my living room there ^{7}_____ two computers and a big TV. I ^{8}_____ very rich. My life ^{9}_____ easy and we ^{10}_____ worried about the future.

6.2 Past simple regular verbs

GR6.2))
1 He **played** football when he was at school.
2 She **lived** in Vietnam ten years ago.
3 I sometimes **studied** all night at university.
4 They **stopped** for coffee at a small restaurant.
5 We **listened** to the radio last night.

- We add -ed to the infinitive to form the past simple of most regular verbs.

post → posted
play → played

- The past simple is the same for all persons.

Positive (+)

I You He/She/It We They	**worked**	yesterday.

Spelling rules
- For verbs that end in -e, we add -d.
  move → moved
  live → lived
- For verbs that end in consonant + -y, we delete -y and add -ied.
  marry → married
  study → studied
- For verbs that end in one vowel + one consonant, we double the consonant and add -ed.
  stop → stopped
- For two-syllable verbs, we only double the consonant when the last syllable is stressed.
  prefer → preferred (but answer → answered)

- We use the past simple to talk about finished actions/states in the past.
  She **finished** work at 7 p.m.
- When we use the past simple, we often say when the action happened, e.g. last winter, in 1999, ten minutes ago, for three days.
  I **returned** your book yesterday afternoon.
  They **moved** to Egypt in 2005.

1 Rewrite sentences 1–8 using past simple verbs and the words in (brackets).

1 Present The hotel room includes breakfast. (yesterday)
  Past *The hotel room included breakfast yesterday.*
2 Present I post our letters every Monday. (last Monday)
  Past _____
3 Present We're waiting for my sister. (for 20 minutes)
  Past _____
4 Present I want a new laptop. (last week)
  Past _____
5 Present They visit my uncle once a year. (in May 2013)
  Past _____
6 Present People use money to buy things. (500 years ago)
  Past _____
7 Present He's shouting at his brother. (for an hour)
  Past _____
8 Present I like dancing. (in the 1980s)
  Past _____

2 Complete the sentences with the past simple form of the verbs in the box.

call carry change ~~chat~~ enjoy listen start stop

1 My friend and I *chatted* for three hours on the phone last Friday.
2 We _____ the film yesterday.
3 She _____ to the radio every morning for 20 years.
4 He _____ my heavy bag to the station for me.
5 They _____ their clothes after work last night.
6 The lesson _____ 20 minutes ago.
7 My boss _____ a taxi for me yesterday morning.
8 The car _____ outside my house for a short time.

3 Complete the text with the past simple of the verbs in (brackets).

Last year, I **1** *worked* (work) in a restaurant for about three months. Some strange things **2**_____ (happen). One night, the restaurant was very busy and I **3**_____ (notice) a woman outside in a very big yellow coat and red gloves. She **4**_____ (wait) outside for about 20 minutes and then she **5**_____ (walk) in and **6**_____ (ask) for a table near the window. There weren't any tables free near the window and she was very angry. I **7**_____ (show) her a different table, but she **8**_____ (stay) next to the door and then **9**_____ (shout) at me for about five minutes. She really **10**_____ (want) a table near the window! Everyone in the restaurant **11**_____ (look) at us. Then suddenly, she **12**_____ (open) her bag, **13**_____ (change) her gloves, **14**_____ (close) her bag and **15**_____ (walk) out!

7.1 Past simple irregular verbs

GR7.1))

1 I **came** home at seven thirty last night.
2 You **did** the housework very quickly yesterday.
3 She **made** dinner for ten people last Saturday.
4 He **ate** a lot at lunchtime.
5 We **drove** to Germany in 2012.

• Irregular past simple verbs are not formed by adding -ed to the infinitive. They all take different forms.

There are no general rules for the formation of irregular verbs.

Regular
walk → walk**ed**   plan → plann**ed**   move → mov**ed**

Irregular
go → **went**   eat → **ate**   write → **wrote**

• The past simple is the same for all persons for both regular and irregular verbs.

Positive (+)		
I You He/She/It We They	**went**	to the park yesterday.

We use the past simple to talk about finished actions in the past states.

He **left** the house an hour ago.
I **had** Salsa lessons last year.

---

1 Match the past simple forms to infinitives 1–18.

ate	chose	did	drank	felt	gave	kept	left	lent
lost	ran	rode	~~slept~~	swam	told	was	went	wrote

1 sleep _slept_
2 drink _____
3 go _____
4 ride _____
5 eat _____
6 give _____

7 choose _____
8 run _____
9 leave _____
10 tell _____
11 do _____
12 swim _____

13 lend _____
14 keep _____
15 lose _____
16 is _____
17 feel _____
18 write _____

2 Complete the gaps using the past simple form of the verbs in the box.

~~come~~	drink	give	have	leave	ride	think	write

1 I _came_ home late last night.
2 He _____ the homework was very difficult.
3 Cynthia _____ a lot of letters to her grandmother.
4 You _____ your passport on the bus.
5 We _____ eight glasses of water yesterday.
6 His parents _____ a lovely weekend.
7 I _____ my bicycle every day when I was at school.
8 Our uncle _____ us lots of fruit for breakfast.

3 Circle the correct option.
1 He run / *ran* / runs to work every day last week.
2 We *went* / *go* / *goes* fishing last weekend.
3 I *chose* / *choose* / *chooses* a good book from the library last Monday.
4 They *swam* / *swims* / *swim* in the sea when they went to Greece.
5 You *win* / *wins* / *won* the race yesterday.
6 She *did* / *do* / *does* a lot of exercise last week.
7 We *have* / *has* / *had* a lot of fun in France last year.
8 He *met* / *meet* / *meets* his friends at the cinema the day before yesterday.

4 Complete the text with verbs in the past simple.

When I lived in Sydney, I didn't have a healthy lifestyle – but then I decided to change my life.

I ¹g_____ up every day at about six o'clock and ²d_____ three cups of coffee. I ³d_____ to the office and ⁴t_____ the lift up to the third floor. At work I ⁵a_____ a lot of snacks and ⁶s_____ in my chair all day. In the evenings I ⁷w_____ to fast food restaurants and then ⁸w_____ TV at home. I ⁹w_____ very unhealthy. So I ¹⁰s_____ to do some exercise. I ¹¹s_____ in our swimming pool every morning before work. I ¹²r_____ to work through the park. I ¹³w_____ to the gym after work. I ¹⁴l_____ weight and learnt that being healthy makes you feel good.

7.2 Past simple negative

> GR7.2)))
> 1 I **didn't drive** to Bristol at the weekend.
> 2 The lesson **didn't finish** at three o'clock.
> 3 We **didn't write** lots of emails yesterday.

- To make the past simple negative we use *didn't* + infinitive without *to*.

Positive (+)	Negative (–)
I **felt** sad when I left home.	I **didn't feel** sad when I left home.
She **walked** at the age of nine months.	She **didn't walk** at the age of nine months.
The match **started** at 7 p.m.	The match **didn't start** at 7 p.m.
We **went** to work yesterday.	We **didn't go** to work yesterday.
They **had** a happy life.	They **didn't have** a happy life.

- We usually use the contracted form (*didn't*), but we sometimes use the full form (*did not*) in formal writing.

> The negative is formed in the same way for both regular and irregular verbs.
> **I didn't play** tennis yesterday.
> **I didn't eat** yesterday. NOT ~~I didn't ate yesterday.~~

1 Write the negatives.

1	thought	*didn't think*	6	looked	_____
2	look	_____	7	brought	_____
3	made	_____	8	paid	_____
4	put	_____	9	waited	_____
5	said	_____	10	sat	_____

2 Correct the information using the word in (brackets).

1 I went shopping two days ago. (swimming)
   No, I didn't go shopping two days ago, I went swimming.

2 She did yoga last Friday. (judo)
   _____

3 He lost his mobile phone yesterday morning. (wallet)
   _____

4 They thought the lesson was easy. (the homework)
   _____

5 We slept at our aunt's house last night. (niece's house)
   _____

6 I borrowed some money from him last week. (last month)
   _____

7 She lent him a book yesterday. (a pen)
   _____

8 I took the bus to work last week. (the train)
   _____

9 My mother made a cake for my birthday last year. (two years ago)
   _____

10 He bought lots of vegetables at the market. (fruit)
   _____

3 Complete the story about Mo Farah's early life with the past simple form of the verbs in (brackets).

> Mo Farah is an Olympic champion runner. In the London 2012 Olympics, Farah ¹ _won_ (win) gold at 5,000 m. He ² _____ (not win) only this race. He also won the 10,000 m.
>
> Farah was born in Mogadishu, in Somalia, on 23th March 1983, but he ³ _____ (not stay) there very long. He ⁴ _____ (move) north to Djibouti with his twin brother and ⁵ _____ (live) with his grandparents. His father ⁶ _____ (not work) in Djibouti – he worked at Heathrow Airport in England. He ⁷ _____ (not earn) much money, but he sometimes ⁸ _____ (visit) the children and ⁹ _____ (bring) them presents.
>
> Farah ¹⁰ _____ (come) to England in 1992 when he was eight years old, but he ¹¹ _____ (not live) with his father. He lived with his aunt in West London. His twin brother ¹² _____ (not come) with him. Farah¹³ _____ (not have) an easy life when he was young.
>
> Farah ¹⁴ _____ (go) to Feltham Community College in London. School was difficult for Farah because he ¹⁵ _____ (not speak) English, but his teachers ¹⁶ _____ (say) he liked sports very much.

8.1 Past simple questions and short answers

Yes/No questions

1 A **Did** you meet any local people?
  B Yes, we **did**.

2 A **Did** she enjoy her last holiday?
  B No, she **didn't**.

- We form past simple yes/no questions with Did + subject + infinitive without to.
- When we answer yes/no questions, we usually use short answers with the auxiliary did or didn't. We don't use the full verb.

  A **Did** you swim in the sea?
  B Yes, I **did**. NOT Yes, I swam.

  A **Did** he visit the whole island?
  B No, he **didn't**. NOT No, he didn't visit.

We can also answer a yes/no question with just yes or no.
Did you go on a tour? Yes.
Did you see the temple? No.

Wh- questions

1 A Why **did** they take the train?
  B Because it was cheaper.

2 A How far **did** we walk?
  B Six kilometres.

We form Wh- questions with a question word and did + subject + infinitive without to.

A What **did** you do there?
B I went sightseeing.

A When **did** she get back?
B At about three o'clock.

A How many museums **did** we visit?
B Nine.

A What time **did** he leave?
B At about ten thirty.

1 Match question words 1–8 to explanations a–h.

1	Who	_g_	a to ask about frequency
2	Where	___	b to ask for a reason
3	When	___	c to ask about a place
4	Why	___	d to ask about quantity
5	How	___	e to ask about manner
6	How many	___	f to ask about a time
7	How often	___	g to ask about a person
8	How far	___	h to ask about distance

2 Make past simple questions using the question words in the box.

How far   How many   How often   ~~What~~   When   ~~Where~~
Who   Why

1 Marco ate his dinner.   _What did Marco eat?_
2 John went to the beach.   _Where did John go?_
3 She met a back packer.   _____
4 He left the apartment.   _____
5 We started at six thirty.   _____
6 He went to six art galleries. _____
7 She trekked a long way.   _____
8 We travelled by public   _____
   transport every day.

3 Put the words in the right order to make questions and short answers.

1 get up / she / Did / early ?   Yes, / did / she
   Did she get up early?   _Yes, she did._
2 map / your / you / lose / Did ?   I / didn't / No,

   _____
3 they / Did / on / go / holiday ?   didn't / No, / they

   _____
4 have / he / Did / fun ?   did / he / Yes,

   _____
5 like / the / Did / food / you ?   didn't / No, / I

   _____

4 Complete the conversation.

Kamran Hi Johan, ¹ _did_ you go out last night?
Johan   Yes, I ² _____ . I went to the cinema.
Kamran What did you ³ _____ ?
Johan   'One Bad Night'.
Kamran I don't know that film. ⁴ _____ you like it?
Johan   Not really. It was very long. How about you?
            ⁵ _____ did you do last night?
Kamran I went to the gym.
Johan   ⁶ _____ did you go there?
Kamran To lose weight and keep fit.
Johan   Did you ⁷ _____ a good time?
Kamran No, I ⁸ _____ !

8.2 Should, shouldn't, have to, don't have to

should and shouldn't

> **GR8.2a** 》)
>
> 1 You **should** wear warm clothes when it's cold.
> 2 He **should** buy his mother a birthday present.
> 3 I have lots of work to do. I **shouldn't** go out tonight.
> 4 She **shouldn't** buy that jacket, it's very expensive.

- We use *should* to talk about things we think are a good idea (the right thing to do) and to give advice. We use *shouldn't* to talk about things that are a bad idea (the wrong thing to do).

- After *should/shouldn't* we use the infinitive without *to*.
  You **should** sleep eight hours a night.
  NOT ~~You should to sleep eight hours a night.~~

- We don't add -s in the third person singular.
  He **should** see a doctor. NOT ~~He shoulds see a doctor.~~

- We don't use *do/does* to make the question forms.
  Should I eat more fruit? NOT ~~Do I should eat more fruit?~~

have to and don't have to

> **GR8.2b** 》)
>
> 1 I **have to** give a presentation next week.
> 2 She **has to** start work at seven.
> 3 The school gives you a coursebook so you **don't have to** buy one.
> 4 You **don't have to** go with me, I can go by myself.

- We use *have to* to talk about rules. (It is necessary.)
- *Don't have to* means that there is a choice. (It isn't necessary.)
- After *have to/don't have to* we use the infinitive form of the verb.
  I **don't have to** work on Saturdays.
- The third person he/she/it form of *have to* is *has to*.
  She **has to** wear a uniform at work.
- The negative form of *has to* is *doesn't have to*.
  He **doesn't have to** work long hours.
- We use *do/does* to make the question forms.
  Where **does** he **have to** go?

> We don't use contractions with *have to*.
> I **have to** call my boss. NOT ~~I've to call my boss.~~
> She **has to** go now. NOT ~~She's to go now.~~

have to or should?

- *Have to* is stronger than *should*.
  We **have to** leave now or we will miss the flight.
  We **should** leave now because we have to get up early tomorrow.

- *Shouldn't* and *don't have to* have very different meanings.
  You **shouldn't** smoke. It's bad for your health. (It's a bad idea.)
  You **don't have to** bring any food to the party. (You can if you want, but it's not necessary.)

1 Circle the correct option.

1 The museum isn't free. We *don't have to / have to* pay to get in.
2 Teachers *don't have to / have to* wear a uniform. They can wear their own clothes.
3 She *doesn't have to / has to* take a bus to the station. It's too far to walk.
4 In England you *don't have to / have to* drive on the left side of the road.
5 She's not hungry. You *don't have to / doesn't have to* make dinner for her.
6 His hair is a mess! He *should / shouldn't* go to the hairdresser's.
7 You *should / shouldn't* believe everything you read on the internet.

2 Rewrite the sentences using *should, shouldn't, have to* or *don't have to*.

1 It's a good idea to drink bottled water in Vietnam.
   You should drink bottled water in Vietnam.
2 It is necessary to show your passport to immigration.
   We _____
3 I think it's wrong for children to eat lots of sweets.
   I think children _____
4 It's not necessary to buy a ticket.
   He _____
5 Her teacher says it's a good idea to read every day.
   Her teacher says she _____
6 It's warm today. It's not necessary to wear a coat.
   She _____
7 It's not a good idea to drive fast in the rain.
   Drivers _____
8 At my school we all study mathematics.
   I _____

3 Complete the conversation using *should, shouldn't, have to* or *don't / doesn't have to*.

Mona   Does your sister like her new job?
Steve No, she ¹ *has to* work twelve hours a day, so she gets really tired and I ² _____ wake her up every morning!
Mona   Does she ³ _____ work at weekends?
Steve No, just Monday to Thursday. So she ⁴ _____ work on Fridays or at the weekend.
Mona   That's not too bad. Is the food in the staff restaurant nice?
Steve It's OK, but they ⁵ _____ pay a lot for it. She doesn't like her boss. He shouts at her.
Mona   He ⁶ _____ do that! I think she ⁷ _____ look for another job.

9.1 Countable and uncountable nouns

There are two types of nouns in English: countable and uncountable nouns.

- Countable nouns are things you can count, so they can be singular or plural. We use *a* or *an* with them.

  a lemon → *two lemons*   *an olive* → *lots of olives*

- Uncountable nouns are things you usually can't count. We don't use *a* or *an* with them and they are never plural.

  rice NOT *a rice*   *lots of bread* NOT *lots of breads*

Some nouns can be countable or uncountable, but the meaning is different.
We don't have time. (Time we measure using a clock.)
We went there four times last week. (We can count each visit.)

some/any

GR9.1))

		Countable	Uncountable
(+)	I'd like	**a** pear. **some** pears.	**some** jam.
(–)	I don't want	**an** olive. **any** olives.	**any** bread.
(?)	Do you have	**a** lemon? **any** lemons?	**any** honey?

- We use *a/an* with singular countable nouns, e.g. *a lemon*.
- We use *some* with plural countable nouns or uncountable nouns in positive sentences, e.g. *some pears, some jam*.
- We use *any* with plural countable nouns or uncountable nouns in negative sentences and questions, e.g. *any olives, any bread*.
- We also use *some* in questions to ask for things or to offer something.

	Countable	Uncountable
Would you like Can I have	**some** noodles? **some** eggs?	**some** coffee? **some** cake?

Drinks are usually uncountable. We say *I'd like some tea*.
But we often say *a tea* as a quick way of saying *a cup of tea*.
Also, *two coffees* (= two cups of coffee), *three orange juices*
(= three glasses of orange juice), etc.

1   Cross out the word that is NOT possible.

1   I'd like *some chicken / a pear / ~~any meat~~*.
2   I don't have *a banana / a lemon / a milk*.
3   Is there any *coffee / olives / honey*?
4   Are there any *pasta / pears / eggs*?
5   Can I have some *knives / spoon / forks*?
6   Would you like some *salad / breads / mushrooms*?
7   She doesn't have a *money / glass / plate*.
8   There isn't any *coffee / vegetable / fruit*.
9   There are four bottles of *oranges / water / milk*.
10 He's got a *pear / biscuit / apples* in his pocket.

2   Complete the sentences using *some, any, a* or *an*.

1   I'd like _some_ honey, please.
2   Can I have _____ eggs, please?
3   Is there _____ milk?
4   We don't have _____ meat.
5   There aren't _____ mushrooms.
6   Are there _____ vegetables?
7   Does he have _____ drink?
8   She doesn't have _____ money.
9   Would you like _____ noodles?
10 There isn't _____ restaurant near here.

3   Complete the sentences with *two, a* or *an*.

1   I'd like _two_ teas and _____ coffee, please.
2   **A** Would you like _____ coke?
    B No, thanks, but I'd love _____ apple juice.
3   Can I have _____ coffees please, with milk?
4   _____ black teas, please, and _____ glass of water.
5   I usually have _____ coffee before breakfast.

4   Complete the message that Alia left for her flatmate.
    Use *some, any, a* or *an*.

Can you buy **1** _some_ food for dinner tonight? There's **2** _____ beef in the fridge, but we don't have **3** _____ vegetables. Can you get **4** _____ sweetcorn and tomatoes? I'd also like **5** _____ salad. Do we have **6** _____ potatoes? Can you check, please? Can you also buy **7** _____ nice big salad bowl? We only have a small one. I left **8** _____ money next to the kettle.

Thanks!

Alia

9.2 Quantifiers – *much/many/a lot of*

GR9.2a))
1 *I have **a lot of** books on my shelf.*
2 *She eats **quite a lot of** rice.*
3 *They drink **lots of** water.*
4 *I don't have **much** coffee.*
5 *We don't have **many** tomatoes.*

- In positive sentences we usually use *a lot of/lots of* for both countable and uncountable nouns to talk about a big quantity.
- We use *quite a lot of* to talk about a medium quantity.
  *He has **quite a lot of** clothes.* NOT ~~He has quite lots of clothes~~.
- In negative sentences we usually use *much* with uncountable nouns and *many* with plural countable nouns.
  *I don't have **much** coffee.* (= I only have a small quantity)
  *They don't have **many** lemons.* (= They have some, but not a lot)
- We can also use *a lot of* or *lots of* in negative sentences for both countable and uncountable nouns.
  *I don't have **a lot of/lots of** time.*
  *We don't have **a lot of/lots of** tomatoes.*

GR9.2b))
1 A ***How many** burgers can you eat?* B *Not many.*
2 A ***How much** bread do you eat?* B *I eat quite a lot of bread.*

To ask questions about quantity, we use …
1 *How many* with plural countable nouns.
2 *How much* with uncountable nouns.

Countable		
How many books are there?	**A lot/Lots.**	There are **a lot of/lots of** books.
	Quite a lot.	There are **quite a lot of** books.
	Not many.	There aren't **many** books.
	None.	There aren't **any** books.
Uncountable		
How much milk do you drink?	**A lot/Lots.**	I drink **a lot/lots of** milk.
	Quite a lot.	I drink **quite a lot of** milk.
	Not much.	I don't drink **much** milk.
	None.	I don't drink **any** milk.

We use *none* in a short answer, but we say *no* with a noun in a full sentence. We often use *no* in sentences with *there is/there are*.
There's no milk. OR *There isn't any milk.* NOT ~~There's none milk~~.
There are no potatoes. OR *There aren't any potatoes.* NOT ~~There are NONE~~.

1 Complete the sentences using *much, many* or *a lot of.*
1 How _many_ glasses of water do you drink a day?
2 I didn't drink _____ water yesterday.
3 How _____ milk is there in the fridge?
4 There's quite _____ milk.
5 How _____ apples did you eat?
6 I didn't eat _____ apples.
7 How _____ time did you spend in the café yesterday?
8 How _____ times did you go back to the same café?
9 I like to drink _____ tea every day.
10 How _____ people are there in this class?
11 There's not _____ juice in my glass.
12 I ate _____ noodles last night.

2 Rewrite the sentences using *no.*
1 There isn't any yoghurt. _There's no yoghurt._
2 There aren't any tomatoes. _____
3 We don't have any money. _____
4 There isn't a living room in my house. _____
5 There isn't any water in the bath. _____

3 Complete the conversation using *much, many, a lot, no* and *none.*

Anas Excuse me. I'm doing some research. Can I ask you some questions?
Berna Yes, OK.
Anas How ¹ _many_ hours do you spend sleeping?
Berna Oh not ² _____ . About five hours a night. I'm always tired!
Anas How ³ _____ time do you think you spend eating and drinking?
Berna Hmm quite ⁴ _____ ! About two hours a day. And, I spend ⁵ _____ of time cooking.
Anas Thank you. OK, next question. How ⁶ _____ kilometres do you drive every day?
Berna ⁷ _____ . I don't drive.
Anas Do you work?
Berna Yes, I do.
Anas How ⁸ _____ hours a week do you work?
Berna About 50.
Anas And how ⁹ _____ time do you spend surfing the internet every day?
Berna Not ¹⁰ _____ . There's ¹¹ _____ internet at my house. So, I think about 30 minutes a day at work. How ¹² _____ questions are you going to ask me? I don't have ¹³ _____ time.
Anas Just one more. How ¹⁴ _____ hours of television do you watch in a week?
Berna Quite ¹⁵ _____ . I usually watch about two hours every day. I love TV.
Anas That's all. Thank you very much.

10.1 Comparative adjectives

1 *Denmark is a **smaller** country **than** Sweden.*

2 *England is **wetter than** Turkey.*

3 *Saudi Arabia is **drier than** France.*

4 *Greece is **more famous** for its beautiful beaches **than** its lakes.*

5 *My new job is **better than** my old one.*

6 *The airport is **further than** the train station.*

• We use comparative adjectives to compare a person, thing, group or situation with another.

• For most one-syllable adjectives and some two-syllable adjectives, we add -er (or -r if the adjective ends in -e).

cool → cool**er**   nice → nic**er**
small → small**er**   safe → saf**er**

• For most one-syllable adjectives ending in one vowel + one consonant, we double the consonant and add -er.

big → big**ger**   wet → wet**ter**
fat → fat**ter**   hot → hot**ter**

• For most one-syllable and two-syllable adjectives ending in -y, we delete the -y and add -ier.

dry → dr**ier**   foggy → fogg**ier**
sunny → sunn**ier**   cloudy → cloud**ier**

• For most adjectives with two or more syllables that don't end in -y, we use more before the adjective.

comfortable → **more** comfortable
interesting → **more** interesting

Irregular comparatives

good → **better**   many → **more**
bad → **worse**   little → **less**
far → **further/farther**

In formal English we use personal pronoun + auxiliary verb after than, e.g. than I am/was/do/did/have, but in informal English we often use an object pronoun, e.g. than me/you/him/her/it/us/them.
*I'm older **than she is** → I'm older **than her**.*
*I was faster **than they were**. → I was faster **than them**.*
*My wife has a healthier lifestyle **than I do**. → My wife has a healthier lifestyle **than me**.*

---

1 Complete the sentences using the comparative form of the adjectives in (brackets).

1 The weather in winter is _icier_ than in summer. (icy)

2 The old town was _____ than the new town. (dirty)

3 My spelling is _____ than my brother's. (bad)

4 Swimming in the sea is _____ than swimming in a lake. (dangerous)

5 Watching a film at the cinema is _____ than watching it on a phone. (good)

6 People in villages are usually _____ than people in cities. (friendly)

7 Today is _____ than yesterday. (foggy)

8 This exercise is _____ than the next one. (easy)

2 Make sentences using comparative adjectives.

1 The sun / bright / the moon.
   The sun is brighter than the moon

2 Canada / big / the UK.
   _____

3 Cooking / difficult / eating.
   _____

4 Planes / fast / trains.
   _____

5 August / windy / July.
   _____

6 Vegetables / healthy / sweets.
   _____

7 Your country / interesting / my country.
   _____

8 His clothes / expensive / her clothes.
   _____

3 Complete the text about Greenland using the comparative form of the adjectives in (brackets).

Greenland has a very cold climate. The country is [1] _more famous_ (famous) for its snow and ice than for good weather. In the summer, the temperature is usually about 5°C in the day. It is [2] _____ (warm) and [3] _____ (dry) inland than it is close to the sea because the sea is very cold all year. The temperatures at night are [4] _____ (cold) than in the day. The air is very dry in Greenland and this means you can see [5] _____ (far) than in other countries.

In the winter, temperatures sometimes go down to -50°C. The middle of Greenland is [6] _____ (icy) and [7] _____ (windy) than the coast. People don't live in the centre of Greenland because it is too cold. The nights in winter are [8] _____ (long) and the days are [9] _____ (short) than in the summer because Greenland is very close to the North Pole. People in Greenland say snow is [10] _____ (beautiful) than rain.

10.2 Superlative adjectives

GR10.2)))

1 Angel Falls in Venezuela is the **tallest** waterfall in the world.
2 The **largest** desert in the world is Antarctica.
3 Yesterday was the **wettest** day of the year.
4 August is the **driest** month of the year.
5 He's the **most famous** football player in the area.
6 It's the **best** restaurant in the city centre.

- We use the superlative form to compare a person or thing to the whole group or category it belongs to. We usually use *the* before superlative + noun.

  The beaches on the north coast are the **most beautiful** on the island.

- For most one-syllable adjectives, we add *-est* (or *-st* if the adjective ends in *-e*).

  cold → colder → cold**est**
  safe → safer → saf**est**

- For most one-syllable adjectives ending in one vowel + one consonant, we double the final consonant and add *-est*.

  wet → wetter → wet**test**
  hot → hotter → hot**test**

- For one- and two-syllable adjectives ending in *-y*, we delete the *-y* and add *-iest*.

  dry → drier → dr**iest**
  easy → easier → eas**iest**

- For most adjectives with two or more syllables that don't end in *-y*, we use *most* before the adjectives.

  famous → more famous → **most** famous
  comfortable → more comfortable → **most** comfortable

- Some superlatives are irregular.

  good → better → **best**
  bad → worse → **worst**
  far → further/farther → **furthest/farthest**
  much/many → more → **most**
  little → less → **least**

After superlatives we often use *in* before a place or a group.
I'm the happiest woman in the world.
He's the funniest person in the office.

1 Write superlative sentences using the words given.

1 This watch / expensive thing / the shop .
   This watch is the most expensive thing in the shop.
2 Mount Everest / high mountain / the world .
   _____
3 My notebook / neat notebook / the class .
   _____
4 The High Street / busy place / my city .
   _____
5 The beaches on the north coast / beautiful beaches / my country .
   _____
6 My frying pan / useful thing / the kitchen .
   _____
7 My house / small house / my street .
   _____
8 Ling–Fan / tall student / my class .
   _____

2 Complete the conversation between Osman and Jitrada comparing Dubai and Rome.

Osman I think Dubai is ¹ _the best_ (good) place ² _____ the world for a holiday.

Jitrada Why?

Osman It has amazing buildings. It has ³ _____ (tall) building ⁴ _____ the world: the Burj Khalifa. It's about 900 metres. It also has ⁵ _____ (large) shopping mall ⁶ _____ the world with more than 1,200 shops. Just outside the mall is a fantastic 'dancing' fountain.

Jitrada I don't really like shopping. I think Rome is ⁷ _____ (interesting) ⁸ _____ Dubai.

Osman No! Why?

Jitrada Rome is ⁹ _____ (old) ¹⁰ _____ Dubai – many of the buildings are more than 2,000 years old. I think they are ¹¹ _____ (beautiful) ¹² _____ tall buildings.

Osman The Burj Al Arab in Dubai is a really beautiful hotel. I think it's ¹³ _____ (beautiful) hotel in the world and it's not ¹⁴ _____ (expensive). You should see it!

Jitrada But I think Dubai is ¹⁵ _____ (hot) ¹⁶ _____ Rome. It's ¹⁷ _____ (comfortable) to walk around Rome ¹⁸ _____ Dubai.

Osman You can drive! The traffic in Rome is ¹⁹ _____ (bad) ²⁰ _____ in Dubai.

Jitrada Well, I don't agree!

11.1 *Going to*

GR11.1 🎵

1 I**'m going to** visit my aunt in hospital this evening.
2 He **isn't going to** give any money to charity.
3 She**'s not going to** have time to visit you.
4 When**'s he going to** organize the football match?
5 **A** **Are** you **going to** cycle to work tomorrow?
   B Yes, I **am**.

We use *to be* + *going to* + infinitive without *to* to talk about future plans and intentions. We often use *going to* with future time expressions, e.g. *tomorrow*, *next week*, *tonight*, *next year*, etc.

Positive (+)	Negative (–)		
I am/I'm You are/You're He is/He's She is/She's It is/It's We are/We're They are/They're	I'm not You aren't He isn't She isn't It isn't We aren't They aren't	going to	drive. cycle.

yes/no questions (?)			Short answers	
Am I Are you Is he/she/it Are we Are they	going to	drive? cycle?	Yes, I am. Yes, you are. Yes, he/she/it is. Yes, we are. Yes, they are.	No, I'm not. No, you aren't. No. he/she/it isn't. No, we aren't. No, they aren't.

Wh- questions

A What **are** you **going to** do this year?
B I'm going to visit my friends in Kenya.

A Why**'s** she **going to** sell her bicycle?
B Because she's going to buy a car.

A How **are** we **going to** celebrate your birthday?
B We're going to have a party.

---

1 Complete the sentences with the correct form of *going to* and the verbs in (brackets).

1 _Are you going to make_ (you/make) a big cake?
2 _____ (my friends/help) me repair my car.
3 _____ (he/plant) a tree in the college garden?
4 _____ (I/run) to work every morning next month.
5 _____ (they/have) dinner with us tomorrow?
6 _____ (I/not work) in Tasmania next month.
7 _____ (we/not play) basketball this afternoon.
8 _____ (she/not learn) a new language this year.

2 Complete the sentences with the correct form of *going to* and a verb from the box.

> eat not come not have ~~repair~~ rent sell start teach

1 I '_m going to repair_ my sister's broken computer next weekend.
2 She _____ a study group with some friends at college.
3 My friends _____ a house in Canberra for $800 a month.
4 The fridge is empty! What _____ we _____ ?
5 She loves her car! Why _____ she _____ it?
6 _____ David _____ his daughter to drive?
7 Katia is feeling ill. She _____ to the party.
8 Sorry, I _____ time to organize a football match. I'm very busy.

3 Complete the conversation using *going to* and the verbs in (brackets).

Adelina So, what ¹ _are we going to do_ (we/do) for Helena's birthday party on Friday?
Carl Well, Pascal and Xian ² _____ (organize) the barbecue and I ³ _____ (buy) the drinks.
Adelina OK, so how many people ⁴ _____ (come)?
Carl About 30, I hope.
Adelina That's a lot of food and drink! How ⁵ _____ (you/carry) it?
Carl Claude ⁶ _____ (lend) me his car.
Adelina OK, that's good! ⁷ _____ (Helena's cousins/ sing)?
Carl No, they ⁸ _____ . But Philippe and his band ⁹ _____ (play). ¹⁰ _____ (you/help) Philippe with the music?
Adelina Yes, I ¹¹ _____ . But I ¹² _____ (not dance) at the party.
Carl Why not?
Adelina You know I don't like dancing. ¹³ _____ (you/ buy) her a present?
Carl Yes, I ¹⁴ _____ . When ¹⁵ _____ (we/make) the birthday cake?
Adelina Tomorrow evening.

11.2 Infinitive of purpose

GR11.2)))

1 *I go on holiday* **to meet** *new people.*
2 *I'm going to the bank* **to change** *some money.*
3 *She went to Spain* **to learn** *Spanish.*
4 **A** *Why are you going to Easter Island?*
   B **To see** *the famous statues.*

- We use *to* + infinitive to express purpose (to say why we want to do something, why we are going to do something, or why we did something).
  We went to the island **to see** *the birds.*
- We can answer a *Why* question with an infinitive of purpose.
  A *Why do you cycle to work?*
  B **To keep** *fit.*
  A *Why did she go to Paris?*
  B **To study** *art.*
  A *Why are you looking at that website?*
  B **To get** *some information about geocaching.*
- We can also use *because* to answer a *Why* question.
  A *Why is he running?*
  B **To catch** *the bus.*/**Because** *he wants to catch the bus.*
  A *Why did you open the window?*
  B **To get** *some fresh air.*/**Because** *I wanted some fresh air.*

The infinitive with *to* does not change form. It always stays the same.
A *Why did you go to Scotland?*
B *To visit my nephew.* NOT *~~To visited my nephew~~.*

1 Complete the sentences using the infinitive of purpose. Use the verbs in the box.

book	buy	improve	invite	make	~~save~~	see	tell

1 I cycle to work *to save* money.
2 She used the internet _____ her flights.
3 They went to London _____ a musical.
4 I'm going to buy some bread _____ some sandwiches.
5 Bob sent everyone an email _____ them to the party.
6 We called my sister _____ her the good news.
7 I went to the mall _____ some new trousers.
8 I'm going to read more _____ my English.

2 Complete the conversation with *to* or *because*.
   A Where's Jane?
   B She's gone to the hospital **1** *to* visit Ellie.
   A Why is Ellie in hospital?
   B She stood on a chair **2**_____ get a bowl from the top shelf, fell and broke her leg.
   A That's terrible!
   B Are you going to visit her?
   A I'm going to the library **3**_____ borrow some books. Then, I'd like to go to bed early **4**_____ I'm very tired, but I can visit her tomorrow morning.
   B You should go today **5**_____ she's very unhappy and she needs to talk to someone.
   A Why don't you go?
   B I'm going to Manchester **6**_____ see my mum **7**_____ she's ill. Remember?
   A Oh, yes. OK. I'll take Ellie some flowers **8**_____ help her feel better.

3 Rewrite the underlined parts of the text using an infinitive of purpose.

Last year, **1** we went to Malaysia because we wanted to go sightseeing. We stayed in a hotel on the beach and went swimming every morning. There was no internet in our hotel, so **2** we sometimes went to the town centre and used the internet café. One night, **3** I went to the café because I wanted to email my sister on her birthday, but the café was closed. **4** I walked around and looked for another café and found a small empty restaurant. **5** I went in and asked them if they had the internet and a very old man said, 'yes' and told me to sit down. The old man went to the back of the restaurant and brought out ten small statues. Suddenly, **6** his wife went to the front of the restaurant and closed the front door. They then spent an hour trying to sell me the statues! I really didn't want to buy one, but I bought two for $20 because I wanted to go back to my hotel. Two weeks later, when we got back to New York, **7** I took the statues to a shop because I wanted to sell them. They gave me $200 for them!

We went to Malaysia to go sightseeing.

12.1 Present perfect simple

We form the present perfect simple with *have/has* and the past participle.

Positive (+)

I/You/We/They	have/'ve	been
He/She/It	has/'s	been

Negative (–)

I/You/We/They	have not/haven't	been
He/She/It	has not/hasn't	been

- Regular verbs have past participles which are the same as their past simple forms.
  We **danced** all night. → She's **danced** all over the world.
  She **played** in a band four years ago. → I haven't **played** in a band.

- Irregular verbs have irregular past participles. Sometimes the past participles of irregular verbs are the same as the past simple forms.
  He **lost** the match last week. → She's **lost** all her photos.
  They **had** dance lessons last year. → We've **had** singing lessons.

- Sometimes the past participle is different from the past simple form.
  I **spoke** to the manager yesterday. → I've **spoken** to the manager.
  She **did** some exercise this morning. → They've **done** lots of exercise.

- The present perfect connects the past with the present. We use the present perfect simple to talk about past experiences and events when …

  1 we don't know when the event happened or it's not important when it happened.

  2 we are interested in what happened more than when it happened.

  I haven't been to a musical, but I've been to a play.

- We don't say when the action happened with the present perfect.
  I've been to Paris. NOT I've been to Paris last year.

The verb *go* has two past participles: *been* and *gone*.
Jacob's *been* to Algeria. (= He went and now he is back.)
Jacob's *gone* to Algeria. (= He went and has not come back yet.)

---

1 Rewrite the <u>underlined</u> part of the sentences using contractions.

1 <u>She has become</u> one the best singers in Italy.
   She's become
2 <u>You have drawn</u> some good pictures. _____
3 <u>He has not opened</u> the café today. _____
4 <u>I have not been</u> to a rock concert. _____
5 <u>We have taken</u> lots of photographs. _____

2 Write infinitives and the past participles of the irregular verbs.

	infinitive	past simple	past participle
1	*give*	gave	*given*
2	_____	put	_____
3	_____	drank	_____
4	_____	went	_____
5	_____	grew	_____
6	_____	heard	_____
7	_____	broke	_____
8	_____	drove	_____
9	_____	woke	_____
10	_____	won	_____

3 Complete the sentences using the present perfect simple form of the verbs in the box.

~~break~~ go not buy not made not see organize
repair swim

1 She*'s broken* her arm. She's in hospital now.
2 I _____ a musical.
3 Lots of people _____ to a salsa class.
4 We _____ in the Pacific Ocean.
5 They _____ a marathon.
6 I _____ a cake for my mother's birthday.
7 He _____ a present for his wife.
8 She _____ lots of broken bicycles.

4 Complete the text using the correct form of the present perfect simple.

My sister and I **1** *have always loved* (always love) music.
I play the piano and she plays the drums. We both sing. We
2 _____ (have) music lessons for many years and **3** _____
(play) in many concerts. I **4** _____ (win) three prizes for
music and I **5** _____ (write) lots of music for films. My sister
6 _____ (not win) any prizes, but she plays in a very famous
rock band. She **7** _____ (give) concerts all over the world
and **8** _____ (earn) quite a lot of money. I **9** _____ (go)
to lots of her concerts. She's fantastic! Our parents are not
musicians, but they **10** _____ (not stop) us from playing
music every day.

12.2 Present perfect questions; Present perfect and past simple

GR12.2a)))

1 A *Has* he *won* the competition? B *No, he **hasn't***.
2 A *Have* you ever *been* to Iceland? B *Yes, I **have***.

- To make *yes/no* questions, we use *Have/Has* + subject + past participle.

Questions (?)			Short answers
Have	I/you/we/they	eaten?	Yes, I/you/we/they **have**. No, I/you/we/they **haven't**.
Has	he/she/it		Yes, he/she/it **has**. No, he/she/it **hasn't**.

Present perfect and past simple

GR12.2b)))

1 A *Have* you ever *seen* a silent film?
  B *No, I **haven't***.
2 A *Did* you *see* The Artist *last weekend*?
  B *No, I **didn't***.
3 *I've* never **driven** a Ferrari.
4 *I **drove*** a Porsche last summer.
5 *She's **been*** to Rio many times.
6 *She **went*** to Rio in 2013.

- We use the present perfect to say something happened before now but we don't know or say when. We often use it with …
  1 *ever* in questions; *ever* means *at any time in your life*. It goes between the subject and the main verb.
    *Has he **ever** written a novel?   Yes, he has./No, he hasn't.*
  2 *never* to talk about experiences that did not happen. It means *at no time in your life* and goes after *have/has* and before the main verb.
    *I haven't acted in a play. → I've **never** acted in a play.*
- We also use the present perfect to talk about the number of times we have done something.
  *They've had dinner at my house **once**.*
- We use the past simple, not the present perfect …
  1 to say something happened before now and we know the time.
    Last May, we went to see a wonderful concert.
  2 with finished time expressions, e.g. *last week, yesterday,* etc.
    I watched lots of horror films when I was a teenager.
    NOT *I've seen lots of horror films when I was a teenager.*
- We often start with the present perfect and then change to the past simple to give more details.
  A *Have* you ever **stayed** in an expensive hotel?
  B *Yes, I **stayed** at the Shangri-La last September.*
  A *Did* you **enjoy** it?
  B *Yes, I **did**. It **was** amazing!*

1 Put the words in the right order.

1 during / you / a film / cried / Have / ever ?
  Have you ever cried during a film?
2 a play / acted / never / in / I've .
3 stayed up / I've / many times / with friends / all night .
4 eight times / She's / the same / film / watched .
5 been / ever / he / to / Has / a big concert ?
6 film / to / never / see / wanted / a horror / I've .
7 been / never / the opera / to / They've .
8 famous / a lot of / You've / people / met .

2 Complete the text with the present perfect or past simple form of the verbs in (brackets).

Andrew ¹ _Have you ever been_ (ever/go) to a comedy club?
Beth   Yes, I ² _____ (go) to one about three weeks ago.
Andrew ³ _____ (enjoy) it?
Beth   Yes, it was very good.
Andrew Who ⁴_____ (go) with?
Beth   Three friends. We ⁵_____ (go) four or five times before.
Andrew I ⁶_____ (never/go) to a comedy club, but I ⁷_____ (watch) lots of comedy on TV.
Beth   You should go. Come with us next time.
Andrew Thanks. ⁸_____ (ever/go) to a circus?
Beth   No, ⁹_____ . Have you?
Andrew Yes, I ¹⁰_____ . Many times. There's one in town at the moment. I recommend it.

3 Complete the email using the present perfect or past simple form of the verbs in (brackets).

Hi Juan

How are you? I'm in Vienna now with Alice. We ¹ _'ve been_ (go) to the opera five times! It's a beautiful city. On Tuesday we ²_____ (see) the palace and ³_____ (walk) around in its large gardens. On Wednesday we ⁴_____ (take) a bus to the Museum of Modern Art and ⁵_____ (swim) in the Danube. It was very cold!

We ⁶_____ (do) a lot of other interesting things, too. Have you ⁷_____ (ever/eat) *Sacher Torte*? It's an Austrian cake. Alice loves it. She also loves German coffee. Yesterday she ⁸_____ (drink) eight cups! We're having a great time, but Alice ⁹_____ (lose) her phone. She ¹⁰_____ (buy) a cheap one on Friday, but it ¹¹_____ (break) the next day.

See you soon,

Ona

Audioscripts

Unit 1 Your world

1.1 🔊

Mexico	Mexican	Spanish
the USA	American	English
Italy	Italian	Italian
China	Chinese	Chinese
Vietnam	Vietnamese	Vietnamese
Turkey	Turkish	Turkish
the UK	British	English
Poland	Polish	Polish
Pakistan	Pakistani	Urdu
the UAE	Emirati	Arabic
France	French	French
Greece	Greek	Greek

1.2 🔊

I So, … Tell us about your life here in Britain. Are you from London?

G Well, my name is Godwin. I'm from Nigeria originally. My wife, Sylvie, is French. Actually, she's half-French: her mother's French and her father's from Brazil. Our two children were born in England, so they're British … We speak English at home. Our home's in north London. Many different nationalities live here. The neighbours are a family from Iraq. Next to our house is a Polish supermarket and the restaurant across the road is Lebanese. I work for an American organization – but my boss isn't American, she's Turkish … What else? … I watch football and I play the saxophone and, oh yeah, my saxophone's Japanese.

1.3 🔊

1 Are you from London?
2 My name is Godwin.
3 I'm from Nigeria.
4 Our two children were born in England, so they're British.
5 The neighbours are a family from Iraq.
6 The restaurant across the road is Lebanese.
7 My boss isn't American.

1.4 🔊

T Come in. Oh, hello. What's your name?
G Hi, I'm Godwin.
T I'm Andy, the saxophone teacher. Are you a student?
G No, I'm not. I have a job.
T No … I mean, are you a student for the saxophone class?
G Oh, sorry, yes. Yeah, I am.
T Where are you from, Godwin?
G I'm from Nigeria, but London's my home now.
T Is it your first class?
G Yes, it is.
T OK. Well, let me introduce you to the other students.
G OK.
T This is Murielle. She's a student here, too.
G Hi, Murielle. Nice to meet you. I'm Godwin.
M Nice to meet you, too.

G Murielle's a French name. Are you French?
M No, I'm from Senegal. But my first language is French.

1.5 🔊

1	brother		c	sister
2	son		f	daughter
3	husband		j	wife
4	father		g	mother
5	uncle		i	aunt
6	grandfather		b	grandmother
7	grandson		h	granddaughter
8	nephew		e	niece
9	stepfather		a	stepmother
10	brother-in-law		d	sister-in-law

1.6 🔊

Zafar and his wife have two children: a son, Hasan, and his twin brother, Tariq. Tariq is married to Rafina. Sahala is Tariq and Rafina's daughter. She's three years old.

1.7 🔊

1	Zafar's wife	Zafar's a doctor.
2	Their daughter	They're happy.
3	I'm his son.	He's my father.
4	Is he your brother?	You're right.
5	She's our teacher.	Are you married?

1.9 🔊

1 I'm Russian.
2 It isn't an Arabic name.
3 That's not a girl's name.
4 They aren't brothers.
5 It's the same.
6 She isn't French.
7 It's a long name.
8 He isn't married.

1.10 🔊

1 It's not a female name.
2 Their name's Spanish.
3 She's called Sara.
4 His family name's Ramirez.
5 That isn't a boy's name.
6 My name isn't very long.
7 Their family's not large.
8 He's my friend.

1.11 🔊

B I'm Bülent and I'm Turkish. In my country we say or write our personal name and then our family name, so I'm Bülent Sadik. It's the same in some other countries for example, the UK, the USA and Thailand.

N Oh, it isn't the same in China. We use the family name first. My first name's Na and my family name's Li. So I'm called Li Na

T Well, I'm not from China but we're the same as you, Na, with names. I'm Hungarian, and my family name's Antalek. So please call me Antalek Tamás.

B So Tamás is your personal name?
T That's right.
M Well … Spanish names are different. I'm Manuela García Gómez. We say our first

name, then our father's family name and then our mother's family name!
T Wow!
M Yes – it isn't short!

1.12 🔊

a name, names
a country, countries
a man, men
a woman, women
a person, people

1.13 🔊

R Hi. Can I help you?
A Yes, I'm here for the 'Create a Website' course.
R Oh yes, at six o'clock. What's your name?
A Antonio Russo.
R Ah, yes. Your name's here on the list. I just need some other details. What's your nationality?
A I'm Italian but my home is here in Toronto.
R OK, and what's your job?
A I'm a restaurant owner.
R Mmm … So, is the website for business or for fun?
A It's for business.
R For your restaurant?
A Yes, that's right.
R And, finally, what's your email address?
A It's antonio@russorest.com.
R Sorry, can you repeat that, please?
T Yes, Antonio – A-N-T-O-N-I-O – at russorest dot com.
R How do you spell russorest?
T R-U-double S-O-R-E-S-T.
R OK. Great. Thanks. Now, the cost of the course is …

1.14 🔊

R Hi. Can I help you?
A Yes, I'm here for the 'Create a Website' course.
R Oh yes, at six o'clock. What's your name?
A Antonio Russo.
R Ah, yes. Your name's here on the list. I just need some other details. What's your nationality?
A I'm Italian but my home is here in Toronto.
R OK, and what's your job?
A I'm a restaurant owner.
R Mmm … So, is the website for business or for fun?
A It's for business.
R For your restaurant?
A Yes, that's right.
R And, finally, what's your email address?
A It's antonio@russorest.com.

1.15 🔊

1 What's your name?
2 What's your nationality?
3 What's your job?
4 Is the website for business or for fun?
5 What's your email address?

1.16)))
A It's antonio@russorest.com.
R Sorry, can you repeat that, please?
T Yes, Antonio – A-N-T-O-N-I-O – at russorest dot com.
R How do you spell russorest?
T R-U-double S-O-R-E-S-T.
R OK. Great. Thanks. Now, the cost of the course is …

1.17)))
Sorry, can you repeat that, please?
How do you spell that?
How do you spell 'russorest'?

1.18)))
A Are you and your wife from England?
B No, we're not. I'm from Edinburgh in Scotland and my wife's Canadian.
A Canadian? Is she from Montreal? My sister's at university in Montreal.
B No, she's from Vancouver. What about you? You're not English. Are you Australian?
A No, I'm not. I'm from Wellington in New Zealand.

1.19)))
1 British
2 the United Arab Emirates
3 Urdu
4 American

1.20)))
Dubai is a very multicultural city in the United Arab Emirates. People come here to work from many different countries. Only 10% of people in Dubai are Emirati: 90% of the city's population are from other countries. Some people come from the UK and the USA, but many people are from Asia. India is home for most of Dubai's workers, but people come from Pakistan and the Philippines, too. The language of the United Arab Emirates is Arabic, but because of its international population, lots of people use English.

1.21)))
1 Your mother's sister.
2 Your father's father.
3 Your sister's daughter.
4 Your son's daughter.
5 Your mother's brother.
6 Your aunt's son.

Unit 2 My day

2.1)))
I'm a scientist. I study penguins on Bird Island and I'm very happy here. In the summer, my days are long. I get up early and go to the beach. I watch the penguins with their babies. I sometimes go out in a boat with the other scientists on the island. We visit different islands and take photos of the birds and animals there.

I often work all day and I only stop in the evening to have dinner. I sometimes go back to the beach after dinner to spend more time with the penguins. Then I work in the lab. I always go to bed late! In the winter, the weather is always very cold, but we usually have more free time and I can relax.

2.2)))
1 Melanie watches penguins.
2 Sven also works on the island.
3 Sven loves his job.

2.3)))
1 goes
2 teaches
3 cooks
4 relaxes
5 makes
6 plays

2.4)))
/s/ cooks, makes
/z/ goes, plays
/ɪz/ teaches, relaxes

2.5)))
1 During the week, he always gets up early and he usually arrives at a volcano at seven o'clock.
2 His work is sometimes dangerous and he never works alone.
3 He usually returns to the research centre at about one o'clock and he always has lunch in the lab.
4 On Friday and Saturday nights he usually relaxes at home. He hardly ever goes out with friends and he often goes to bed early.

2.6)))
1 get up
2 have a shower
3 make breakfast
4 go to work / go to college
5 have lunch / have dinner
6 go home
7 watch TV / watch a film
8 read a book
9 listen to music
10 play video games
11 go to bed
12 see friends

2.7)))
All astronauts in Europe learn their job at the European Astronaut Centre in Cologne in Germany. The training is hard, but it's interesting and I love it. My day starts at ten to seven when I get up. I have a shower and then have breakfast in the canteen at quarter to eight. Classes begin at half past eight. In the morning, we study things like engineering and physics. At quarter past eleven, we stop and have a break. I usually have a coffee and I also try and learn some Russian vocabulary. We all learn Russian here. Classes start again at half past eleven.

Lunch is at one o'clock, and in the afternoons we have more classes from quarter past two. We learn to use the space equipment and machines and we also have language classes. Classes finish at quarter to six. I always feel really tired, but I often go to the gym in the evening. I'm in bed by ten o'clock and by five past ten I'm usually asleep.

2.8)))
1 three o'clock
2 five past three
3 ten past three

4 quarter past three
5 twenty past three
6 twenty-five past three
7 half past three
8 twenty-five to four
9 twenty to four
10 quarter to four
11 ten to four
12 five to four

2.9)))
1 half past eight
2 quarter to three
3 ten to ten
4 five to six
5 twenty past three
6 twenty-five to four

2.10)))
1 They don't have a lot of free time.
2 I don't go to classes in the evening.
3 Chris doesn't have a shower in the morning.
4 Sanaa doesn't sleep in a sleeping bag.
5 They don't speak to their families every day.
6 He doesn't work eight hours a day.

2.11)))
1 Most astronauts don't feel well when they first go into space. Space sickness is very common.
2 Astronauts don't wear special clothes in the space station. They only need a space suit when they go on a spacewalk.
3 Astronauts don't change their clothes every day. It isn't possible to wash clothes in space.
4 Astronauts usually exercise for two hours a day.
5 Usually, an astronaut doesn't go on a spacewalk more than once a week.
6 Most astronauts sleep for less time in space but they don't feel very tired.

2.12)))
1 I have lunch at one or two in the afternoon.
2 I wake up and have breakfast.
3 People eat because they're hungry.
4 I try to wake up early, but it's difficult!

2.13)))
1
A I watch the news on TV every morning.
B I listen to it on the radio.
2
A It's a good idea.
B I agree with you.
3
A Do you pay for tea and coffee at work?
B No, they're free, but we buy sandwiches at lunchtime.
4
A Do people often wait for buses and trains in your city?
B No, not often. They're usually on time.
5
A I'd like to talk to you before the meeting tomorrow.
B OK, are you free after lunch?
6
A Do we have a reply from them?
B No, they want more time to think about it.
7
A It's not nice to laugh at other people.
B I know, my grandmother always says that!

8
A Do students often ask for a discount?
B Yes, but they need to show their student card.

2.14 🔊
1 Tarik talks to his family on the phone every day.
2 Kristofer never laughs at funny films. He doesn't enjoy them.
3 My sister never waits for people who are late.
4 I usually agree with my friends, but we sometimes have different ideas.
5 Gregorja listens to pop and classical music.
6 When he's alone, he thinks about his friends and family.
7 We always pay for our shopping with cash.
8 Intira always asks for help when she doesn't understand something in class.

2.15 🔊
BDK ... So, welcome to Seoul, Mr Schmidt. Nice to meet you.
KS Thank you, Mr Kim. Nice to meet you, too.
BDK How was your journey?
KS It was fine, thanks.
BDK Good. I'd like to take you to dinner. Are you free tonight?
KS Um ... yes, I am. But what time is our first meeting tomorrow?
BDK It's at nine thirty.
KS OK, that's fine, then.
BDK Great! Would you like to go for dinner at Jinju Jip? They do very good Korean soup there ...
KS Yes, that sounds nice. What time do you want to eat?
BDK Well, I usually go at about midnight.
KS Er ... I'm sorry, but I'm usually in bed at that time. Can we go a bit earlier?
BDK OK, no problem. It's open 24 hours. Let's go at half past nine.
KS Right ...
BDK And do you want to do some shopping while you're here?
KS Yes, I'd love to.
BDK Great! Let's do that after dinner.
KS After dinner? What time do the shops close?
BDK Oh, very late! Some shops close at 5 a.m. People say that in Seoul, everything is open all the time!
KS 5 a.m.? Wow! OK, then. Where shall we meet?
BDK I'll pick you up from your hotel. It's not very far ...

2.16 🔊
1 British people never have fish for breakfast. They usually have toast or cereal.
2 They are hardly ever late for meetings. They like to arrive on time.
3 British people sometimes go to a different city to study at university.
4 British people often have more than one TV at home: some people have three or four.
5 They usually eat lunch at work. They don't have time to go home.
6 And British people always, always talk about the weather!

2.17 🔊
A Are you free after class today?
B I'm sorry, but I'm busy this evening. But I don't have any plans tomorrow.
A Would you like to go out for a pizza?
B Yes, I'd love to. What time shall we meet?
A Eight o'clock at Gino's? Or do you want to meet at the station?
B Yes, let's meet there at 7.45.
A OK, see you then!

Unit 3 Work

3.1 🔊
1 She has her own company. She's a businesswoman.
2 My son fixes a lot of different machines. He's a mechanic.
3 Manu takes pictures with his camera. He's a photographer.
4 My brother flies planes for a Japanese airline. He's a pilot.
5 She washes hair, cuts it, and dries it. She's a hairdresser.
6 Ekaterina writes for the newspaper. She's a journalist.
7 Sameeha cleans and fixes people's teeth. She's a dentist.
8 My cousin sings and plays the guitar in a band. He's a musician.
9 He studies at university. He's a student.
10 She works in a hospital and helps sick people. She's a nurse.
11 Daniela cooks food in a restaurant. She's a chef.
12 My best friend cleans offices and people's houses. He's a cleaner.

3.2 🔊
businessman   mechanic
businesswoman   musician
chef   nurse
cleaner   photographer
dentist   pilot
hairdresser   student
journalist

3.3 🔊
M I work at a cinema in town, but I don't sell tickets, I'm the piano player! At my cinema they have a lot of old, silent movies so they need someone to play music. I watch the film and decide what type of music to play. If it's a sad part of the film, I play slow music; but if it's an exciting part, I play it fast.
D I am a 'fire lookout' and I work in a big forest. Fire can be very dangerous here, so my job is to make sure no fires start. I work in a very high tower, so I can see very far. I check the weather on the internet every morning because strong winds can be a big problem. I like my job because the forest is beautiful and quiet.

3.4 🔊
1
A Does Máté work at the cinema?
B Yes, he does.
2
A Does he always play fast music?
B No, he doesn't.

3
A Is Dana a police officer?
B No, she isn't.
4
A Does she work in a big office?
B No, she doesn't.
5
A Does she enjoy her job?
B Yes, she does.
6
A Do Dana and Máté have unusual jobs?
B Yes, they do.

3.5 🔊
1
A Do they like their jobs?
B Yes, they do.
2
A Does he play the piano?
B Yes, he does.
3
A Does he sell tickets?
B No, he doesn't.
4
A Do you have a job?
B No, I don't.

3.6 🔊
1 work for a big company, work freelance, work for a fashion magazine.
2 work in a hospital, work from home, work in a factory, work in a big office.
3 salary, earn.
4 work full-time, work part-time, work long hours.
5 retired, unemployed.
6 colleagues, manager/boss.

3.7 🔊
1 Where do you live?
2 What do you usually wear to work?
3 Why do you want to learn English?
4 What time do you start work or class?
5 When do you take breaks?
6 Who do you live with?
7 What do you do when you're bored?
8 How often do you check your emails?

3.8 🔊
1 Where do you live?
2 What do you usually wear to work?
3 How often do you check your emails?

3.9 🔊
author   mechanic   pilot   teacher

3.11 🔊
address, after, again, answer, breakfast, clever, daughter, internet, forget, later

3.13 🔊
1 a recent report
2 one job that makes people very happy
3 there are three reasons
4 work for a company
5 a lot of different people

3.14 🔊
A new book by author and mechanic Matthew Crawford says that people who work with their hands are often happy in their jobs. The great thing about working with your hands is that you can see the result very quickly – you fix a bike and it works ... or it doesn't! It's not the same for

people in office jobs. For them, success often comes after weeks or months of hard work, which can make them feel unhappy.

Not everyone agrees with the author. They say that office workers are happy because they usually work as part of a team, and that spending time with other people can help them to be happy. But people who work with their hands, like cleaners, mechanics, farmers and artists, often work on their own and can have a lonely life.

A recent report says that there is one job that makes people very happy. And who are these lucky people? Hairdressers! Researchers say that when they ask people in different jobs how happy they are, hairdressers usually answer they're 'very happy'. The report says there are three reasons why hairdressers are so happy. They don't usually work for a company, so they don't have a boss. They see a lot of different people every day. And they make their customers look good and feel good. So, because they see a lot of happy people every day, they're happy, too.

3.15)))

A Hello and welcome, everyone. Before we begin, I'd like to tell you a few things about the course.

B Excuse me. Could I open the window?

A Yes, of course. It's really hot in here, isn't it? So ... class is at 2 p.m. every Thursday and Friday in the room next door. You can use the computers there ... Yes, do you have a question?

C ... Er, yes ... Can we use the computers after class?

A Yes, of course, but you need a password. It's 'student451'.

C Sorry, can you repeat that, please?

B Sure. It's student451. That's S-T-U-D-E-N-T-4-5-1.

B And can we leave our books and bags in the computer room?

A I'm afraid not. There are evening classes in that room from 6 p.m. Now, if there's nothing else ... Oh, before you leave today, could you give your personal details to the administrator, including your bank details, please?

C Sorry, but I don't have them with me today. Could I send them by email later?

A That's fine. Just tell the administrator before you leave. OK, our first lesson is ...

3.16)))

1
A Could I open the window?
B Yes, of course. It's really hot in here, isn't it?

2
A Could you give your personal details to the administrator?
B Sorry, but I don't have them with me today.

3
A Could I send them by email later?
B That's fine. Just tell the administrator before you leave.

4
A Can you repeat that, please?
B Sure. It's student451. That's S-T-U-D-E-N-T-4-5-1.

5
A Can we use the computers after class?
B Yes, of course, but you need a password.

6
A Can we leave our books and bags in the computer room?
B I'm afraid not. There are evening classes in that room from 6 p.m.

3.17)))

1
A Can I sit here, please?
B Of course you can.

2
A Could I leave early tomorrow?
B I'm sorry, but that's not possible.

3.18)))

1 She teaches in a school or university.
2 He paints people's houses.
3 Her job is to sing songs.
4 You use this thing to play DVDs.
5 He builds houses.
6 She makes bread.

Unit 4 Places and things

4.1)))

airport	library
campsite	museum
chemist	railway station
hairdresser's	restaurant
hospital	swimming pool
hotel	theatre

4.2)))

F I'm so hot! I'm so happy to be at the hotel at last. Is there a swimming pool? I'd like to have a swim.

R No, I'm sorry, there isn't. It doesn't rain a lot here, so there aren't many swimming pools.

F You mean there aren't any swimming pools at all?

R No, don't worry! There's a big swimming pool in the town centre if you want to go swimming. There just isn't one at the hotel.

F Are there any museums near the centre?

R Yes, there are. There's the opal mine museum. Look, here's some information about it.

A Thank you. That looks interesting. And are there any underground buildings we can visit?

R Yes, there are lots of beautiful underground buildings in Coober Pedy. They aren't very far from the hotel, so you can walk up to most of them. I'll show you on the map.

A OK, I see. And is there a theatre in Coober Pedy?

R No, there aren't any theatres here, I'm afraid. But there is a cinema just near the hotel.

A Great, thank you very much. Well, I'm really hungry, so I think we should find a restaurant and have lunch.

R There are some really nice restaurants in the town centre. And they're quite cheap, too.

F Great! And after lunch we could go to the swimming pool.

4.3)))

1
A Is there a swimming pool?

B No, I'm sorry, there isn't. It doesn't rain a lot here, so there aren't many swimming pools.

2
A Are there any museums near the centre?
B Yes, there are. There's the opal mine museum.

3
A Is there a theatre in Coober Pedy?
B No, there aren't any theatres here.

4.4)))

I live in New York City in the Lower East Side District. My flat is very small, but the rent is $800 a month. It's a studio flat. There isn't a kitchen, dining room, living room, or bedroom. I cook, eat, relax and sleep in one room.

4.5)))

The flat's on the 4th floor of a building between Delancey Street and Grand Street. The building is opposite a 24-hour garage and next to an Indian restaurant, so there are always lots of cars and people in the street. The cars are quite noisy.

It's a studio flat with only one room. My bed is on a shelf above the kitchen. The toilet and shower are under the shelf. In the kitchen there's a sink, a fridge and a cooker, but there isn't a dishwasher or a washing machine – I go to the launderette on Grand Street to wash clothes. In front of the window, there's a red carpet on the floor and there's an armchair and table with a television on it. From the window, I can see the East River. It's behind the building.

4.6)))

It's very difficult to find a flat in New York. I'm very lucky. I like my flat because it's in the centre of the city. There are shops and restaurants all around me. The Lower East Side isn't the best district in the city, but my flat is near a theatre and it's also near the East River and a small park. One of the things I don't like about my flat is that there isn't a lift. Also, unfortunately, I'm not near the underground station, but there's a bus stop opposite the door of my building.

4.7)))

1 It's in the centre of the city.
2 It's near a theatre.
3 It's difficult to find a flat.

4.8)))

1 I live in a flat.
2 My flat is on the 5th floor.
3 There's a supermarket opposite my house.

4.9)))

1	difficult	h	easy
2	big	f	small
3	new	b	old
4	good	c	bad
5	clean	j	dirty
6	long	a	short
7	heavy	d	light
8	quiet	i	noisy
9	ugly	g	beautiful
10	old-fashioned	e	modern

4.10)))

S Excuse me, could you give me some directions, please?

A Yes, of course! How can I help you?
S Thanks! So, is there a chemist near here?
A Yes, there is. It's in the town centre.
S How do I get there?
A OK, well go out of the main door and turn left. Then go to the end of the road and turn left again.
S OK.
A Go straight on for about five minutes. Go past the internet café and the bank, and then turn left into Raya Andong. It's on the left, next to the supermarket.
S OK, thanks. Oh, and where's the palace?
A That's easy. It's at the end of this road on the corner. Here, take one of these maps. It has all the important places on it.
S Good idea!
A And we are just here.

4.11 》
1 Excuse me, is there a bank near here?
2 Excuse me, where's the library?
3 Excuse me, how do I get to the post office?
4 Go past the café.
5 It's on the left.
6 Turn right into Albert Street.
7 Take the second right.
8 Go straight on for about ten minutes.
9 Go to the end of this street.
10 It's on the corner.

4.12 》
A What's special about Neft Daşhlari?
B It's a town on an oil platform in the Caspian Sea.
A A town in the sea? Is it very small?
B No, not really. There are 300 km of streets and 2,000 people. And there are lots of things to do.
A Really? Are there any restaurants?
B Of course! There are some nice restaurants and hotels, and there's a cinema and a park, too.
A What about education? Is there a school?
B Yes, there's a school, but there isn't a university.
A So can people visit the place?
B No, there aren't any tourists. Only people who work on Neft Daşhlari can go there.

4.13 》
1 You go here when you are ill.
2 You can study here or take books home.
3 You can see a film here.
4 You usually need your passport to travel from here.
5 You can sleep here on holiday.
6 You can go here to have dinner.
7 There's lots of water and you can swim here.

4.14 》
1 modern
2 cheap
3 ugly
4 easy
5 quiet
6 long
7 big
8 clean

Unit 5 Clothes and shopping

5.1 》
1 I buy bread from the baker's.
2 I spend a lot of money at the weekends.
3 I buy magazines and newspapers from the newsagent's.
4 I buy meat from the butcher's.
5 I do a lot of my shopping online.
6 I get a discount because I'm a student.
7 I go shopping to a shopping centre. I prefer them to small shops.
8 When I buy something I don't like, I return it to the shop.
9 I stand outside and wait for the shops to open on the first day of the sales.
10 I pay for small things with cash.

5.2 》
Today the typical town centre is very different from in the 1970s. Then, you couldn't buy everything from one shop. People needed to go to different shops: the butcher's for meat, the baker's for bread and the newsagent's for their newspapers. Shopping took a long time! But there were good things. You could TALK to the people in the shops. Now it's easy to buy everything in the supermarket and in the shopping centre. But customers can't ask for information and chat to the shop assistant like they could in the past. In the 1970s you couldn't go shopping on the internet, but now you can buy almost everything online. Online shopping is cheap and easy, so it's difficult for the high street shops. Lots of them closed. I can't buy my bread and meat in the town centre now. But there are some things customers can't buy online. The internet can't cut your hair, for example, and it can't give you a cup of coffee. In the 1970s you couldn't get a cup of coffee on the high street, but there are five cafés here now – and three hairdresser's!

5.3 》
In positive sentences and questions *can* is pronounced /kən/ e.g.
A *Can you use euros in Norway and Sweden?*
B *I think you can use euros in Sweden but not in Norway.*
In short answers *can* is pronounced /kæn/.
Yes, you can.

5.4 》
A Can you use Euros in Norway and Sweden?
B Yes, you can.
C I think you can use them in Sweden but not in Norway.

5.5 》
1 People could buy things online in 1994. The first thing they could buy was pizza.
2 In the 1990s, rich people couldn't buy trips into space. But in 2001 Dennis Tito paid to visit the International Space Station.
3 Today you can buy eggs from vending machines in Japan. And you can also buy flowers, fruit and umbrellas and many other things.
4 You can buy a bottle of rainwater for $11 these days. The water comes from the sky, into a bottle and then you drink it. It never touches the ground.

5 You can't use euros in Norway and Sweden. They use the Norwegian Krone and the Swedish Krona.
6 People could buy things from machines in 1890. The first vending machines were in London in the 1880s and they sold postcards.
7 In the 1960s, you couldn't buy petrol at supermarkets. They started to sell petrol in the 1970s.
8 You can't buy clothes online from all the big fashion companies. For example, Chanel don't sell their clothes online because they believe customers need to try everything on.

5.6 》
1 Paul is wearing a suit.
2 Anita and Paul are having a meeting with their boss.
3 They aren't working today.

5.7 》
… And, of course, we don't all wear the same clothes every day. But most of us have a colour, or two colours, that we wear more than others. And the colours you choose to wear can say a lot about you as a person. Let's start with a very common colour: are you wearing black? People who often wear black like to be the boss. It can make you look serious and important. But what about the opposite? I'm wearing white today. If you often wear white clothes, there's a good chance that you like things to be tidy and clean, and you enjoy a simple life. Yes, that's true – I am a tidy person.

Another popular colour is blue. This means you are a peaceful person and you don't like change …

Now, how about some less common colours? Are you wearing red today? Do you often wear red? Well, the good news is that you are probably a strong person and you always try hard at everything you do.

Finally, who is wearing yellow? You are the good students because you love learning … and – this is important – you are a lot of fun! So, does any of this sound true to you? …

5.8 》
L Hello?
M Where are you?
L I'm in a clothes shop. Why?
M Because I need your help. What are you doing?
L What am I doing? What do people usually do in clothes shops? I'm buying clothes, of course.
M Well, are you nearly finished? I'm trying to cook a meal for six people, and the kids are making a lot of noise and the dog's running around and …
L Why are the kids there? They go to tennis practice on Thursdays.
M Not today because it's raining. They never play in the rain.
L OK, I'm paying now. I'll be back in an hour.
M An hour? Why …

5.9 》
hat	hate
not	note
man	main

5.11 🔊
1 That man is her husband.
2 Can I sit here?
3 He's not a teacher, he's a student.
4 I met my wife at university.
5 I have a red jacket.
6 Take off your coat, it's hot in here.

5.12 🔊

hate	main	sells
man	text	tin
boat	long	one
shop	jeans	thing
shut	take	page
cheap	stand	not
eat	press	note
live	sales	coat

5.13 🔊
/æ/ hat, man, stand
/eɪ/ play, hate, main, take, sales, page
/ɒ/ lot, shop, long, not
/ʌ/ cut, shut, one
/əʊ/ home, boat, note, coat
/e/ set, text, press, sells
/ɪ/ sit, live, tin, thing
/iː/ seat, cheap, eat, jeans

5.14 🔊
I hate shopping. Maybe it's because I'm a man, but I usually walk into a shop, choose something cheap, pay for it and leave quickly. The main problem is that it takes such a long time. But I'm here today to try the 'virtual mirror'. It's a new way to shop and it might change my life! I'm in a clothes shop and I need some jeans. But I don't need to take five pairs of jeans to the changing rooms. Instead, I just stand in front of this 'virtual mirror', press a button and it shows me in every pair of jeans the shop sells. I choose a pair, press a button and the mirror shows me wearing them! I press another button and the next pair appears. I can see myself in ten pairs in just one minute! And another thing: if I'm not sure, I press a button and a picture of me wearing the jeans goes to my Facebook page and my friends can say what they think. It's not difficult to use, and I can find the right jeans easily. So I make a note of the jeans I like, pay for them and go home!

The company behind the virtual mirror plans to put them in shops all around the world. So next time you need a new hat, top or coat, go to a shop with a virtual mirror!

5.15 🔊
1
A How much money do you earn?
B Not much, so I try to spend it carefully.
2
A What's the matter? Why do you look so scared?
B Because you're driving dangerously! Be careful!
3
A Why are you talking so quietly?
B Shhhh! Because we're in the library!
4
A I always get up late at weekends.
B Me too, at about ten o'clock.
5
A I can't see the television clearly.
B I think you need glasses.
6
A Maria answers every question correctly.
B I know. She's the best student in the class.
7
A Did you do well in your exam?
B I got an 'A'.

5.16 🔊
1
C Excuse me?
A Yes? How can I help?
C How much is this magazine?
A It's £4.99.
C Right ... and do you offer a student discount?
A Yes, we do. You get 20% off.
C Oh, that's good. Do you sell batteries?
A Yes, we do. What kind do you need?
C Erm ... AA, please. Just one packet.
2
A Can I help you?
C No, thanks. I'm just looking.
A Well, if you need anything, just ask.
C Can I try this hoodie on, please?
A Yes, of course. The changing rooms are over there.
3
C Two egg and tomato sandwiches and two coffees.
A That's £10.98, please.
C Can I pay by card?
A No, I'm afraid we only take cash.
C OK, that's fine.
A Would you like a bag?
C Yes, please. Just a small one.
A And would you like a receipt?
C Yes, please. Just put it in the bag.

5.17 🔊
1
A Can I help you?
B No, thanks. I'm just looking.
2
A Do you need a bag?
B Yes, please. Just a small one.
3
A Can I try this on, please?
B Of course. The changing rooms are over there.
4
A Can I pay by card?
B No, I'm afraid we only take cash.
5
A How much is this magazine?
B It's £4.99.
6
A Do you offer a student discount?
B Yes, we do. You get 20% off.
7
A Would you like a receipt?
B Yes, please. Just put it in the bag.
8
A Do you sell batteries?
B Yes, we do. What kind do you need?
9
A What time do you close?
B At eight o'clock.

5.18 🔊
1 I'm a student. Do I pay less?
2 Could I have a small chocolate cake, please? And what types of bread do you have?
3 I don't think we need to go to any other shops. This place has everything we need.
4 Excuse me, but these jeans are too small for me. Could you give me my money back, please?
5 Do you sell a magazine called 'Garden World'?
6 Look at this. It's half-price. Everything is so cheap!

Unit 6 The past

6.1 🔊
People were surprised to see a bobsleigh team from Jamaica at the 1988 Winter Olympics in Canada. It wasn't very easy for the team to practise in Jamaica before the Olympics because there was no ice and there were no bobsleighs for them to use. They weren't successful in their races, but they were very popular with the people watching because they tried so hard. There was a film telling their story in 1993 called *Cool Runnings* and it was a huge success, making $150,000,000 around the world.

6.2 🔊
1
A Was there a bobsleigh team at the Olympics?
B Yes, there was.
2
A Was it easy for them to practise?
B No, it wasn't.
3
A Were there bobsleighs for them to use?
B No, there weren't.
4
A Were they popular?
B Yes, they were.

6.3 🔊
1 The first football World Cup was in the last century, in 1930.
2 The first Olympic Games were about 2,800 years ago, in 776 BCE.
3 The first dishwasher was in the 19th century.
4 The first Sony Walkman was in 1979.
5 The first talking film was in 1927.
6 The first Oscars ceremony was in 1929.

6.4 🔊
Welcome to *The Money Programme*. Today we're talking about the history of money. These days most people use notes, coins and credit cards to buy things. But people in the past used different ways of paying for things.

The Ancient Egyptians liked wearing their money on their fingers as rings. The rings were made of gold. When they wanted to pay for something they pulled a ring or two off their fingers.

People in ancient Turkey were some of the first to use coins as money in the 7th century BCE. The Romans also used coins but added pictures of their emperors to them in the first century BCE. The Chinese put their coins on a piece of string to make them more valuable.

For hundreds of years, people around the world paid for things with salt. In fact, the word 'salary' comes from a Latin word that means 'money used to buy salt'. This is because the Romans sometimes paid their soldiers with salt.

The Lobi people of Ancient Ghana in Africa lived as farmers. Because they worked in the fields and there were a lot of snakes, they decided to make metal snakes and use them as money. They believed their snake money helped them to stay safe.

6.5 》
/d/ opened, returned, called
/t/ finished, looked, thanked
/ɪd/ started, collected, visited

6.6 》
copied   prepared
believed   received
liked   shouted
loved   used
moved   waited
noticed   wanted
posted   worked

6.7 》
/d/ copied, believed, loved, moved, prepared, received, used
/t/ liked, noticed, worked
/ɪd/ posted, shouted, waited, wanted

6.8 》
1
wait for a long time
wait for a friend
2
post a letter
post a comment on a webpage
3
enter a race
enter a competition
4
move to the countryside
move house
5
visit a museum
visit a relative
6
shout at your dog
shout at someone
7
prepare a meal
prepare for an exam
8
receive an email
receive a phone call
9
call a taxi
call an old friend
10
use a dictionary
use a tablet

6.9 》
1
A When was the last time you moved house?
B In 2010. From an apartment to a house.
2
A When was the last time you received an email?
B This morning. It was from my boss.

3
A When was the last time you prepared a meal?
B Last night. I cooked spaghetti for my housemate.
4
A When was the last time you posted a letter?
B A month ago. It was to my friend in Australia.
5
A When was the last time you shouted at someone?
B About a week ago. My son was very naughty.
6
A When was the last time you visited a relative?
B Last summer. I travelled to Kenya to see my grandmother.
7
A When was the last time you called a taxi?
B Yesterday. I was late for work.
8
A When was the last time you entered a competition?
B When I was a child. I was in a swimming race.
9
A When was the last time you used a dictionary?
B Last week. I checked the meaning of 'coin'.
10
A When was the last time you waited for a long time?
B Two hours ago. My bus was very late.

6.10 》
1 When was the last time you moved house?
2 When was the last time you received an email?
3 When was the last time you prepared a meal?
4 When was the last time you posted a letter?
5 When was the last time you shouted at someone?
6 When was the last time you visited a relative?
7 When was the last time you called a taxi?
8 When was the last time you entered a competition?
9 When was the last time you used a dictionary?
10 When was the last time you waited for a long time?

6.11 》
1 Five thousand people visited this gallery last month.
2 Fifty thousand people visit this gallery every year.

6.13 》
1 cooked
2 carried
3 change
4 helped
5 wait
6 listened
7 chatted
8 dance
9 enjoyed

6.14 》
1 My friends cooked a great meal for me last night.
2 A lot of people at work listen to the radio these days.

3 I helped my parents a lot when I was a child.
4 We dance a lot when we go out.
5 I waited a long time for the bus last Monday.
6 I washed the car carefully, it was really dirty.

6.15 》
From a distance, Inhotim looks like typical Brazilian countryside, but as you get closer, you notice something a bit unusual. There are hundreds of tourists walking through the fields and gardens! This beautiful place started as a farm and for many years only farmers lived here. They worked in the fields and looked after the animals. But that all changed in the 1990s when billionaire Bernardo Paz decided to use the space for something very different. He created a 'Disneyland for art lovers'! Today, people travel from around the world and they look at the art. The spaces of Inhotim include more than 500 sculptures by Brazilian and international artists. As well as being important culturally, it is really important for the local area because Inhotim creates a lot of jobs – 1,000 people work here in the museum, gardens and restaurant. Although it is quite far from the usual tourist spots of Brazil, it is now a very successful and popular 'outdoor museum'. In 2011, nearly a quarter of a million people visited Inhotim. Mr Paz believes there will soon be a million visitors a year.

6.16 》
S1 I visited Inhotim last week. My main reason for going was the art, and the sculptures were very interesting. The gardens were quite nice, too. However, the restaurants were really expensive. It was a bit difficult to find, too, and the journey was quite long.
S2 I travelled to Inhotim a couple of months ago. I thought the sculptures in the park were a bit boring, actually, but the gardens were really beautiful. The food was quite good at the restaurants. Oh, and the journey to the park was really long and I was very tired when I arrived.

6.17 》
1 … the sculptures were very interesting.
2 The gardens were quite nice, too.
3 I thought the sculptures in the park were a bit boring …
4 … the journey to the park was really long …

6.18 》
A … It was my Business Management class dinner on Saturday.
B That's great! How was it?
A I don't know. I didn't go.
B Oh no! Why not?
A Well, first I couldn't find my shoes.
B Really?
A Yeah … I looked everywhere. In the end I used my ordinary shoes. Then the bus was late. I waited for half an hour, but it never arrived!
B Oh no! That's awful!
A I know. After that it started to rain … so I called a taxi. And I waited and I waited… In the end I decided to walk home. I was just so wet by the time I got home.
B What a nightmare! Poor you!
A I know. I was really angry about it …

6.19 〕)
Responding to good news
That's brilliant! That's great! That's amazing!
Responding to bad news
That's terrible! That's awful! What a nightmare!
Oh no! Poor you!
Responding to interesting news
Really? That's interesting!

6.20 〕)
I remember my eighteenth birthday very well. It was on a Friday and I was really excited when I got home from college. I called out 'Mum? Dad?' But there was no answer. I walked into the living room. It was completely dark – I couldn't see anything! Then suddenly the lights came on and everyone was there! All my family and friends! And there was a huge birthday cake. I was really happy, but I couldn't see any presents. Then my dad told me to look behind the sofa and there they were – all my presents. A new tablet and a new suit – for my first job interview!

6.21 〕)
1 I passed my driving test!
2 I don't have a television.
3 My brother goes to a lot of job interviews, but he can't find a job.

Unit 7 Health and fitness

7.1 〕)
1 eat lots of fruit and vegetables
2 take the stairs, not the lift
3 walk to work
4 ride a bicycle
5 drink eight glasses of water a day
6 do an hour of exercise each day
7 sleep seven to eight hours a night
8 go to the gym or an evening class
9 do physical jobs around the house

7.2 〕)
come	came
make	made
do	did
eat	ate
drive	drove
give	gave
write	wrote
have	had
tell	told
take	took
think	thought

7.3 〕)
1 thought/bought/taught
2 got/chose/wrote
3 sat/went/had
4 came/made/ate
5 flew/took/put
6 met/said/slept

7.4 〕)
1 jog/run
2 go fishing
3 play football
4 play tennis
5 ski
6 swim
7 do yoga
8 go to the gym

9 do athletics
10 play basketball
11 cycle
12 do judo

7.5 〕)
In April 2011, Fauja Singh celebrated his 100th birthday. In October 2011, he ran the Toronto marathon and became the first person aged 100 years old to finish a marathon. But Fauja didn't run his first marathon until the year 2000. Why not? This is his story.

Fauja was born in Punjab in India. He grew up on the family farm with his parents and brothers and sisters. He wasn't a strong child and he had problems with his legs. He didn't walk before he was five years old. But he was happy and life was good after he learnt to walk. Later, Fauja got married and had six children. But his happy life didn't continue. Unfortunately, his wife and two of his children – a daughter and a son – died.

Fauja then moved to London to live with another son, but he wasn't happy. It wasn't easy to forget about his life in India. So he started to go running. When he ran, he didn't think about the past and didn't feel sad. Then in 2000, at the age of 89, he ran his first London Marathon in a time of 6 hours and 54 minutes. And he didn't stop then. From 2000 to 2011 he ran eight marathons. He said marathons changed his life and helped him feel happy again.

7.6 〕)
He didn't walk …
He didn't feel sad …

7.7 〕)
Fauja didn't run marathons when he was young.
He didn't have a lot of problems when he lived on his family's farm.
His happy life didn't continue after he had a family.
He didn't stop after his first marathon.

7.8 〕)
1 When he was a young boy, Usain Bolt didn't do athletics all the time. He played cricket and football.
2 In 2008, when he won the Olympic 100m final, he slowed down at the end and he broke the world record. His time was 9.96 seconds.
3 When he won the 100m final at the 2012 London Olympic Games, two billion people watched him on TV. American TV didn't show the race when it happened. They showed it later in the evening.
4 There was a thunderstorm during the 100m World Championship final in 2013. Lightning didn't hit him, but there was lightning in the sky.

7.9 〕)
1 Can you lend me your car for the weekend?
2 They watched basketball on TV last night.
3 Come here! I want to speak to you.
4 My colleague told me about a new restaurant in town.
5 Can you take this book to the library for me?
6 'I'm lost,' he said.

7 When Jacek looked at his phone during the meeting, I got very angry.
8 I didn't have a pen, so I borrowed one from my friend.
9 When you come to the party, can you bring something to drink?
10 Let's go to the beach tomorrow.

7.10 〕)
P People usually think that video games are bad for children's health. But new research says that perhaps this isn't true. At a school in Hedgesville, West Virginia, in the USA, students played video games in their gym class every week. Some children didn't enjoy exercise before, but with games like *Just Dance* and surfing on *Wii Sports Resort*, they started to enjoy their gym classes. Jan Hamilton and Sarah White, two local parents, are in the studio with me to discuss this.

7.11 〕)
P Jan and Sarah, you're both parents, what do you think of this idea?
J I think it's great. And it's a fun way to do exercise, too.
S Hmm … I don't know about that. Some video games aren't OK for children because they're very violent.
J Yes, but they didn't use violent games like that at the school. They were exercise games, like *Just Dance*.
S Well, for me, it depends on the game. But you're right, some games can be good. My son plays the football video game *FIFA* for hours and hours sometimes. But then he goes out to the park and plays football with his friends, and they try to do things they see on the video game.
P Yes, my son is the same. What's your opinion, Jan?
J Well, they want to be like their heroes.
S I agree with that. They certainly do. But do we want our children to be like their heroes?
P Well, an interesting discussion, but I'm afraid that's all we have time for today.

7.12 〕)
1 What do you think of this idea?
2 I think it's great.
3 I don't know about that.
4 Yes, but they didn't use games like that at the school.
5 Well, for me, it depends on the game.
6 You're right.
7 What's your opinion?
8 Yes, I agree with that.

7.13 〕)
The most popular sport in Argentina is football. People like playing it, going to games and watching it on TV. The Argentinian team won the World Cup in 1978 and 1986, and came second in 2014.

Basketball is also very popular, especially after Argentina won the semi-finals against the NBA players in 2004, and then took the Olympic gold home.

Tennis was a sport for rich people in the past, but now lots of people play it. The best Argentinian player, Juan Martín del Potro, is world number 8.

Winter sports are also very popular in Argentina, people often ski in the Andes Mountains. And of course lots of people jog in local parks or go to the gym to keep fit!

Unit 8 Travel and transport

8.1 》

1   I love lazy holidays. I normally rent an apartment by the sea with my family. We lie on the beach most of the day and go swimming in the sea. For me, the most important thing to do on holidays is to relax and have fun.

2   For me, holidays are about culture, and I enjoy visiting all the art galleries and museums. Sometimes I go on a tour with a guide because it's a great way to learn about a place and its history. I also like going out on my own and looking around the town without a map. I always get lost, but I think it's the best way to find interesting places.

3   We stay in cheap hotels and guest houses, and travel by public transport so we can meet local people. We don't go sightseeing. We prefer to trek in the mountains and visit places that tourists don't often see.

8.2 》

1   Do you like lying on the beach?
2   Do you visit art galleries and museums?
3   Do you usually take a map or do you get lost?
4   Do you like going on a tour of places you visit?
5   Do you prefer to stay in a hotel or rent an apartment?
6   Do you ever stay in expensive hotels?

8.3 》

K   Hey, Tom. So you went to Guatemala on holiday this time? Where is it exactly?
T   It's in Central America, to the south of Mexico.
K   Why did you go there?
T   Because it's a really interesting country. I wanted to go sightseeing and see some of the famous ruined Mayan cities and temples.
K   I see. And whereabouts in Guatemala did you go?
T   I visited the whole country. I started in Antigua – it's the historic capital – and then I went to Lake Atitlán, a beautiful lake in the mountains.
K   So what did you do and see?
T   I went on lots of tours, and I went trekking in the rainforest. My favourite thing was the ruins of a Mayan city in Tikal. They're in the middle of the rainforest and they're really beautiful. I climbed to the top of a temple at sunrise.
K   Wow! It sounds fantastic.
T   It was. I took a lot of pictures!
K   And how long did you stay?
T   About six weeks.
K   Did you stay in hotels?
T   No, mostly guest houses, and I also stayed with a Guatemalan family. They were lovely and it really helped me with my Spanish.
K   Did you go on your own?
T   Yes, I did, but I met lots of local people and I made lots of new friends.

8.4 》

1
K   Why did you go there?
T   Because it's a really interesting country.
2
K   Whereabouts in Guatemala did you go?
T   I visited the whole country.
3
K   What did you do and see?
T   I went on lots of tours and I went trekking.
4
K   How long did you stay?
T   About six weeks.
5
K   Did you stay in hotels?
T   No, mostly guest houses.
6
K   Did you go on your own?
T   Yes, I did, but I met lots of local people.

8.5 》

1   Where did you go on your last holiday?
2   Did you go with a friend?
3   What did you do?
4   Did you have a good time?
5   How long did you stay?
6   Where did you stay?
7   Did you like the food?

8.6 》

In past simple questions did + pronoun subject is usually unstressed.

We pronounce *did you* /dɪdʒə/, and *did he* /dɪdi/.

8.7 》

How long did you stay?
Did you like the food?
Did he stay in hotels?

8.8 》

1
M   I get the bus and the underground to work. It takes about forty minutes.
2
W   Most of the time, I go to work on foot. But if it's raining, I drive.
3
M   I go to work by car and it takes about an hour because there's a lot of traffic. I listen to music during the journey or I sometimes listen to CDs in English.
4
W   I go by bike to work. It's great exercise! But when it rains, I take the bus.
5
M   I usually take the train. Sometimes I get up late and I miss my train, so I have to get a taxi. I should get up earlier!

8.9 》

1   You take or get the train, the underground, a taxi or the bus.
2   You can miss the bus, your plane or your train.
3   You go on foot.
4   You go by public transport, by bike or by car.

8.10 》

1   You should have a map.
2   You shouldn't take a taxi.
3   You have to wear it.
4   You don't have to pay.

8.11 》

1   Did you have fun there?
2   How often do you have a sleep in the afternoons?
3   How many text messages do you get?
4   Do you want to get something to eat now?
5   Did he get a taxi last night?
6   Did it take her a long time to learn English?

8.13 》

1   Where did you have lunch?
2   Does he get lots of emails every day?
3   Why did you take the stairs?
4   Did he take photos last week?
5   How often do you get a taxi?
6   Did you take the bus on Sunday?

8.14 》

G   Guess what? I'm going to Moscow for two months.
H   Really? Is it for fun or do you have to work?
G   Well, a bit of both. You went to Moscow a few years ago, didn't you?
H   Yes, I did. I even lived there for a while.
G   How long did you live there?
H   Three years.
G   Oh, wow! And do you speak the language?
H   Yes, a little. I can buy things in shops and order food in restaurants.
G   And did you like the city?
H   Yes, it's great. I had a really good time.
G   What about things like accommodation and transport? What did you think of the transport system?
H   Well, the Underground is just … fantastic! It's really famous! It was built in the 1930s, and every station is a work of art.
G   But is it a good way to travel around Moscow?
H   Well, local people complain about it a lot, but I always thought it was very good. And it's quite cheap.
G   What about the buses? Do the local people use the buses?
H   Oh yes, the buses are usually full. But to be honest, I got taxis quite a lot to my lessons. I taught in companies and local businesses, so I didn't want to be late! You know, Moscow's like lots of other big cities: lots of traffic, really busy, sometimes the transport is good, other days not so good. But there is one great thing: you can simply stand in the street and stop any car, like a taxi, and they give you a lift for money.
G   Oh wow, that's cool! OK, so moving on to accommodation …

8.15 》

1   Do you have to work? (present)
2   How long did you live there? (past)
3   Do you speak the language? (present)
4   Did you like the city? (past)
5   What did you think of the transport system? (past)
6   Do the local people use buses? (present)

8.16 》

T   Hello. Can I help you?
M   Yes, please. I need to get to New Delhi.
T   OK. When would you like to travel?
M   Later today or tomorrow. When's the next train?
T   The next one leaves at 18.40 p.m.

M OK, and how long does it take?
T About seventeen hours. It arrives at 11.25 a.m. tomorrow.
M Right. How much is a sleeper ticket?
T Would you like a single or a return?
M Just a single, please.
T OK, then. That's 775 rupees.
M 775 rupees … OK. Which platform does it leave from?
T Platform 7.
M Thank you.

8.17 》
1 Can I help you?
2 When would you like to travel?
3 When's the next train?
4 How long does it take?
5 How much is a sleeper ticket?
6 Would you like a single or a return?
7 Which platform does it leave from?

8.18 》
1 You don't have to leave a tip in restaurants.
2 You shouldn't forget your umbrella.
3 Australians don't have to have a visa to visit.
4 You shouldn't go to Myers Park at night.
5 You have to get a student visa to study for more than 3 months.
6 You should visit the islands in the Hauraki Gulf.

8.19 》
A Hello. Can I help you?
B Yes, please. When's the next bus to Manchester?
A There's one at 4.00.
B How much does it cost?
A Do you want a single or return ticket?
B A return, please.
A And when would you like to come back?
B Next Sunday.
A OK, that's £32, please.
B How long does it take?
A Two hours 45 minutes. Here's your ticket.
B Where does it leave from?
A Bay six. It's just over there.

Unit 9 Cooking and eating

9.1 》
1 yoghurt
2 bread
3 a bottle of lemonade
4 salad
5 jam
6 chicken
7 honey
8 noodles
9 lemons
10 beef
11 rice
12 olives
13 sweetcorn
14 pasta
15 mushrooms
16 a pear

9.2 》
L Wow! Look at all this different food!
C I know. I can't decide what I want.
L Well there's some pizza over there.
C No! We can have pizza any day. Let's try something different.
L OK, what about this place?
C Mmm … that looks delicious, but what is it?
L Excuse me, what is this?
M It's Kung Pao chicken.
C It smells so good! What does it come with?
M It comes with some noodles.
C I don't really like noodles. Is there any bread?
M No, we don't have any bread, sorry. But we

have some rice.
C Great. So could I have a small Kung Pao chicken with some rice, please?
L And the same for me, but I'd like some noodles, please.
M OK, and would you like any drinks?
L Can I have a bottle of lemonade?
M We don't have any bottles of lemonade, I'm afraid. We have Coke or water.
L OK. Well, just a Coke, please.
C And for me, too.

9.3 》
1 It comes with some noodles.
2 Is there any bread?
3 We don't have any bread.
4 We have some rice.
5 Would you like any drinks?
6 We don't have any bottles of lemonade.

9.4 》
S Hello. Can I help you?
C Hi. Yes, please. Do you have any beef?
A Yes, we have some nice steaks here. We also have some small beef cubes.
B OK. Can I have some beef cubes? About a kilo, please. And I'd also like a small steak.
A Just one?
B Yes, just one. Thanks. Also, do you have any yoghurt?
A No, I'm afraid we don't.
B What about rice? Do you have any rice?
A Yes, we have some bags of rice, but we also do rice salad.
B No, I'll just have a bag of rice, please.
A OK. Anything else?
B Yes, do you have any lemons?
A No, we don't sell any fruit or vegetables, I'm afraid.
B OK. That's everything then, thanks.

9.5 》
1 Do you have any meat?
2 We have some beef.

9.6 》
1 I'd like some beef, please.
2 Do you have any mushrooms?
3 Can I have some sweetcorn?
4 We don't have any sweetcorn.

9.7 》
B Um … what do I have in my kitchen? Not much really! I have a kettle because I make a lot of tea. And I have one frying pan and two saucepans. I don't really need anything else. Oh! I forgot the most important thing in my kitchen – the microwave!
L Well there's nothing special about my kitchen. I have all the usual things. Oh, but I have a beautiful old set of plates and bowls for when people come for dinner. I have a lot of dinner parties!
J I love my kitchen. It's my favourite room in the house! I have a very modern oven and I use it a lot. I have an expensive food-processor, too – I use it to make soup. My flatmates sometimes get angry with me because I spend hours in the kitchen and they can't come in to cook their dinner!

9.8 》
1 an oven
2 a food-processor

3 a frying pan
4 a saucepan
5 a microwave
6 a kettle
7 a fork
8 a knife
9 a spoon
10 plates
11 bowls

9.9 》
1 You boil water in a kettle to make tea.
2 For breakfast I often fry eggs, mushrooms and tomatoes together in a big frying pan.
3 To roast meat, you need a very hot oven.
4 Mix the water and flour together in a bowl with a spoon.
5 Not many people bake their own bread or cakes at home these days.
6 You need to use a sharp knife to chop the onions.

9.10 》
1 Papua New Guinea is 160 kilometres north of Australia.
2 Singapore grows less than 10% of its food.
3 Papua New Guinea grows about three-quarters of its food.
4 Singapore got independence in 1965.
5 The coldest temperature ever recorded in Singapore was 19.4 degrees Celsius.
6 Less than a quarter of people in Papua New Guinea live in cities.

9.12 》
The first country we're going to look at today is Indonesia in South East Asia. It became independent in 1945 and now one of the most important days for the country is Independence Day on 17th August. There are 240 million Indonesians, and they live on 6,000 of its 18,110 islands. Java is only the fourth largest island, but 60% of Indonesians live on it. Two of the main cities are on Java: Jakarta, the capital of Indonesia, with 9.6 million people, and Surabaya, the second largest city, with 2.7 million.

9.13 》
Now, moving on, the country is 5,120 kilometres from east to west and 1,760 kilometres from north to south. Forty million Indonesians work on farms, which is 1/6 of all Indonesians. The climate is perfect for growing rice because the temperature is usually between 25 and 35 degrees Celsius, and there is 3,175 millimetres of rain a year. In mountain areas this can be 6,100 millimetres. Indonesia is the third largest rice growing country in the world, but it still imports about three million tonnes of rice a year.

9.14 》
Vocabulary Focus saying numbers
Fractions: a quarter (¼), a third (1/3), a half (½), three-quarters (¾), two-thirds (2/3), two fifths (2/5),
Percentages: fifteen per cent (15%), four point seven per cent (4.7%)
Decimals: two point eight nine (2.89), nought point three (0.3)
Temperatures: twenty-two degrees Celsius (22°C), minus seven (−7°C) / minus seven degrees Celsius

Dates: the first of September (1/9), the twenty-sixth of March (26/3)

9.15 》
1 seven point three five
2 the third of October twenty sixteen
3 four-fifths
4 sixteen point one degrees / sixteen point one degrees Celsius
5 eighty-two point four per cent
6 the twelfth of May nineteen eighty-six
7 minus fourteen / minus fourteen degrees Celsius
8 one and three-quarters

9.16 》
1 We're looking for a Thai restaurant.
2 You can sit outside on the roof.
3 What's your favourite café for lunch?
4 Do I need to book online?
5 Where's a good place to have some cake?
6 It has a wonderful menu.
7 You don't need to call them and book.
8 Do you know anywhere that has a garden?
9 There's a place called the Riverside with a nice view.
10 My favourite place is Café Blanc because it sells French food.

9.17 》
S Excuse me?
W Hi, would you like to order?
S Yes, please.
W OK. So, would you like a starter?
S No, thanks. Just a main course, please. Could I have the grilled chicken?
W Certainly. And would you like any side dishes with that?
S Um ... yes. Can I have some roast potatoes and some mixed green vegetables, please?
W Of course. And for you, madam?
M Could I have some fish cakes, please? This one ...
W The fish cakes, OK. And anything else?
M A tomato, olive and onion salad, thanks.
W And would you like something to drink?
M Yes, some sparkling water, please.
S And the same for me. Oh, and another question. Can we pay by credit card?
W Yes, of course. No problem!
S Oh, good. Thank you very much.

9.18 》
1 Would you like to order?
2 Could I have the grilled chicken, please?
3 Would you like any side dishes with that?
4 Can I have some roast potatoes?
5 Would you like something to drink?
6 Can we pay by credit card?

9.19 》
P Welcome to the program, Dr Zhang from the National Food and Health Group.
D Thank you.
P So, you're here today to talk about some interesting numbers about food.
D That's right. Firstly, do you know how many different types of tomato there are in the world? Well, some people say 10,000, but other people say there are about 25,000.
P Oh, really?
D Yes. And staying with fruit, when you're watching your calories, try a lemon. There

are only 17 calories in a lemon.
P Only 17? And what about milk?
D Well, it's surprising to hear that a cup of 2% fat milk contains 12.3 grams of sugar – that's about 50 calories.
P That's a lot of calories. How much does the average American eat every year?
D The answer to that was 891 kilograms of food in 2011.
P Wow! That's huge. And there's time for just one more fact.
D Well, I think we should finish in Italy – a country of coffee lovers. They drink 14 billion cups every year. That's over 200 cups for every man, woman and child in the country.
P Well, some of those numbers are amazing. Dr Zhang, thank you very much for coming today ...

9.20 》
1 twenty-one degrees Celsius
2 two-thirds
3 forty-five point five per cent
4 two million four hundred and seventy-eight thousand

9.21 》
W Would you like to order?
C Could I have the baked fish, please?
W Would you like a side dish with that?
C Could I have some roast potatoes, please?
W And would you like something to drink?
C Do you have any apple juice?
W No, we don't.
C OK, just a bottle of water, please.

Unit 10 The world around us

10.1 》
1
So, in Lisbon today it's cloudy this morning but dry, and we don't expect any rain. By the afternoon it's going to be warm and sunny, but not really hot, with temperatures of around 20 degrees Celsius.

2
It was great. We loved Malaysia. We went in the wet season, so we had some storms. The first night we arrived, it was really windy and there was a big storm with very loud thunder and lightning. But most of the time during the day it was lovely.

3
N Let's now go to Rupinder in Chicago. Hello, Rupinder. How's the weather there?
R Well Mike, it's freezing here today. There was a lot of snow last night and the roads are very icy. It's cold and foggy now, and there is more snow to come later today.

10.2 》
snow, to snow, snowy
rain, to rain, rainy
sun, to shine, sunny
wind, to blow, windy
ice, to freeze, icy/freezing
fog, foggy

10.3 》
When we make a comparative sentence, we say *than* with a weak sound /ðən/.

The nights are colder than the days.
Is spring wetter than summer?

10.4 》
1 Is Dublin drier than Paris?
2 Is Sydney bigger than Cairo?

10.5 》
1
A Which city is drier, Dublin or Paris?
B It's close: both cities have a lot of rain, but Dublin's wetter.
2
A Which is bigger, the population of Sydney or Cairo?
B Well, Cairo's population is bigger than Sydney's. Cairo has a population of over nine million, but Sydney's is smaller at just over four and a half million.

10.6 》
1
A Are Indian elephants heavier than African elephants?
B No, they aren't. African elephants are heavier than Indian elephants.
2
A Is Tokyo more expensive than Singapore?
B Yes, it is. Both places are quite expensive, but Tokyo is more expensive than Singapore.
3
A Are giraffes faster than humans?
B Yes, they are. Giraffes can run at 35 miles an hour which is faster than any human being.
4
A Is Canada bigger or smaller than the USA?
B Canada is slightly bigger than the USA.
5
A Is the North Pole colder than the South Pole?
B No, it's warmer. The South Pole is colder than the North Pole.

10.7 》
a Mount Kilimanjaro is in Tanzania in East Africa. Its name means 'mountain of light' and it's a very beautiful place. It's the highest mountain in Africa, but it's not difficult to climb.
b Victoria Falls are beautiful! It's a very big waterfall on the Zambezi River between Zimbabwe and Zambia.
c Lake Baikal is in the south of Siberia in Russia. It's the biggest and deepest lake in the world, but it often freezes in winter because Siberia has a very cold climate.
d The Amazon Jungle is the biggest area of rainforest in the world. It is mostly in Brazil, but some parts of it are in other South American countries such as Ecuador, Peru and Bolivia. About half the world's plants and animals live in rainforests.
e The Andaman Sea has some very beautiful tropical islands, with white sandy beaches, near the west coast of Thailand. The biggest and most famous is Phuket.
f The Gobi Desert is a very large desert in north-west China and Mongolia. It's a cold desert because it's so far north and it sometimes snows there.

10.8 》
1 Lake Baikal is in the south of Siberia.
2 The Gobi Desert is in north-west China and Mongolia.
3 Phuket island is near the west coast of Thailand.

10.9))
Lake Baikal in Siberia is the biggest, deepest and oldest lake in the world. It's more than 1,600 metres deep and more than twenty-five million years old. It has almost twenty per cent of the world's freshwater, and thousands of different kinds of plants and animals live there.

Mount Kilimanjaro, in Tanzania, is one of the largest volcanoes in the world. It's 5,895 metres tall – the highest mountain in Africa. It's sometimes called the 'Roof of Africa'. It's also one of the easiest mountains in the world to climb, even for tourists. The oldest person ever to climb to the top was a Frenchman, Valtee Daniel, who was eighty-seven years old.

An oasis is an area of water in a desert, and Al Hasa is the largest oasis in Saudi Arabia. It covers over 12 km² and gives water to over three million trees and a million people, even at the hottest times of the year. Many Saudis believe Al Hasa is the most beautiful and best area to visit in the country.

10.10))
We say *the* in superlatives with a weak sound /ðə/ when the following adjective starts with a consonant. We say the ending *-est* with a schwa sound /əst/.

10.11))
A Which river's the longest in the world?
B I think the Nile's the longest.
C Maybe, but I think the Amazon is longer than the Mississippi.

10.12))
1 The busiest airport of the three is Beijing, then Dubai and then Los Angeles.
2 Of these islands, Greenland is the biggest, and Madagascar is bigger than Sumatra.
3 The Great Pyramid of Giza isn't the oldest monument in the world, but it's the oldest in this group. It's older than the Parthenon, and the Parthenon's older than the Colosseum.

10.13))
1 Is there usually heavy traffic on your way to this class?
2 Did you have a high score in your last test?
3 Do you like strong coffee?
4 Which jobs usually have the lowest salaries?
5 Are you a deep sleeper?

10.14))
A OK, so we can take a tent and sleeping bag each and we need to decide on the five most important things to take as well.
T Well, we need cooking equipment – we have to eat – but I think we should take one stove instead of three because we don't need one each.
A I think a lighter is more important than a stove because we can make a fire for cooking with wood from the forest.
Z I'm sorry, but I don't agree. Taking a stove is a better idea than making a fire because what happens if it rains? If we have the lighter and the stove – then we can cook inside the tent.
A OK, so a stove, lighter and cooking equipment makes three things. We can have two more.

Z Well, we need to find our way to the camp. I think a map and compass are the most useful things for this because a GPS could break or run out of battery.
A But that's two more things and we can't have any more than that. What happens if we need the first-aid kit? I'd prefer to take the GPS instead of the map and compass because then we can have the first-aid kit.
T But what about the torch? I don't like the forest at night time!
A It gets dark quite late, and we should to go bed early after a long day walking in the forest, so I don't think we need the torch.
Z OK, let's take the GPS and the first-aid kit.
T OK.
A Good idea.

10.15))
1 I think a compass is better than a GPS.
2 I'd prefer to stay in a hotel.
3 The most important thing to take is food.
4 I think we should take only one torch.
5 Taking a first-aid kit is more important than taking a knife.
6 I'd prefer to have my own tent.

10.16))
1 Bangkok is hotter than Cairo.
2 Canberra is foggier than London.
3 The pollution is worse in New Delhi than in Beijing.
4 Damascus is older than Rome.
5 Ottawa is snowier than Moscow.
6 Tokyo has a bigger population than Mexico City.

Unit 11 Working together

11.1))
1 organize a party
2 give a present to someone
3 repair your friend's bike
4 visit someone in hospital
5 make a cake for a colleague's birthday
6 help a classmate with their homework
7 plant some flowers
8 look after a friend's children for the evening
9 teach someone to drive
10 improve your local area by picking up rubbish

11.2))
1 We aren't going to use any electricity or use the car tomorrow. I'm going to walk to work and … Arturo? Are you going to cycle to work tomorrow morning? Yes, my husband's going to work by bike.
2 Next Saturday, I'm going to organize a game of football for the kids around here. We're going to sell tickets and give all the money to charity.
3 What am I going to do on Mandela Day? Well, I've got a neighbour and he's unemployed at the moment. I know he's a bit unhappy about it so I'm going to help him find work. We're going to improve his CV and spend the day sending emails to companies.

11.3))
I So, how are the plans for this year's Mandela Day?

O Great, thanks! We're getting emails from people all around the world telling us how they're going to celebrate the day.
I That's good to hear. So what is everyone going to do?
O Oh, all sorts of things. A lot of people are going to make soup and sandwiches and give them to homeless people. I had an email from a man yesterday – he isn't going to eat for 24 hours and he's going to collect money for his local hospital. And, of course, we're going to post everything on our website for people to see.
I Are you going to have time to do something yourself?
O No, I'm afraid I'm not going to have much time at all. But we are going to have a big party here at the office and everyone needs to buy a ticket to come. And all the money goes to charity, of course.

11.4))
In sentences with *going to* we do not usually stress *to*.
We're going to /tə/ *look after a friend's daughter.*
Are you going to /tə/ *visit someone in hospital?*
In negative sentences, we stress *not/aren't/isn't*.
I'm not going to /tə/ *organize an event.*

11.5))
1 We're going to organize a party.
2 I'm not going to visit my family this weekend.
3 What are you going to do for Mandela Day?

11.6))
1 I have a smartphone, so I can use the internet when I'm out.
2 I often buy apps for my phone.
3 I take my tablet everywhere, so I can work or study when I'm not at home.
4 I check the news every day on my favourite newspaper website.
5 I have GPS on my phone because I drive to lots of different places for work.

11.7))
www.allinoneshopping.hu/personal
www.thefamouswebsite.org/join-in
k.m.customer-contact@cateringbizz.com
ania_cart9219@yahoo.co.uk

11.8))
1 I go geocaching to keep fit. I choose caches in the countryside and I walk for miles to find them! It's better than going to the gym.
2 I do it to meet new people. I go on to the website and I arrange to meet them in a café in town and then we look for the cache together. I met my best friend geocaching!
3 Well, it's a good way to find some interesting places. Yeah, I go geocaching to see different places.
4 Why do I go geocaching? That's a good question. Um … because I really enjoy it. I love running around looking for presents. It's like being a kid again!

11.9))
1 I go geocaching to keep fit.
2 I do it to meet new people.
3 I go geocaching to see different places.

11.10))
1
A Were you very glad to get the job?
B Of course! I was really delighted!
2
A Was the weather very nice on your holiday?
B Yes, it was really lovely! We were very lucky.
3
A Is she very good at tennis?
B Yes, she's really excellent! She always wins.
4
A What's wrong? You don't look very happy.
B It's really awful! I failed my driving test.
5
A Let's use my car. Your car is too small for five people.
B You're right. My car is really tiny!

11.11))
Conversation 1
A So, Ryan and Jan made a list of questions to ask Dr Pedersen.
B Oh, that's great. Can I see it?
A Yeah, of course. We've got five main questions so far …
B I see, yes, these are really good. I'd like to know about the types of questions in the exam too. Shall I write that down?
A Yes, good idea. And when are we going to ask Dr Pedersen about all this?
C I'm going to have a meeting with him this afternoon. Why don't I give him the list then?
A Yes, that's perfect, Shaz. Then we can talk about it in class tomorrow. Now, the next thing is the homework …
Conversation 2
A So I'll read the list and if anyone would like to do something, please just say. Is that OK?
B I'll take notes so we don't forget.
A Thank you. That's very helpful. OK, first there's the problem with rubbish in the park.
C Oh, shall I do that? I go to the park every day anyway.
A Thank you, Janek.
B Let me help you with that, Janek. It's a big park.
C Thanks.
A Great! What's next? Ah yes, we need someone to paint the walls of the school.
D Oh, my husband and his brother could probably do that. Would you like me to ask them?
A Yes, that would be very helpful, thank you. Now, then …

11.12))
1 Shall I write that down?
2 Why don't I give him the list then?
3 I'll take notes so we don't forget.
4 Let me help you with that.
5 Would you like me to ask them?

11.13))
M Do you have any New Year's Resolutions this year?
W Yeah, I'm going to spend less time at work.
M Really? Are you going to spend more time with your friends and family?
W Yes, I want to spend more time with my brother because he's going to move next year.
M Really? Is he going to look for a new apartment?

W Oh, I didn't tell you. He's going to move to Italy.
M Wow! Great! Are you and Johan going to visit him?
W That's my other resolution. We're not going to join a gym this year because it's too expensive. So we're going to save some money for a trip to Italy instead!

11.14))
1 He got up early to paint the living room.
2 She's going to move to Greece to teach English.
3 I go to Bob's house every weekend to look after his dog.
4 I went to my parents' house to repair my Mum's car.
5 I'm going to call all our friends to organize a birthday party for my best friend.
6 We're going to buy some eggs and sugar to make a cake.
7 I'm going to take the afternoon off work tomorrow to visit my aunt in hospital.
8 I went to the garden to plant some flowers.

11.15))
1 What are we going to have for lunch?
2 I want to go out tonight, but I can't.
3 I can't speak much Japanese.
4 I'm really busy at the moment.
5 I broke my washing machine last night.

Unit 12 Culture and the arts

12.1))
Nobuyuki Tsujii was born blind, but he started playing on a toy piano at the age of just two. He began learning the piano two years later, and he gave his first big concert in Tokyo when he was twelve years old. He's in his twenties now, but he has given concerts all over the world, and he has won many prizes and international competitions. He has written music for film and TV, too. He hasn't seen the written music, but he has learnt to play some of the most difficult pieces of music in the world only through sound. His classical music fans have said this is amazing.

12.2))
In the present perfect, the stress is on the past participle in positive sentences, and on *haven't/hasn't* in negative sentences.
1 *He's given concerts …*
2 *… he hasn't seen the written music …*

12.3))
1 He's sold them all over the world.
2 He hasn't opened a gallery in New York.
3 This hasn't stopped her dream of dancing.
4 Thousands of people have watched her.

12.4))
P I've always loved music. I don't play an instrument, but I've always wanted to play in a band. I like pop music, rock and jazz, and since I was a child I've had a big music collection. In my free time I often go to rock concerts and I usually go to two or three music festivals a year. I haven't been to a classical music concert before, but I'm going to my first one next week!
J My parents are artists, so I've had lots

of drawing and painting lessons. I enjoy painting a lot and I often do it in my free time. I like going to art galleries, too. I also like writing – I've started writing two or three books, but I haven't finished any of them!
A I had dance lessons at school, but I wasn't very good, so I stopped going. But I've always wanted to dance, so I've started going to salsa classes. I love it! I also enjoy going to the theatre to see plays, and especially to see musicals. I live in a big city, so I've been to see all the big musicals – they're fantastic!

12.5))
1 go to the cinema / go to the theatre
2 go to a music festival
3 go to a salsa class
4 go to art galleries
5 go to a rock concert / go to a classical music concert
6 go to the opera
7 see a film / see a movie
8 see a play
9 see a musical
10 play the guitar
11 play in a band
12 have music lessons
13 have painting lessons
14 have dance lessons
15 have drawing lessons
16 have singing lessons

12.6))
1 Sometimes you don't want to look because they are scary, e.g. *The Blair Witch Project*, *Dracula* films.
2 They tell a love story e.g. *Titanic*, *Gone with the Wind*.
3 You laugh at them because they are funny, e.g. *Mr Bean*, *The Mask*.
4 They tell a story about something that happens in people's lives and sometimes they are very sad e.g. *The Help*, *Forrest Gump*.
5 People fight and drive fast cars, e.g. *Speed*, *James Bond* films.
6 They have spaceships and are set on other planets or they're about the future, e.g. *Avatar*, *Star Wars* films.
7 They don't have real people and nowadays they're usually made with computers, e.g. *Shrek*, *Finding Nemo*.
8 People sing and dance, e.g. *Mamma Mia*, *Grease*.

12.7))
1 horror films
2 romantic films
3 comedies
4 dramas
5 action films
6 science fiction films
7 animations
8 musicals

12.8))
1 My favourite film is *Titanic*. It's a drama, but also a love story, and it stars Kate Winslet and Leonardo DiCaprio. It's about a huge ship and all the people on it.

2 The film that's made more money than any other in the world is *Avatar*. It's a science fiction film and it's set in the future.

12.9))
I Have you ever left the cinema early?
S1 Oh yes! I've left in the middle of a lot of films. I don't want to sit in a cinema watching something really bad – life's too short!
S2 I've never left the cinema early, but I've often wanted to. A few months ago, I went to see a terrible film. Someone walked out every five minutes. At the end of the film, I was the only person left! But I think you have to watch the whole film or you don't know if it's good or bad!
S3 Yes, I have. I walked out once – it was last summer and it was a beautiful day. The film was really boring, so I just decided to leave.
S4 No, I haven't, but I've fallen asleep in a lot of cinemas! When the lights go out, and the seats are comfortable, and the film is slow, then I just can't stay awake! I've never walked out of a film, though. I think it's rude to other people who are watching.

12.10))
1
I've never left the cinema early, but I've often wanted to.
2
A few months ago, I went to see a terrible film.
3
A Have you ever left the cinema early?
B Yes, I have. I walked out once – it was last summer and it was a beautiful day.

12.11))
I So Pavel, you're here for the Rio de Janeiro film festival. Have you visited Brazil before?
P Yes, I have – twice. Actually, I came here when I was a child and I was here three years ago for work, too.
I Interesting. And what about you, Wanda? Have you ever been to Rio before?
W No, I've never been here before, but it's a beautiful city.
I I'm very pleased to hear that! So, I saw your latest film *Inbox Me* last night and I thought it was really wonderful.
P Well, thank you very much!
I And everyone else in the cinema enjoyed it, too. When it finished, people stood up and clapped – I couldn't believe it!
P Really? I'm delighted to hear that. A lot of people have said some lovely things about it.
W Last week someone told me it was their favourite film of the year!
I Great! So, tell me …

12.12))
1 I opened the door.
2 I've opened the door.
3 She's run a marathon.
4 She ran a marathon.
5 We've met him.
6 We met him.
7 I've watched *Star Wars* twice this month.
8 I watched *Star Wars* twice last month.

12.14))
P Good evening. Our guest tonight is Mark Russell, who is going to talk about the Indian film industry, Bollywood, and one of its biggest stars. Mark, welcome.
M Thanks, Steffi.
P Tell us a little bit about Bollywood. Many of us have heard of it, but perhaps we don't all know much about it. Is it bigger than Hollywood these days?
M Yes, it is. In the last ten years, Bollywood has made more films and it's sold more tickets, too. For example in 2009, Bollywood produced over 1,200 films and Hollywood made only about 500. Also, Bollywood films have become popular all over the world and they've made them in lots of countries.

12.15))
M One of the biggest names in Bollywood is Hema Sardesai.
P I've never heard of her. Is there a reason for that?
M Well, she's a playback singer. This means that she records the songs that other actors use in their films. The actors move their mouths, but they are not singing. The voice is really the voice of a playback singer like Hema.
P So we never see her.
M Not exactly. She's recorded playback songs for over sixty Bollywood films, but she's also had a few successful albums. Also, she's been in shows all over India, and she's visited a lot of different countries.
P So, she's quite famous in India outside Bollywood?
M Oh, yes. When India celebrated fifty years of independence, she sang her own song and three million people watched her live.

12.16))
F Hello?
M Hi Francis, it's Marcus. Is Caitlin there?
F She's not here at the moment.
M OK, well can you tell her to call me back, please?
F Yes, sure. Oh wait, she's just come back. Hang on a minute. I'll just get her.
C Hi, Marcus.
M Hi, Caitlin. Have you booked tickets for the comedy club tonight?
C No, I haven't. Their website said they're sold out tonight.
M Oh no. Well why don't you call them and ask about returned tickets? Sometimes people return tickets because they can't go.
C Oh yes, I didn't think of that. Good idea! I'll call them now and I'll call you back in a minute.
M Thanks, Caitlin. Speak soon.
C OK. Bye.
R Good afternoon, Phoenix Comedy Club. How can I help you?
C Hello. Could I speak to the ticket office manager, please?
R I'm afraid he's not available at the moment. Can I help?
C Maybe. I'm calling about the show tonight. Your website says it's sold out, but has anyone returned any tickets?

R Oh, I'm not sure. You'll need to speak to the ticket office manager about that.
C Right, well could you ask him to call me back, please?
R Yes, of course. Could I have your number, please?
C Yes, it's 0 … 7 … 5 …

12.17))
1 Hi Francis, it's Marcus. Is Caitlin there?
2 Hello. Could I speak to the ticket office manager, please?
3 She's not here at the moment.
4 I'm afraid he's not available at the moment.
5 Can you tell her to call me back, please?
6 Could you ask him to call me back, please?
7 Could I have your number, please?
8 Hang on a minute. I'll just get her.

12.18))
A Right Insurance. How can I help you?
B Hello. Could I speak to Ms Martinez, please?
A One moment, please. I'm afraid she's out of the office at the moment. Would you like to leave a message?
B No, that's fine. I'll call back later.
A Ok, thank you.
B Thanks. Bye.

12.19))
These days, Verona coliseum is famous for its opera festival, but it has been a place to see other types of entertainment over the years. The Romans built the coliseum almost two thousand years ago for sports and games called 'ludi'. The most famous of these games were fights between gladiators. These events were very popular and people came from far away to see them. In 1117, there was a big earthquake in Verona and people didn't use the coliseum for a long time. However, centuries later, the Venetians decided to repair the building and use it for concerts. From that time, hundreds of thousands of people have come to Verona to listen to music and many famous opera singers and ballet dancers have performed there.

173

Irregular verbs

Infinitive	Past simple	Past participle
be	was/were	been
become	became	become
begin	began	begun
break	broke	broken
bring	brought	brought
build	built	built
buy	bought	bought
can	could	been able to
catch	caught	caught
choose	chose	chosen
come	came	come
cost	cost	cost
cut	cut	cut
do	did	done
draw	drew	drawn
drink	drank	drunk
drive	drove	driven
eat	ate	eaten
fall	fell	fallen
feel	felt	felt
find	found	found
fly	flew	flown
forget	forgot	forgotten
get	got	got
give	gave	given
go	went	gone/been
grow	grew	grown
have	had	had
hear	heard	heard
keep	kept	kept

Infinitive	Past simple	Past participle
know	knew	known
learn	learnt/learned	learnt/learned
leave	left	left
lose	lost	lost
make	made	made
meet	met	met
pay	paid	paid
put	put	put
read	read	read
ride	rode	ridden
run	ran	run
say	said	said
see	saw	seen
sell	sold	sold
send	sent	sent
sing	sang	sung
sit	sat	sat
sleep	slept	slept
speak	spoke	spoken
spend	spent	spent
stand	stood	stood
swim	swam	swum
take	took	taken
teach	taught	taught
tell	told	told
think	thought	thought
understand	understood	understood
wear	wore	worn
win	won	won
write	wrote	written

Phonemic symbols

Single vowel sounds

/iː/	tree /triː/	/ə/	computer /kəmˈpjuːtə/
/ɪ/	his /hɪz/	/ɜː/	learn /lɜːn/
/i/	happy /ˈhæpi/	/ɔː/	four /fɔː/
/ʊ/	good /gʊd/	/æ/	hat /hæt/
/u/	usual /ˈjuːʒuəl/	/ʌ/	sunny /ˈsʌni/
/uː/	school /skuːl/	/ɑː/	car /kɑː/
/e/	ten /ten/	/ɒ/	clock /klɒk/

Diphthongs (double vowel sounds)

/ɪə/	near /nɪə/	/ɔɪ/	boy /bɔɪ/
/ʊə/	tour /tʊə/	/aɪ/	try /traɪ/
/eə/	wear /weə/	/əʊ/	so /səʊ/
/eɪ/	train /treɪn/	/aʊ/	out /aʊt/

Consonant sounds

/p/	pen /pen/	/s/	see /siː/
/b/	big /bɪg/	/z/	lazy /ˈleɪzi/
/t/	tea /tiː/	/ʃ/	shower /ˈʃaʊə/
/d/	do /duː/	/ʒ/	television /ˈtelɪvɪʒn/
/tʃ/	children /ˈtʃɪldrən/	/m/	man /mæn/
/dʒ/	journey /ˈdʒɜːni/	/n/	never /ˈnevə/
/k/	cat /kæt/	/ŋ/	sing /sɪŋ/
/g/	go /gəʊ/	/h/	hot /hɒt/
/f/	fly /flaɪ/	/l/	like /laɪk/
/v/	very /ˈveri/	/r/	river /ˈrɪvə/
/θ/	thing /θɪŋ/	/w/	water /ˈwɔːtə/
/ð/	this /ðɪs/	/j/	yes /jes/

OXFORD
UNIVERSITY PRESS

Great Clarendon Street, Oxford, OX2 6DP,
United Kingdom

Oxford University Press is a department of the
University of Oxford. It furthers the University's
objective of excellence in research, scholarship,
and education by publishing worldwide. Oxford
is a registered trade mark of Oxford University
Press in the UK and in certain other countries

© Oxford University Press 2015

The moral rights of the author have been asserted

First published in 2015

2019 2018 2017 2016 2015

10 9 8 7 6 5 4 3

ISBN: 978 0 19 456523 3

Printed in China

This book is printed on paper from certified
and well-managed sources.

ACKNOWLEDGEMENTS

*The publisher would like to thank the following for
permission to reproduce photographs*: Alamy Images
pp.6 (London skyline/Stefano Baldini), 6 (Dubai/
Gavin Hellier), 11 (pencil/incamerastock),
11 (watch/Zoonar GmbH), 11 (dictionaries/David
Lee), 11 (businessmen/Juice Images), 11 (shoe
box/travellinglight), 11 (kids/Blend Images),
11 (hairbrush/Stock Experiment), 11 (glasses/
Digifoto Sapphire), 11 (knife/Winston Link),
11 (umbrella/Andrzej Tokarski), 12 (word cloud/
Marek Uliasz), 14 (Brighton Pavilion Royal
pavilion/eye35.pix), 15 (young man outdoors/
Maria Vazquez), 16 (seals on iceberg/Niebrugge
Images), 18 (Euro Space Centre/Falkensteinfoto),
19 (striped flannel/Dorling Kindersley ltd), 19 (red
sleeping bag/Oleksiy Maksymenko), 19 (sunrise
from space/Johan Swanepoel), 22 (Seoul, South
Korea/age fotostock Spain, S.L.), 23 (Paris cafe/Ian
Dagnall), 23 (Lagos harbour/Prisma Bildagentur
AG), 24 (Obelisk, Buenos Aires/Keren Su/China
Span), 26 (woman holding briefcase/OJO Images
Ltd), 26 (man repairing car/Wavebreak Media
ltd), 26 (photographer Celal Teber/Emin Ozkan),
26 (aeroplane pilot/ambrozinio), 26 (hairdresser/
Keith Morris), 26 (boy studying/TongRo Images),
29 (sticky note ideas/Image Source), 30 (senior
woman on laptop/B.A.E. Inc.), 31 (teacher in
classroom/Stockbroker), 32 (man in wheelchair in
library/Blend Images), 36 (underground living room/
Andrew Watson), 37 (underground city, Montreal/
Forray Didier/Sagaphoto.com), 39 (downtown
Manhattan/Kevin Browne), 43 (Garden Denpensar),
44 (Dubai/imageBROKER), 49 (young woman
portrait/Glow Asia RF), 49 (businesswoman at
desk/Norman Pogson), 49 (senior man portrait/

CCGP), 49 (full-length portrait man/Hongqi Zhang),
49 (confident man portrait/Andres Rodriguez),
53 (mountain bike/Oleksiy Maksymenko),
54 (Primark store/Kathy deWitt), 54 (vintage
market/Don Tonge), 54 (Camden Lock Market/
LH Images), 59 (man unloading lorry/Richard
Wareham Vervoer), 61 (sculptures, Brazil/Arcaid
Images), 62 (taxi roof sign/Russell Kord), 62 (man
sheltering rain/Cultura Creative), 63 (young
woman portrait/fotofreaks), 63 (using laptop as
shelter/Radius Images), 63 (man funny face/Hongqi
Zhang), 63 (scared face/Franck Camhi), 63 (wacky
headshot/Eric Anthony Johnson), 63 (portrait
man/Franck Camhi), 63 (funny face/Jeff Smith),
64 (cruise ship/Jake Lyell), 67 (vitamin supplements/
Keith Leighton), 74 (gym/Emmanuel Lattes),
74 (highline/Stacy Walsh Rosenstock), 78 (traffic/
Caro), 78 (woman/Sarah Hadley), 79 (traffic jam,
Hanoi/Tom Corban), 79 (Rickshaw in Vietnam/LOOK
Die Bildagentur der Fotografen GmbH), 81 (metro
station, Moscow/Dominic Harris), 82 (Kolkata
railway station/Neil McAllister), 83 (fishing nets,
Kerala/Robert Preston Photography), 87 (Italian
pizza stall/Michael K Berman-Wald), 87 (Chinese
food stall/Peter Phipp/Travelshots.com), 88 (woman
looking at recipe book/ONOKY – Photononstop),
91 (3d red figures/Sergey Nezhinkiy), 94 (pizza/Liv
Friis-Larsen), 94 (bread ingredients/Bon Appetit),
96 (lightning strike/Dennis Hallinan), 100 (polar
bear/IML Image Group Ltd), 103 (elephant safari/
John Warburton-Lee Photography), 103 (Victoria
Falls/Gary Cook), 104 (Grand Canyon/RGB Ventures/
SuperStock), 104 (Grand Canyon/AlamyBest),
106 (planting tree/Richard Levine), 107 (football/
Frank Paul), 109 (Easter Island statue/Galina
Barskaya), 113 (group Bible study/Design Pics Inc.),
113 (planning meeting/Jason Smalley Photography),
114 (wheat field/Nigel Cattlin), 114 (King's College/
John Kershaw), 114 (PCB repair/Sergey Kuznetsov),
120 (Glastonbury festival/Roger Cracknell 16/
Glastonbury), 120 (receptionist working at
computer/Hero Images Inc.), 120 (university
students studying/Ammentorp Photography),
122 (red retro telephone/stockshot), 123 (young
band/Datacraft – QxQ images), 123 (circus acrobats/
Larry Lilac), 124 (Theatre of Dionysos/North Wind
Picture Archives), 124 (Globe Theatre interior/
Bob Masters), 124 (Globe Theatre/Anne-Marie
Palmer), 125 (Shakespeare Globe Theatre/Peter
Phipp/Travelshots.com), 125 (dance class/Oliver
Knight), 125 (Death Cab for Cutie concert/Martin
Thomas Photography), 125 (Tate Britain Gallery/
Brian Harris), 125 (marching band/B Christopher),
125 (Roman Arena, Venice/EmmePi Images);
Barcroft Media p.8 (Twins/Niklas Halle'n); Corbis
pp.19 (astronaut Chris Hadfield/Sergei Ilnitsky/
epa), 28 (vintage camera/Ashley Corbin-Teich),
56 (Vera Wang/Fairchild Photo Service/Condé
Nast), 66 (Michael Bloomberg/Ramin Talaie),
72 (family playing video game/KidStock/Blend
Images), 75 (basketball Olympic champions/
Marcos Brindicci/Reuters), 76 (mountains hikers,
Nepal/John Carr/Eye Ubiquitous), 77 (Mayan ruins/
Ivan Vdovin/JAI), 77 (Lake Atitlan,Guatemala/
Frank Krahmer), 96 (Lisbon/Wiktor Szymanowicz/
Demotix), 97 (snowstorm in desert/STRINGER/
Reuters), 97 (sand skiing/STRINGER/Reuters),
111 (driver at pit stop/Randy Faris), 116 (Chinese
dancers/Guo Jian She/Redlink), 125 (watching 3D
film/Andersen-Ross); Getty Images pp.6 (Golden
Gate Bridge/Uschools University Images),
6 (Melbourne, Australia/Bjorn Holland), 7 (man
laughing/Kevin Russ), 13 (young woman portrait/
Juanmonino), 13 (man using laptop/Blend Images/
Hill Street Studios), 15 (business meeting/Celia
Peterson), 16 (king penguins/Michael Nolan),
23 (beach, Brazil/Sergio Pitamitz), 26 (reporter
holding microphone/Dave & Les Jacobs), 26 (dentist/
Fuse), 26 (man playing guitar/Digital Vision),
26 (woman in hospital/Blend Images – Jose Luis
Pelaez Inc), 26 (chef in kitchen/ColorBlind Images),

26 (young caretaker/XiXinXing), 27 (man playing
piano/Hal Bergman), 27 (park ranger/Blend Images
– John Lund/Sam Diephuis), 36 (kangaroo road sign/
scibak), 42 (woman on hike/Phil Boorman), 45 (Neft
Dashlari floating town/Reza), 47 (travel shopping/
filo), 53 (laptop/CostinT), 56 (Sony President Akio
Morita/The LIFE Images Collection), 57 (1930
World Cup/Bob Thomas/Popperfoto), 62 (brown
leather shoes/Sjo), 62 (London bus/Lluis Real),
65 (chair, Vincent Van Gogh/The Bridgeman Art
Library), 69 (Fauja Singh/Bloomberg), 70 (eyelashes/
Gamma-Rapho), 74 (cafe/Image Source), 77 (street in
Guatemala/Cultura Travel/Ben Pipe Photography),
78 (businessman getting out of taxi/DreamPictures),
78 (woman on bicycle/Felbert+Eickenberg),
78 (getting off bus/UpperCut Images), 79 (taxis in
Hanoi/AFP), 79 (street in Hanoi/AFP), 83 (Old Delhi
market/Mike Powles), 85 (Auckland from above/
Matej Pribelsky), 92 (Edinburgh panorama/Travelpix
Ltd), 96 (snowy street, Chicago/Christopher
Arndt), 98 (Mount Kilimanjaro/Charles Bowman),
98 (Victoria Falls/Peter Bischoff), 98 (snowy
landscape, Russia/AFP), 98 (Amazon River/Eurasia),
98 (beach in Thailand/Sarun Laowong), 98 (Gobi
Desert/Per-Anders Pettersson), 101 (Sand Marathon
cooling off/AFP), 106 (Nelson Mandela/The LIFE
Images Collection), 117 (classical concert/Hiroyuki
Ito), 121 (Hema Sardesai/AFP), cover (blue light
trail/teekid); iStockphoto p.36 (three opal rings/
Imagesbybarbara); Mary Evans Picture Library
p.46 (1960s Camden/John Gay/English Heritage.
NMR); Max Tuta Noronha p.60 (Brazil); Norbert
Michalke p.50 (virtual mirror); Oxford University
Press pp.44 (dirty dishes/Image Source), 104 (white
water rafting/David Maddison); Oxford University
Press video stills pp.14 (classroom), 24 (TV, family),
34, 44 (top), 54 (top), 94 (restaurant); 84; Rex
Features pp.69 (Usain Bolt/Chamussy/Niviere/SIPA),
116 (Stephen Wiltshire sketching/REX), 118 (The
Artist poster/Weinstein/Everett); Shutterstock
pp.9 (family tree/Kudryashka), 14 (Brighton Pier/
Philip Bird LRPS CPAGB), 30 (pilot's shoulder/
Victor Torres), 31 (car mechanic/Andrew
Lam), 44 (pearl neckalce/Gabriel Georgescu),
58 (Chinese ancient coins/HomeStudio), 58 (pile
of salt/Monkey Business Images), 62 (blank card/
Mega Pixel), 62 (rain on water/Dmitry Naumov),
64 (Hagia Sophia, Istanbul/guroldinneden),
64 (Grand Bazaar, Istanbul/photo.ua); David
Veszelovszki p.82 (ticket office).

Cover: Getty Images

Illustrations by: Tatiana Arocha/Bernstein & Andriulli
pp.21,80; Paul Boston pp.38, 119; Vicki Gausden
p.10, 51, 71, 110; Dylan Gibson pp.55, 128 (right),
129, 133 (right), 134; Kerry Hyndman pp.42 (town);
45, 128 (map), 133 (map); Marianne Karlssen at
Molly&Co Agency p.48; Joanna Kerr/New Division
pp.17, 18, 36, 42 (directions), 68, 98, 102, 105, 108,
130 (compass); Script & Seal (Gavin Potenza and
Liz Meyer)/Bernstein & Andriulli pp.16; 60, 77, 90,
109,130 (2 maps), 135; Phil Schramm/New Division
pp.58 (a+c), 73, 89, 127, 132.

Commissioned photography by: Gareth Boden pp.40,
52, 86, 95.

With thanks to Sarah Kay Walker for the video
pages.

With thanks to Jeanette Lindsey-Clark for the
Grammar Reference pages.

Oxford University Press would like to thank: Five
Corners, Peoples Television, Central Films,
Alamy Images, Park Theatre, La Cucina,
Sarah Darby, p.8 http://abcnews.go.com, p.73
www.sciencedaily.com, p.88 www.telegraph.co.uk,
pp.108–9 www.geocaching.com